THE GREAT COMMISSION

A Closer Look at Why Discipleship Cannot Be Ignored

VALY VADUVA

Author of the *Fullness of Christ*

The Great Commission: *A Closer Look at Why Discipleship Cannot be Ignored*

Published by Upper Room Fellowship Ministry (URFM)
Livonia, MI 48150
www.urfm.org

978-1-930529-41-0 (sc)

Library of Congress Control Number: N/A

This book is a work of non-fiction. Unless otherwise noted, the author and the publisher make no explicit guarantees as to the accuracy of the information contained in this book and in some cases, names of people and places have been altered to protect their privacy. The views expressed in this work are solely those of the author and do not necessarily reflect the views of the publisher.

Because of the dynamic nature of the Internet, any web addresses or links contained in this book may have changed since publication and may no longer be valid. Cover image royalty-free from iStockphoto.com, and compass graphic free from Pixabay.com used for illustration purposes only.

DEDICATION

To Jesus Christ—my Lord and my Master
To the Church—the Bride of Christ
To all believers who are embracing the cross and following Jesus
To all mentors who are committed to invest in discipleship

CONTENTS

PREFACE

I am so glad that you hold this book in your hands! I am praying that your heart will be touched by God, you will hear with clarity the voice of the Great Shepherd, and your life will be transformed by the Holy Spirit.

Let me share a few things about me. I was born and raised in Romania. I did not grow up in a Bible-believing family. Even though my parents considered themselves Christians, they did not have a personal relationship with Jesus. They did not read Bible stories to me before tucking me in bed. You can read more details in the "Meet the Author" section of this book.

When I was twelve years old, I received a small New Testament with a burgundy imitation leather cover. I literally devoured that little book during my summer break. In fact, I read it three times. I guess it was during that time that I fell in love with the Word of God.

While in High School, before my second summer break, a colleague gave me a small Bible with a green vinyl cover. I could not wait for summer vacation to start reading it! Before the summer break was over, I finished reading the entire Bible, from Genesis to the Revelation. During the fall semester, my colleague invited me to go to his church. My heart was ready to accept Jesus as my Lord and Savior. The Holy Spirit renewed my heart in a visible way. My water baptism was a powerful experience for me. I felt so happy and fulfilled, that for a few weeks I thought I was on cloud nine—I felt so light, and so free.

February 20th, 1976 marked the beginning of my journey as a disciple of Christ. Why do I remember that date? Because my baptism was about two weeks before the devastating earthquake on March 4, 1977, that literarily mutilated the *face* of downtown

Bucharest.

Reading the Bible, studying the Word of God, fellowshipping with my fellow believers, and witnessing to my family, relatives, and colleagues, felt so natural to me. God orchestrated the circumstances in such a way that I was asked to preach the gospel of Christ when I was only seventeen years old. After my first sermon, people came to me and told me that I have a gift. That stuck with me and motivated me to kindle afresh the gift, immerse myself in the Bible, study the Scriptures with other believers, while trying my best to prepare to share my faith, and continue preaching the gospel at every opportunity.

In the meanwhile, I was intentional on spending quality time with a few more mature believers who knew the Bible much better than me. I met with them regularly, asked questions, confessed my sins to them, and prayed together. With every session and every meeting, the Holy Spirit transformed my life and grew me more in the grace and knowledge of our Lord and Savior, Jesus Christ. Looking back, I cannot imagine the Christian life any different than that. I guess I was blessed to have godly mentors around me who kept me accountable and challenged me to become the disciple who Jesus called me to be.

I married young. Shortly after our marriage, the Holy Spirit called my wife and I into ministry. We just had our first child, but God considered us to be ready for the task. So, we opened our apartment for Bible studies, prayer meetings, and weekend fellowship with other believers from all over the country. All those experiences strengthened our faith and matured us even more. The Bible was and remains central to our ministry. Fulfilling the Great Commission, making disciples, and equipping God's children for the ministry, despite hardship, persecution, even one arrest, were very normal to us.

At age thirty, God led our family of four children, ranging in age from four to nine, to immigrate to the United States. We were excited that from then on, we could freely do what we liked most—*making disciples*, in a free country, without fearing any raids of the secret police. We imagined that everybody would be as thrilled and as excited as we were to gather to study God's Word, to pray, and to fellowship. But it did not take too long to realize that things were not the way we hoped. Christians in the United States were busy, stressed, and being intentional about discipleship was not a priority for many of them. Only by the grace of God and guided by the Holy Spirit were we able to continue to do what we knew we were called to do—*making disciples*. Within a few years, the Holy Spirit directed our steps to obtain more training in the discipleship counseling ministry. Shortly after that God led us to establish a nonprofit organization. You can read more about this in the "About Upper Room Fellowship Ministry," (URFM) section of this book.

Shortly after we founded URFM, we started offering more Bible studies and family seminars. We even took a group of fifteen families through a two-year long family seminar. Mainly we met in the finished basement of our home, or in a large living room of any family who wanted to host our meetings.

In parallel, my wife invested in teen girls. Even now, after twenty plus years, they still call her their spiritual mother. She also started investing in younger women who were eager to know more from the Bible and to grow in Christ. This kind of ministry, based on Titus 2:4, continues even today.

Twenty plus years ago I offered a Discipleship 101 seminar. It was a joy to take young believers through two years of basic discipleship training about the Bible and fundamental principles of the Christian faith.

From 2010 onward, the Lord directed my steps to offer Advanced Discipleship Training (ADT), a solid platform for equipping future mentors for the ministry of disciple-making. You can read more about ADT in the last chapter of this book.

Why am I sharing all these things with you? First, to encourage you to keep on keeping on as a follower of Christ. Second, to motivate you to start to be more intentional about your relationship with God. Third, to direct your steps to become a mentor—a person fully equipped to disciple other believers. Fourth, to cheer you on to start investing in the lives of other people. I can tell you that this is not a simple task. It is, however, one of the most rewarding things you can do here on earth. Keep in mind that this type of ministry is rewarded by the Lord in eternity. I have a suspicion that a lot of believers who heard about the Great Commission, never heard that the heart of Jesus is one hundred percent for the ministry of discipleship. His promise is so strong: "I am with you always, even to the end of the age" (Matthew 28:20b).

I hope and pray that the concepts and ideas contained in this book will build you up, will encourage you to become the best disciple Jesus called you to be, and will equip you with more tools to use as you mentor other believers.

May God bless you and empower you to fulfill Christ's vision and mission—*be discipled* and *make disciples.*

Have a great personal spiritual journey!

Valy Vaduva

Ordained Minister/Life Coach/Spiritual Mentor

CHAPTER 1
A Closer Look at The Great Commission

And Jesus said to them; therefore, every scribe who has become a disciple of the kingdom of heaven is like a head of a household, who brings out of his treasure things new and old.
— Matthew 13:52

One of the great scholars of the Renaissance, Erasmus[1], told a mythical tale about Jesus' return to heaven after His time on Earth. The angels gathered around Him to learn what happened. Jesus told them of His miracles, His teaching, and then of His death and resurrection. When He finished, Michael the archangel asked: *"But Lord, what happens now?"* Jesus answered: *"I have left behind eleven faithful men who will declare My message and express My love. These faithful men will establish and build My Church." "But,"* responded Michael, *"what if these men fail? What then?"* Jesus answered, *"I have no other plan."*[2]

Hmm! Jesus has no Plan B! According to the Great Commission stated in Matthew 28:18–20, it is clear that Christ relies one hundred percent on His discipleship vision to be carried out by His original disciples, followed by the next generation of faithful men, and so forth, until His second coming. No other plan—*just discipleship.*

Think about this! God created the entire universe and governs it so everything runs according to His plan. Part of the universe is the planet Earth inhabited by us. Even before sin entered into this world, God commanded the first family to multiply—"Be fruitful and multiply, and fill the earth, and subdue it; and rule over the fish of the sea and over the birds of the sky and over every living thing that moves on the earth" (Genesis 1:28). If we search the entire Bible, we cannot find any verse in which God canceled His first commandment given to humanity. We can conclude that even after the Fall, this commandment was to be carried forward. The fact that people are still living in the twenty-first century is a testament that God's first commandment still stands. In other words, reproduction is in the genes of human beings. Is physical reproduction essential for the survival of the human race? Absolutely! How much more important is spiritual multiplication?

The Great Commission Cannot be Evaded

My heart is passionate about the *Great Commission*. We all know that the Great Commission is the last message Christ gave to His first-century disciples before He ascended to heaven. Every Christian, at least in theory, knows it:

> Go therefore and make disciples of all the nations, baptizing them in the name of the Father and the Son and the Holy Spirit, teaching them to observe all that I commanded you; and lo, I am with you always, even to the end of the age. (Matthew 28:1–20)

In a sense, similarly to the commandment—"Be fruitful and multiply" God gave the first family in Genesis, Christ commands His apostles to make disciples according to His discipleship model. In other words, spiritual reproduction is in the *"spiritual genes"* of the Church.

Jesus' method of discipleship is people. His discipleship model is personal, relational, life-on-life, and experiential. His focus is on transformation, not mere information.

Christ's "manual" of discipleship is the Word of God. And the transforming power is the Holy Spirit. The process of discipleship implies a *willing mind*, a *listening ear*, and an *obedient heart.*

In his book, "*Follow Me: A call to die, A call to live*," David Platt writes:

> He has woven into the fabric of every single Christian's DNA a desire and ability to (spiritually) reproduce. More than a married couple longs to see a baby naturally born; every Christian longs to see sinners supernaturally saved. All who know the *love* of Christ yearn to multiply the *life* of Christ. God has formed us, fashioned and even filled Christians with His own Spirit for this very purpose.[3]

If we search the entire New Testament, we cannot find a single verse that states otherwise. **Therefore, the Great Commission is still in effect today.** We can conclude that Jesus Christ is expecting His discipleship vision to continue. Back then, He was looking for disciples; now He looks for disciples; and, I am confident that, even within seconds before His return, Christ will draw disciples to Himself. David Plat writes:

Jesus' method of discipleship is people. His discipleship model is personal, relational, life-on-life, and experiential. His focus is on transformation, not mere information.

> Every disciple of Jesus has been called, loved, created, and saved to make disciples who make disciples of Jesus who make disciples of Jesus until the grace of God is enjoyed, and the glory of God is exalted among every people group on the planet. And that day every disciple of Jesus—*every follower of Christ and fisher of men*—will see the Savior's face and behold the Father's splendor in a scene of indescribable beauty and everlasting bliss that will never, ever fade away.[4]

The bottom line is this: The Church of the twenty-first century is not exempt from the Great Commission. On the contrary, today's Church is called to be actively part of it, *here* and *now*.

Hudson Taylor, (21 May 1832 - 3 June 1905), the famous missionary to China, once said, "The *Great Commission* is not an option to be considered; it is a command to be obeyed." Let's ask ourselves: How are we supposed to respond today in regard to the Great Commission? David Livingstone (19 March 1813 - 1 May 1873), the great missionary to Africa, once said, "If a commission by an earthly king is considered an honor, how can a *commission* by a Heavenly King be considered a sacrifice?" Therefore, it is an honor to make disciples for our King Jesus. Howard Hendricks, (5 April 1924 - 20 February 2013), a longtime professor at Dallas Theological Seminary and speaker for Promise Keepers, in the foreword to "*Disciples, are Made not Born,*" wrote, "*'Make disciples'* is the mandate of the Master (Matthew 28:19–20). We may ignore it, but we cannot evade it."[5] The questions for us today are: What are we doing? Are we ignoring it? Knowing that we cannot evade the Great Commission, what are we waiting for? In the same book cited above, David Platt writes: "God has commanded every disciple to make disciples. No Christian is excused from this command, and no Christian would want to escape this command."[6]

Simple Exegesis of The Great Commission

By undertaking a simple exegesis on Matthew 28:16–20, any serious student of the Bible can easily observe that Jesus was not asking the apostles just to spread the gospel through evangelism, or just to make converts. Rather, He emphasized *"making disciples."* In other words, the Great Commission is about spiritual reproduction according to Christ's model of discipleship. If we read the book of Acts carefully, the discipleship aspect becomes very clear. In this chapter, we are not going to analyze it in detail; we are just highlighting some crucial elements pertaining to discipleship.

First, we observe that the apostles took to heart what Jesus commanded and immediately started making disciples, thus fulfilling the Great Commission in their generation. Luke writes: "The word of God kept on spreading; and the number of the disciples continued to increase greatly in Jerusalem, and a great many of the priests were becoming obedient to the faith" (Acts 6:7). This speaks clearly of multiplication not just *proselytism*[7] or just making a few *converts*[8]. As Jesus commanded them in Acts 1:8—which sounds similarly to the Great Commission, the apostles started in Jerusalem, continued spreading the Way in Judea, then moved into Samaria, and later on, they made disciples in the farthest parts of the Roman Empire.

Second, the apostles spent quality time making disciples. "He—*the apostle Paul*—withdrew from them and took away the disciples, reasoning daily in the school of Tyrannus" (Acts 19:9. *Emphasis mine*). Dr. Luke traveled with Paul and he shared from his personal experience: "This—*making disciples*—took place for two years, so that all who lived in Asia heard the word of the Lord, both Jews and Greeks" (Acts 19:10. *Emphasis mine*). What caused *"all"* who lived in Asia to hear the Word of God? An organic multiplication. This organic increase can only result from the process of discipleship. In the introduction to "*Follow Me*," Francis Chan writes:

> The Church began in Acts 2 when three thousand people were converted. By AD 100, estimates claim twenty-five thousand followers. By AD 350, estimates claim over thirty million followers... How could the Church grow at this incredible rate, especially under persecution? The followers saw their obligation to make disciples.[9]

The first-century church, empowered by the Holy Spirit, made disciples, not just converts. Are we, the believers of the twenty-first century, settling for less? I am not too fond of the fact that we are lowering the standard. Today we are still called to ***make disciples***. Richard Foster writes: "Perhaps the greatest malady in the Church today is converts to Christ who are not disciples of Christ—*a clear contradiction in terms*. This malady affects everything in church life."[10] Dallas Willard, an expert in spiritual formation and a very well-known Christian author, writes:

> The last command Jesus gave the Church before he ascended to heaven was the **Great Commission**, the call for Christians to "*make disciples of all the nations*." But Christians have responded by making "*Christians*," not "*disciples*." This has been the Church's Great Omission.[11]

I hope you agree with me that we are challenged to reverse this *omission*. For the first century Christians, "The Great Commission was not a choice for them to consider, but a command to obey."[12] Should we continue to perpetuate the current statistics or decide to obey God? You and I have a choice to make.

Make Disciples, Not Converts

Making disciples should be the driving force of everything the local Church is doing. See diagram 1.

Diagram 1

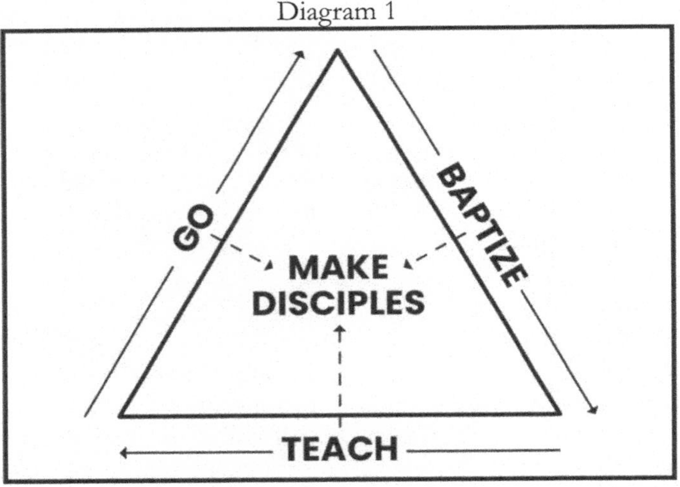

Dr. Robert E. Coleman writes:

> The Great Commission of Christ given to His Church summed it up in the command to *"make disciples of every creature"* (Matthew 28:19). The word here indicates that the disciples were to go out into the world and win others who would come to be what they themselves were—*disciples of Christ*. This mission is emphasized even more when the Greek text of the passage is studied, and it is seen that the words "*go*," "*baptize*," and "*teach*" are all participles which derive their force from the one controlling verb ***make disciples***. This

> means that the Great Commission is not merely to go to the ends of the Earth *preaching the gospel* (Mark 16:15), nor *to baptize* a lot of converts in the Name of the Triune God, *nor to teach* them the precepts of Christ, but to "make disciples"—to build men like themselves who were so constrained by the Commission of Christ that they not only followers but led others to follow His way. Only as disciples were made could the other activities of the commission fulfill their purpose.[13]

Interesting, isn't it?

Scott Hildreth, Director of the Center for Great Commission Studies (CGCS), writes:

> The main verb of the sentence that makes up **Matthew 28:19-20** is μαθητευσατε (***make disciples***), followed by descriptive phrases βαπτιζοντες αυτους (***baptizing them***) and διδασκοντες αυτους (***teaching them***). According to Blomberg, this command calls for a kind of evangelism that does not stop after someone makes a profession of faith. **The truly subordinate participles explain what *making disciples* involve:**
>
> – The first of these will be a once-for-all decisive initiation into the Christian community.
> – The second proves a perennially incomplete lifelong task. This includes coming to faith, identifying with the Christian community, **and growing in faith throughout the life of the believer**.
>
> Rengstorf[14] notes that μαθητευσατε (make disciples) always implies the existence of a personal attachment, which shapes the whole life of the one described as μαθητης (Gr. mathétés—a disciple—a learner, disciple, pupil). These descriptions highlight that the command of the **Great Commission** is for followers of Jesus to introduce unbelievers to the faith; **however, the work is not finished until the whole of life is affected**."[15]

I hope that everybody agrees that the Great Commission requires thinking beyond *evangelism* and *missions.* The Great Commission challenges every one of us to think radical discipleship and spiritual transformation; to think spiritual growth and maturity; to think multiplication and spiritual reproduction. This is the kind of discipleship Christ is expecting. I am sure that when He returns, Jesus expects to find mature disciples—*a people transformed into His likeness.*

The Four Dimensions of the Great Commission

Many years ago, when I began studying this topic, I knew only the traditional format of the Great Commission from Matthew 28:19–20. At that time, I did not realize that the Great Commission is stated, in one form or another, in every gospel. However, after reading and re-reading the New Testament text and listening several times to various audio versions of the gospels, it occurred to me that every gospel writer stated the Great Commission in his unique way. So, the Great Commission has four (4) dimensions. (See diagram 2).

Diagram 2

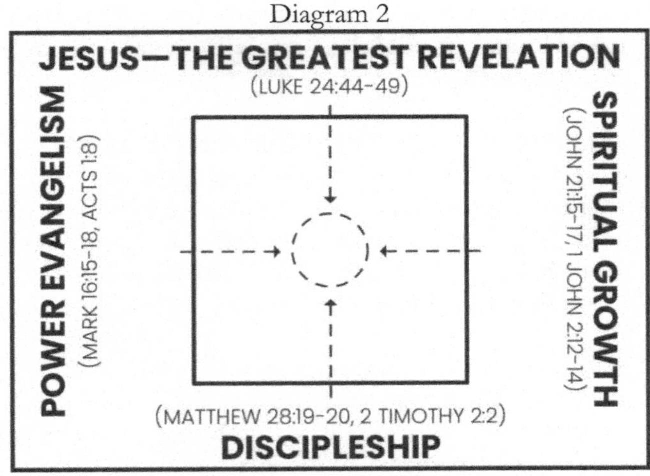

1. *Make Disciples*
2. *Power Evangelism*
3. *Jesus—the Highest Revelation*
4. *Spiritual Growth for every category of believers*

1. Make Disciples—The Great Commission according to Matthew

We already discussed the traditional format. Now, let us take a closer look at the other three formulations of the Great Commission found in the other gospels.

2. Power Evangelism—The Great Commission according to Mark

In his gospel, after the resurrection account, Mark states that the Lord Jesus appeared to the eleven and commissioned them to preach the gospel under the endowment of the Holy Spirit. The Bible tells us:

> He said to them, "Go into all the world and preach the Gospel to all creation. He who has believed and has been baptized shall be saved; but he who has disbelieved shall be condemned. These signs will accompany those who have believed: in My name, they will cast out demons, they will speak with new tongues; they will pick up serpents, and if they drink any deadly poison, it will not hurt them; they will lay hands on the sick, and they will recover. (Mark 16:15–18)

The first line: "Go into all the world and preach the gospel to all creation," sounds very similar to the traditional version from the Gospel of Matthew. The second line: "He who has believed and has been baptized shall be saved; but he who has disbelieved shall be condemned" emphasizes the faith-based-baptism, and the reason for people's condemnation—*disbelief*. However, after this line, Mark's version of the Great Commission is radically different. In verses 17 and 18, Mark states that the preaching of the Gospel is going to be followed by all sorts of signs and wonders, from casting out demons to the healing of the sick. In my Bible, all these verses are in red, which indicates that Mark reproduced the very words of Jesus before His Ascension to the Father.

Verse 20: "And they went out and preached everywhere, while the Lord worked with them, and confirmed the word by the signs that followed," speaks about their immediate obedience. The only thing I have to say to this is a sincere, Amen. The world today, especially in the west, needs this kind of preaching followed by miracles. Nobody can argue that *power evangelism* was crucial for fulfilling the Great Commission in the early part of the Church history. I believe *power evangelism* is as essential today as it was then.

3. Jesus—the Highest Revelation—The Great Commission according to Luke

At first, it was difficult for me to see the Great Commission in the Gospel of Luke. However, after praying and reading it many times, the Holy Spirit enabled me to discover it. Because Luke, the beloved physician, wrote two books: *The Gospel of Luke* and *the Book of Acts*, the last chapter of his gospel has a different ending than the Gospel of Matthew and Mark. In chapter 24, Luke describes some of the post-resurrection events. The bulk of this chapter revolves around the trip of two disciples from Jerusalem to Emmaus. We know the name of one is Cleopas, but we do not know who the second disciple is. However, this detail is not essential. The distance between these two places, according to Luke, is about 60 stadia. Depending on what definition we use for "stadia," it represents approximately 12 km. What is important here is that the Resurrected Jesus considered essential to give those disciples a condensed version of the "Old Testament Survey." Listen to these words:

> Was it not necessary for the Christ to suffer these things and to enter into His glory? Then beginning with Moses and with all the prophets, He explained to them the things concerning Himself in all the Scriptures. (Luke 24:26–27)

If they walked with an average speed of 4 km/hour, it took them approximately 3 hours to reach Emmaus. Instead of immediately revealing Himself to them, Christ considered it essential to provide them with an in-depth Bible study regarding

Himself. I am not sure about you, but I found this very interesting. The resurrected Christ used key references from the Torah, the Major Prophets, and the Minor Prophets to cause their hearts to burn inside their chests with wonder (Luke 24:32). I believe Christ used many passages from the Book of Psalms, especially from Psalm 22 and 69. During their journey, their eyes were prevented from recognizing Jesus (Luke 24:16). However, when they broke bread in their house, Jesus revealed to them His true identity (Luke 24:31).

After this extraordinary experience, Cleopas and the unnamed disciple could not stay in Emmaus anymore. Filled with unspeakable joy, despite the outside darkness and danger, they returned to Jerusalem and shared their extraordinary experience with the eleven. What was their experience? It was the experiential knowledge of the Resurrected Christ at the end of a compelling Bible study. As they finished the story, Christ appeared to all of them. He told the disciples:

> These are My words which I spoke to you while I was still with you, that all things which are written about Me in the Law of Moses and the Prophets and the Psalms must be fulfilled. (Luke 24:44)

Trust me, when I studied this portion of Luke's Gospel, my heart was burning and pounding in my chest. I exclaimed, "*Christ is the Supreme Revelation.*" The entire Old Testament points to Christ. The world today, Jews and Gentiles alike, need to know Christ by revelation. This is Luke's version of the Great Commission. In fact, in his second book—Acts, Luke testifies that the apostles preached Christ everywhere they went. Below are some accounts of this:

> And every day, in the temple and from house to house, they kept right on teaching and **preaching Jesus as the Christ**. (Acts 5:42)

Saul of Tarsus, after his powerful encounter with the Resurrected Jesus on Damascus road, started preaching Jesus.

And immediately, he began to **proclaim Jesus** in the synagogues, saying, "He is the Son of God." (Acts 9:20)

But there were some of them, men of Cyprus and Cyrene, who came to Antioch and began speaking to the Greeks also, **preaching the Lord Jesus**. (Acts 11:20)

Explaining and giving evidence that the Christ had to suffer and rise again from the dead, and saying, "This Jesus, whom I am **proclaiming to you is the Christ**." (Acts 17:3)

And also some of the Epicurean and Stoic philosophers were conversing with him. Some were saying, "What would this idle babbler wish to say?" Others, "He seems to be a proclaimer of strange deities,"—because he was **preaching Jesus and the resurrection**. (Acts 17:18)

But when Silas and Timothy came down from Macedonia, Paul began devoting himself completely to the word, solemnly **testifying to the Jews that Jesus was the Christ**. (Acts 18:5)

For he powerfully refuted the Jews in public, **demonstrating by the Scriptures that Jesus was the Christ**. (Acts 18:28)

Solemnly <u>testifying</u> to both Jews and Greeks of **repentance toward God and faith in our Lord Jesus Christ**. (Acts 20:21)

But I do not consider my life of any account as dear to myself, so that I may finish my course and the ministry which I received **from the Lord Jesus**, to testify solemnly of the Gospel of the grace of God. (Acts 20:24)

> Preaching the kingdom of God and teaching **concerning the Lord Jesus Christ** with all openness, unhindered. (Acts 28:31)

In conclusion, the book of Acts is a powerful testimony on how the first-century church fulfilled the Great Commission—*proclaiming to the world that Jesus is the Christ.*

4. Spiritual Growth for every category of believers—The Great Commission according to John

The apostle John wrote his gospel towards the end of the first century, probably 90–100 AD. He could refer to Matthew's version of the Great Commission, but he did not. Instead, in the last chapter of his gospel, John gives us the history of Peter's restoration back into the ministry. Let us review the context. Towards the end of His earthly ministry, Jesus shared with His disciples: "He must suffer many things and be rejected by this generation" (Luke 17:25). Before His arrest, Jesus told His disciples that all of them would "fall away" (Mark 14:27). Peter took a boastful stand: "Even though all may fall away, yet I will not" (Mark 14:29). He even insisted that he was ready to die for Him. "Even if I have to die with You, I will not deny You!" (Mark 14:31) We know the story. The very night Jesus was arrested, Peter denied Jesus three times before the rooster crowed two times (Mark 14:72), precisely as Christ predicted.

After His resurrection, Christ had a heart-to-heart conversation with Peter. Here is how that conversation went:

> So when they had finished breakfast, Jesus said to Simon Peter, "Simon, son of John, do you love Me more than these?" He said to Him, "Yes, Lord; You know that I love You." He said to him, "*Tend My lambs.*" He said to him again a second time, "Simon, son of John, do you love Me?" He said to Him, "Yes, Lord; You know that I love You." He said to him, "*Shepherd My sheep.*" He 'said to him the third time, "Simon, son of John, do you love Me?" Peter was

> grieved because He said to him the third time, "Do you love Me?" And he said to Him, "Lord, You know all things; You know that I love You." Jesus said to him, "*Tend My sheep.*" (John 21:15–17)

In his first epistle, John wrote about three categories of spiritual growth in the Church:

> I am writing to you, **little children**, because your sins have been forgiven you for His name's sake. I am writing to you, **fathers**, because you know Him who has been from the beginning. I am writing to you, **young men**, because you have overcome the evil one. I have written to you, **children**, because you know the Father. I have written to you, **fathers**, because you know Him who has been from the beginning. I have written to you, **young men**, because you are strong, and the word of God abides in you, and you have overcome the evil one. (1 John 2:12–14)

Christ wanted Peter to take care of His **lambs**, His **young sheep**, and His **adult sheep.**

Diagram 3

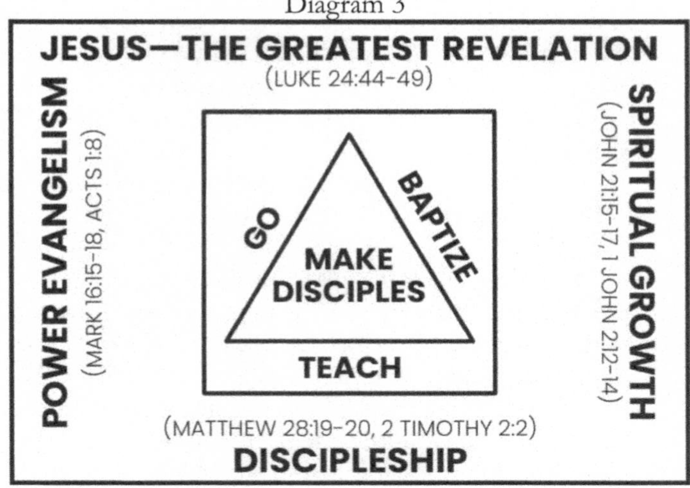

Without unpacking this great Scripture passage, I am hearing John saying that part of the Great Commission is providing spiritual growth to all categories of believers in the local Church. To me, the passage in John 21:15–17, is John's version of the Great Commission—*providing spiritual growth to all categories of believers:* **children, youth, and adults**. See diagram 3.

Discipleship—The Greatest Need of the Church Today

Rick Knoth, the managing editor of *Enrichment Journal,* visited with McNeal[16] to discuss insights from *The Present Future* and *Missional Renaissance* as they relate to church revitalization and transformation. When asked: **What has been the number one failure of the Church in the past twenty-five years?** Reggie McNeal responded: **To create genuine followers of Jesus.**[17]

We can conclude that generally speaking, the Church, at large—***is lacking discipleship***. I hope that all my readers will consider this a shocking realization! We must stop hiding our heads in the sand like an ostrich, pretending that everything is fine in our churches. If we look closely at the Great Commission, we shall realize that discipleship cannot be ignored.

While serving as Assistant General Superintendent in the Assemblies of God, Charles Crabtree[18] said: "I believe that our discipleship, at this point right now, is ineffective."[19] Another leader within the same organization declared:

> There is no greater need in the Assemblies of God today than for personal, ongoing Pentecostal discipleship of believers.[20]

Furthermore, according to the Assemblies of God News Service:

> Unless we, as a Fellowship, passionately pursue discipleship, the Assemblies of God will continue to lose millions of converts and, ultimately, our distinctive Pentecostal heritage.[21]

Do we need another warning much clearer and more direct than this? Moreover, Crabtree said:

> I pray that the Lord will awaken pastors and churches to the crisis,... We can provide all of the best resources we want, but without spiritual insight in local situations and the willingness to obey the Lord's command of the ***Great Commission*** ... without quality disciples; we simply aren't going to have quality churches."... *Churches need to be prepared for spiritual* ***babies*** *by training up* **spiritual mothers** *and* **fathers** *who understand the significance of their commitment.*[22]

Amen brother Crabtree! I second this prayer with all my heart. Do you?

Moreover, David Platt challenges us to embrace the vision of discipleship wholeheartedly:

> "I want to be part of a people who have forsaken every earthly ambition in favor of one eternal aspiration to see disciples made and churches multiplied from house to house to our communities to our cities to the nations. ... This is God's design for His Church, and disciples of Jesus must not settle for anything less."[23]

Mature Disciples, Not Just Better Programs

It seems that thirty or forty years ago, the priority of Christian leaders shifted from spiritual growth via discipleship, to creating better programs. By doing this, the emphasis moved from the inside transformation of church members to the outside *"show"* put together by the Church. This situation has made the discipleship vision, stated so clearly in the **Great Commission,** the *"elephant"* of the local Church. In most local churches, the best efforts, energies, and budgets are invested not in the genuine inner spiritual transformation of the believers, but in creating the best programs for Sunday morning church service. Winfield Bevins, in his essay *The Discipleship Challenge* writes: "There is a lack of biblical discipleship in the North American Church. Dallas Willard calls it, "*Non-discipleship the elephant of the church.*"[24]

I suspect that most local churches are aware the elephant is in the room but for whatever reason, they are not willing to radically change their view on the Great Commission. Instead, many churches continue to perpetuate the same statistics.

Furthermore, Knoth asked McNeal, "You state that church leaders are asking the wrong questions to solve today's church problems. What should they be asking?" McNeal responded, "Church leaders are asking, '*How can we get people to come to church?*'" He continues:

> To me, the most important questions are: "How can we create better followers of Jesus rather than thinking about simply creating better churches? How can we have better communities rather than simply creating better churches? We have shrink–wrapped our notion of what God is doing in the world by assessing the health of the gathering. Did the worship go well? How many showed up? Did the choir get their stuff done? Did the band do well? Was the PowerPoint good? Was the sermon good? We act as if these things have an impact on the health of the Kingdom and God's activity in the world."[25]

I suspect many aspects raised by McNeal are typical of most churches.

Glenn McDonald, the author of "*The Disciple Making Church: From Dry Bones to Vitality*," explains:

> Most churches measure success using the ABC formula: A—*Attendance,* B—*Building,* and C—*Cash.* Please, I beg you, do not misunderstand me. We need people to *attend* our churches; we need *buildings* to conduct our meetings, and we need *cash* to support our churches and ministries, but the "ABC" based–success is *alive* and *well* in the United States, if we can bring ourselves to use the words "*alive*" and "*well.*" It's safe to say that a vast majority of Protestant congregations

> have made *attendance, building,* and *cash*—as opposed to Christ's Great Commission in Matthew 28:18–20 **to be** and **to make disciples**—*their organizational bottom line.* Programs are poor substitutes for vision, and utterly unacceptable as any Christian group's reason for existence.
>
> A second standard feature of the ABC church is the tendency to rely on hard work as the way to go forward. **If the program isn't producing, we'll step up our efforts.** If the goals aren't being reached, our leaders will simply have to keep a few more balls in the air. ABC churches, in summary, are more preoccupied with:
>
> (1) Structural issues than with spiritual vitality,
> (2) Tend to seek programmatic solutions to problems,
> (3) Rely on the gifts, energy, and over functioning of one or just a few key leaders,
> (4) Value an environment of command and control more than giving permission,
> (5) And expect little more than compliance from church attendees instead of world-changing personal transformation.[26]

These observations made by McDonald should give us plenty of food for thought.

David Platt writes:

> Imagine your Church. Don't picture the building, or parking lot, and don't envision the activities and programs. Just the people. Whether there are fifty, one hundred, five hundred, or five thousand of them, simply imagine the people who comprise your Church. So if you had nothing but the people—no buildings, no programs, no staff, and no activities—and you were in charge with spreading the Gospel to the whole world, where would you begin? Would you get the best speaker, the greatest musicians, and the most talented staff in order to organize the presentations and programs that appeal to your families and your

> children? Would you devote your resources to what is most comfortable, most entertaining, and most pleasing to you?
> I don't think your Church would do these things—and neither would mine. Not if we totally believe God's Word, and we were honestly looking at God's world.[27]

Greg Hawkins, one of Bill Hybels' senior assistant pastors, became aware that **the effectiveness of the church service was wanting**, and that Willow Creek Community Church [Willow] had become more of the place to be than a place to follow Christ. He approached Hybels (Willow's Senior Pastor) and asked for funds to conduct an in-depth study of membership to determine:

> (a) Their state of maturity
> (b) Their satisfaction with teaching and programs
> (c) Their feelings about their church journey in general.

The study was based on more than 11,000 individuals who completed the survey from Willow Creek and six additional churches of various sizes from different geographical locations. This research totaled 2.6 million points of data. I read somewhere that Hybels said this was, "The biggest wake–up call of my life, and the worst day of my life." In the summer of 2007, Willow published the results of that self–study under the title: "*Reveal: Where Are You?*" The report's front cover says that readers will learn *"surprising research findings that rocked Willow."*

The findings are astonishing! The results indicated:

> 1. Involvement in externally and internally focused church programs didn't necessarily translate into spiritual growth.
> 2. Spiritual growth is all about increasing relational closeness to Christ. Why is this? Very simple: "Because God "wired" us first and foremost to be in a growing relationship with Him not with the church."
> 3. More than 25 percent of those surveyed described themselves as spiritually "*stalled*" or "*dissatisfied*" **with the role of the Church in their spiritual growth**.

> (This should make every pastor and church leader think deeply about what type of spirituality they promote.)

There was much more information that surfaced, but the exciting aspects were as follows:

> (i) Far too much emphasis was put upon church involvement, and **far too little on encouraging personal growth** through a personal and growing relationship with Jesus Christ. (Does this sound familiar in your Church too?)
> (ii) The Church spends far too much time catering to seekers with their teaching and programs, what they called the "spiritual equivalent of diaper-changing" while letting "spiritual adolescents" fend for themselves.
> (iii) We have been wrong. We need to rethink the coaching we give you as you pursue your spiritual growth.[28]

Here is my summary based on their research published in *Reveal*:

> We should give Hybels credit for his sincerity. He agreed that the emphasis on programs and meetings did not produce disciples. Of course, the study does not address the considerable need for spiritual growth and maturity in Christ in all churches. However, Willow displayed much humility to undertake self-study and genuine vulnerability to publicize the results. Still, this should provoke all of us to think more deeply about what it means to be *The Church*. It is admirable that Hybels admitted that while they have "*spruced up the worship, spiked up the sermons, and become great at organization*" at the same time **they were failing to produce disciples**. The real question is: Would there be more congregations with such passion and humility? I pray and hope that churches across America and the world would wake up and re-connect

> with Christ's original vision—*Go, therefore, and make disciples?*[29]

May the vision of Jesus stated in Matthew 28:19–20, spread like wildfire from disciple to disciple, Church to Church, country to country, until Christ's return. May the promise of Christ that **He is** (present continuous) (Matthew 28:20) **with us** within the process of fulfilling the Great Commission, powerfully encourage us to keep on keeping on: *go, baptize, teach*—**make disciples**.

Radical Obedient Discipleship Leading to Maturity

I am encouraged to see that more and more church leaders, presidents of Bible schools and seminaries, and ministry organizations recognize openly that in the past few decades, the Church at large did not have the **Great Commission**—*making disciples*—as their number one priority. Not only that, but in recent years more and more church leaders and ministry organizations are calling the entire membership back to *discipleship* and the *disciple-making* vision and strategy. This should be very simple and straight-forward, as Dallas Willard wrote:

> When Jesus walked among humankind, there was a certain simplicity to being His disciple. Primarily, it meant to go with Him, in an attitude of study, obedience, and imitation. **There were no correspondence courses.** One knew what to do and what it would cost.[30]

Making disciples was never intended for programs and church marketing. Authentic discipleship is relational; it is the result of mature disciples—spiritual mentors, investing their lives into the lives of others. I like the way George Barna underlines the problem of the contemporary Church. He wrote: "Discipleship is not a program. It is not a ministry. *It is a life-long commitment to a lifestyle*."[31] Let me share with you the conclusions of The Third Lausanne Congress on World Evangelization, which took place in Cape Town, on October 16-25, 2010. This prestigious event of the

Christendom brought together 4,200 evangelical leaders from 198 countries, and extended to hundreds of thousands more, participating in meetings around the world, and online. What was the goal of this Congress? The goal was to bring a fresh challenge to the global Church of the *Great Commission*—**to bear witness to Jesus Christ and all His teaching**—*in every nation, in every sphere of society, and the realm of ideas*. Here they are:

> God was in Christ reconciling the world to Himself. God's Spirit was in Cape Town, calling the Church of Christ to be ambassadors of God's reconciling love for the world. God kept the promise of his Word as his people met together in Christ's name, for the Lord Jesus Christ himself dwelt among us, and walked among us (2 Corinthians 10:4-5). We sought to listen to the voice of the Lord Jesus Christ. And in His mercy, through His Holy Spirit – Christ spoke to His listening people. Through the many voices of Bible exposition, plenary addresses, and group discussion, two repeated themes were heard:
>
> (1) The need for radical obedient discipleship, leading to maturity, to grow in depth as well as in numbers.
> (2) The need for radical cross-centered reconciliation, leading to unity, to grow in love as well as in faith and hope.
>
> Wait! There is more. Are you ready for this?
>
> ***Discipleship*** and ***reconciliation*** are indispensable to our mission. We lament the scandal of our ***shallowness*** and ***lack of discipleship*** and the scandal of our ***disunity*** and ***lack of love***. For both seriously damage our witness to the Gospel."[32]

In my opinion, the conclusions of The Third Lausanne Congress on World Evangelization are monumental!

Conclusion

Here is my grand conclusion: *It is all about Jesus, and Jesus is all about discipleship*. The Great Commission challenges all of us once again to think beyond *"just evangelism" and "just missions";* instead, think *radical discipleship* and *spiritual transformation; think spiritual growth* and *maturity; think multiplication* and *spiritual reproduction*. As David Platt wrote: "This is a call worth dying for. This is a call worth living for."[33]

I wholeheartedly invite all of you to pray that all of us who call ourselves Christians, all over the world, would get out of our comfort zone of lukewarm religion and became disciples, get adequately equipped, and start *making disciples*. I am fascinated by Paul's boldness and faithfulness before his martyrdom to transfer his godly legacy to his son in the faith—*Timothy*: "The things which you have heard from me in the presence of many witnesses, entrust these to faithful men who will be able to teach others also" (2 Timothy 2:2). Should we do less than that? You be the judge.

Discussion Question:

– What is your personal view on the Great Commission?

– How does your local community of believers consider the Great Commission? Optional? Required? Please elaborate.

– Were you surprised to see that each gospel has its own version of the Great Commission?

– What does Christ's discipleship model require you personally to do?

– Do you take discipleship seriously? What specific steps are you taking to grow as a disciple of Christ?

– What plans do you have to fulfill the Great Commission?

– Are you properly equipped to make disciples? Please elaborate.

Notes

1. The Great Commission: A Simple Exegesis

[1] Erasmus of Rotterdam, (27 October 1466–12 July 1536), or simply Erasmus, a great scholar of the Renaissance is believed to be writing about Archangel Michael talking with Lord Jesus about His plan of saving the world.
[2] L. Alton Garrison, *Transforming a Church — the Acts 2 Way*, Accessed on April 29, 2013. http://enrichmentjournal.ag.org/.
[3] David Platt, *Follow Me: A Call to Die, A Call to Live*, (Tyndale House Publishers, Carol Streams, IL, 2013) 207.
[4] David Platt, 226.
[5] Walter A. Henrichsen, *Disciples are Made not* Born, (Victor, Colorado Springs, CO, 1988) 4.
[6] David Platt, 222.
[7] Proselytism (pron.: /ˈprɒsɨlaɪtɨzəm/) is the act of attempting to convert people to another religion or opinion. Historically in the Koine Greek Septuagint and New Testament, the word proselyte denoted a gentile who was considering conversion to Judaism. (http://en.wikipedia.org/). Accessed on April 29, 2013
[8] Convert: to bring over from one belief, view, or party to another. (www.merriam-webster.com/). Accessed on April 29, 2013.
[9] David Platt, p. XV.
[10] Richard Foster, *Devotional Classics*, ed. by Richard Foster & James Bryan Smith (Harper San Francisco, 1993), 18.
[11] Dallas Willard, *The Great Omission: Reclaiming the Essential Teachings on Discipleship*, (New York, NY: Harper Collins Publishers, 2006). Page #?
[12] David Platt, 179.
[13] Robert E. Coleman, *The Master Plan of Evangelism*, (Ravell, Old Tappan, NJ), 2006, 108-109.
[14] Karl Heinrich Rengstorf (1903-1992), German theologian.
[15] Scott Hildreth, *Contextualization and Great Commission Faithfulness*, (Published in the Contemporary Practice section, October 2010). Accessed on May 1, 2013. www.globalmissiology.org.
[16] Reggie McNeal, Ph.D., is missional leadership specialist for Leadership Network, Dallas, Texas. For over a decade McNeal was a denominational executive, leadership development coach, and has been the founding pastor of a church.
[17] Reggie McNeal was interviewed in *Engaging the Church in God's Redemptive Mission*, Enrichment Journal, Winter 2010. (http://enrichmentjournal.ag.org/). Accessed it on April 29, 2013.
[18] Charles Crabtree is the president of the Northpoint Bible College (NBC), formerly known as Zion Bible College, in Haverhill, Massachusetts. Crabtree served AG as Assistant General Superintendent for 14 years (1993 to 2007).
[19] "Pentecostal Discipleship" –between 18 and 21, not italicized the same a desperate need in the AG, Friday 08, Sep 2006. Accessed on May 1, 2013. http://ag.org/).
[20] Thomas E. Trask was elected General Superintendent of the Assemblies of God in August of 1993. Trask serves presently on the boards of the Assemblies of God Theological Seminary, Central Bible College and Evangel University.

http://leadershipblog.blogspot.com (Accessed on May 1, 2013).
[21] Assemblies of God Makes Desperate Changes for Pentecostal Discipleship. http://www.christianpost.com/news. Mon, Sep. 11, 2006 Posted: 08:18 AM EDT. (Accessed it on April 19, 2011).
[22] *Pentecostal Discipleship* – a desperate need in the AG. http://ag.org/ (Fri, 08 Sep 2006 - 4:53 PM CST). Accessed it on May 1, 2013.
[23] David Platt, 180.
[24] Winfield Bevins, *The Discipleship Challenge*, (2008). http://www.acts29network.org/ (Accessed on April 25, 2010).
[25] *Engaging the Church in God's Redemption Mission*. http://enrichmentjournal.ag.org/ (Accessed on April 29, 2013).
[26] Glenn McDonald, *The Disciple Making Church: From Dry Bones to Vitality*, (Faith Walk Publishing, Grand Rapids, MI, 2004), 4, 5, 6, 13.
[27] David Platt, p. 176.
[28] Greg Hawkins and Cally Parkinson, *REVEAL: Where are You?* (Willow Creek Resources, Barrington, IL), 2007.
[29] Valy Vaduva, *Lack of Spiritual Maturity among Christians*, (MSFL: Spiritual Formation Research Program Paper, Spring Arbor University (SAU), Spring Arbor, MI: 2011).
[30] Dallas Willard, *Discipleship: For Super-Christians Only?* (Christianity Today, October 10, 1980).
[31] George Barna, *Growing True Disciples: New Strategies for Producing Genuine Followers of Christ,* (Colorado Springs, CO: Water Brooks Press, 2001), 19.
[32] "The Cape Town Commitment," © 2011 The Lausanne Movement. http://www.lausanne.org/en/documents/ctcommitment.html. Accessed on May 1, 2013.
[33] David Platt, 226.

CHAPTER 2

Discipleship—The Greatest Need of the Church Today

And He was saying to them all, "If anyone wishes to come after Me, he must deny himself, and take up his cross daily and follow Me."
— Luke 9:23

In 1883, the US Marine Corps adopted this motto: "Semper Fidelis—*Always Faithful.*" Since then, they have lived up to this motto. "There has never been a mutiny, or even the thought of one, among U.S. Marines."[34] Using a 29-second video clip depicting the process of making a sword from the raw steel to a laser-polished final product, the Marines' commercial, tries to attract new candidates into their program. The narrator ends the commercial with these famous words: "We're looking for a few Good Men."

Dare to Be a Disciple

The Resurrected Christ is still looking for faithful men and women to follow Him as disciples. This is the highest calling in life. In Luke 9:23, the gospel writer, captures His calling: And He was saying to them all: "If anyone wishes to come after Me, he must deny himself, and take up his cross daily and follow Me" (Luke 9:23).

Let's look closely at this verse: "He was saying to them all." In other words, Christ addresses this calling to **all** born-again believers. It suggests that disciples are not born; they are made. "If anyone **wishes**"—expresses a powerful inner desire.

Please allow me to ask you a couple of questions:

– Do you desire Jesus more than anything in this world?
– Do you wish to be with Him more than with anyone else?

I think it is clear that one becomes a disciple of Christ because of a sincere desire burning in his or her heart. "To come after Me." The discipleship calling offers the best **pathway**—*walking in the footsteps of Jesus.* This doesn't mean belonging to a specific religion, or being part of a particular denomination, or following a famous person. Not at all! It refers to following Christ and Him alone. "He must deny himself." It is evident that this verse includes the most **challenging condition**—*denial of self.* Discipleship asks for total abandonment of self. Let's face it—this is the hardest thing to do, especially in our times. Not seeking any personal ambitions anymore? Not pursuing success? Not looking for fame? Wanting to elevate Jesus, and Him only? Who would want to do this in the 21st century? Counting everything as a loss for Christ's sake? No kidding! This is hard! Discipleship calling is extraordinary despite its difficulties! Only a true disciple would do something like this. The apostle Paul declares:

> Although I myself might have confidence even in the flesh. If anyone else has a mind to put confidence in the flesh, I far more: circumcised the eighth day, of the nation of Israel, of the tribe of Benjamin, a Hebrew of Hebrews; as to the Law, a Pharisee; as to zeal, a persecutor of the church; as to the righteousness which is in the Law, found blameless. But whatever things were gain to me, those things I have counted as loss for the sake of Christ. (Philippians 3:4–7)

The Cross

"*Take up his cross daily.*" Discipleship implies the most **austere**

discipline. In Luke 9:23 for the first time, the word—*cross*, is mentioned. I consider this fact important. During the time of Jesus, the cross was very well known as an instrument of death. I like the way the well-known author, A. W. Tozer writes about the cross:

> [The] cross is a symbol of death. It stands for the abrupt, violent death of a human being. The man in Roman times who took up his cross and started down the road had already said good-bye to his friends. He was not coming back. He was going out to have it ended. The cross made no compromise, modified nothing, spared nothing; it slew all of the man, completely and for good. It did not try to keep on good terms with its victim. It struck cruel and hard, and when it had finished its work, the man was no more.[35]

I hope we all see this! In the context in which Christ addressed His calling, He did not have to explain or define the meaning of the cross because everybody witnessed or heard of crucifixions done by the Romans. Our supreme example of accepting the cross is none other than Jesus. Paul writes: "Being found in appearance as a man, He humbled Himself by becoming obedient to the point of death, even death on a cross" (Philippians 2:8). In other words, the cross represents a model of **surrender** and **obedience** motivated by pure love. Our Savior modeled for us this type of surrender—absolute submission to the Father's will. (See Philippines 2:5—11). Most of us are not going to die on a physical cross, and this is not even the main point of the verse. The point is that discipleship implies a full understanding of the **concept of crucifixion**—*total surrender, total commitment,* and *willing obedience*. Let's understand this clearly: The Lord Jesus asks you and me to obey until death, and, if needed—martyrdom. It is crucial to realize that there is no such thing as a disciple without the cross. Therefore, giving ourselves to God means carrying the cross **voluntarily** and **consistently**. This is precisely the context in which the Lord Jesus Christ made this high calling. A disciple must willingly accept every suffering, hardship, persecution, loss, denigration, and so forth, motivated by his or her love and devotion for Christ. Believers from the first church understood this concept clearly—following Jesus may eventually cost them even their life. Dietrich Bonhoeffer wrote: "When Christ calls a man, he bids him come and die."[1] For the first-century disciples, more often than not, the cross implied the supreme sacrifice for the cause of Jesus. The church tradition tells us that all of Christ's disciples died as martyrs. They understood the secret of all secrets. Spiritual victory and abundant life are discovered when people accept the cross. Walter A. Henrichsen writes: "In no way can a person get without giving or truly live without dying." The Lord Jesus Christ is our perfect example.

When His love motivates us, we too can live for God to the point of death. Paul writes:

> For the love of Christ controls us, having concluded this, that one died for all; therefore all died, and He died for all so that they who live might no longer live for themselves, but for Him who died and rose again on their behalf.
> (2 Corinthians 5:14–15)

The point is that discipleship implies a full understanding of the concept of crucifixion—*total surrender, total commitment,* and *willing obedience.*

Walking as disciples requires the most precise direction—*follow Me.*

In verse 24, Christ explains that following Him is more precious than life itself. Luke writes: "For whoever wishes to save his life will lose it, but whoever loses his life for My sake, he is the one who will save it" (Luke 9:24). In direct connection with the concept expressed in this verse, in his journal entry from October 28, 1949, Jim Elliot, writes one of his most famous statements: "He is no fool who gives what he cannot keep to gain that which he cannot lose."[36] This reminds me of an interesting verse from Psalms: "Because Your lovingkindness is better than life, My lips will praise You" (Psalm 63:3).

In his book, "*Disciples are Made, Not Born,*" Walter A. Henrichsen writes:

> The key to being first is to be the last. The key to

> living is to die. The key to being free is to be a slave for Christ. The key to receive is to give. The key to being a leader is to be a **servant**. The key to being exalted is to live a life characterized by humility.
> Everyone wishes to live, but no one wants to die. Everyone wants to be free, but no one wants to be a slave. Everyone wants to receive, but no one wants to give. This is precisely the situation where we are in conflict with God's plan.[37]

As we can see in the statement above, Henrichsen gives us a pretty good picture of Christian discipleship.

Disciples are Made not Born

In Matthew 28:19–20 the Lord Jesus says: "Go therefore and make disciples of all the nations, baptizing them in the name of the Father and the Son and the Holy Spirit, teaching them to observe all that I commanded you; and lo, I am with you always, even to the end of the age." We all know, at least theoretically, that this is *The Great Commission*. Please observe that in Matthew 28:19, Christ did not commission the apostles to convert the nations but specifically told them to **make disciples**. In other words, disciples do not come out of the blue. Disciples are **made** not **born**. Disciples are the fruit of the discipleship process conducted by spiritual mentors, guided by the Holy Spirit.

There is a difference between someone who is ***converted*** in the name of Jesus Christ and someone who is a **disciple** of Christ. In Acts 11:26b, it is written: "...The disciples were called Christians first at Antioch." If the disciples were called Christians in Antioch, it does not mean that all believers who identified themselves as Christians today are disciples. We shall be cautious not to make this incorrect assumption. I repeat: disciples are **made** not **born**.

Genuine Disciples

Shortly after Jesus began His mission on this earth, He selected twelve men. He discipled them in the secrets of God's Kingdom and appointed them to preach the gospel. One gospel writer recorded:

> And He went up on the mountain and summoned those whom He Himself wanted, and they came to Him. And He appointed twelve, so that they would be with Him and that He could send them out to preach, and to have authority to cast out the demons. (Mark 3:13–15)

Jesus wants us to be with Him (Mark 3:14), to spend time with Him (1 Corinthians 1:9), and to know Him intimately (John 17:3, Philippians 3:10). **This is essential in discipleship.** This is the way Jesus started His discipleship ministry. The word disciple comes from the Latin word *"discipulus,"* and the Greek word *"mathetes."* In essence, it means a student who studies at the feet of a teacher or a follower of a religious movement. Cambridge English Dictionary defines disciples as follows: "a person who believes in the ideas of a leader, especially a religious or political one, and tries to live according to those ideas."[38] Previous definitions do not give us the full meaning of a disciple. I like the definition given by Spiros Zodhiates, a Greek Bible scholar and editor of the "Hebrew-Greek Key Word Study Bible." According to Zodhiates, *mathetes* means: "more than a mere pupil or learner. It means an adherer who accepts the instruction given to him and makes it his rule of conduct."[39] The "International Standard Bible Encyclopedia provides another good definition." It describes the disciple of Christ as "one who believes His doctrines, rests upon His sacrifice, imbibes His spirit, and imitates His example."[40]

When I put my heart into digging deeper into the theme of discipleship, I found it interesting that the concept of disciple-mentor is also present in the Old Testament. For the first time in the Bible, the word **follower** is found in Isaiah 8:16: "Bind up the testimony, seal the law among my disciples." Furthermore, in Isaiah 54:13, the Bible tells us: "All your sons will be taught of the LORD; and the well-being of your sons will be great." Isn't it amazing that Isaiah, prophesized that God's children will be taught of the LORD? In Isaiah, there is a more direct reference regarding disciples: "The Lord GOD has given Me the tongue of disciples, that I may know how to sustain the weary one with a word. He awakens Me morning by morning, He awakens My ear to listen as a disciple" (Isaiah 50:4). I realized that the process of discipleship implies a *willing mind,* a *listening ear,* and an *obedient heart.*

The Lord Jesus did not write any books with His hand, but during the three and a half years of ministry He "wrote" in the hearts of His disciples. His "writing" left deep marks within their souls for the rest of their lives, to the point of dying for Christ. This is amazing! This is the most significant testimony for the process of discipleship. Our Lord left us only one method through which we shall influence the whole world, all generations, all cultures, and all ethnic groups. This method is discipleship. **Discipleship is Jesus' Plan A**. Christ did not leave us any other way.

A disciple of Christ is a person called to know Jesus, to follow Him, and to make disciples of all ethnic groups. In the process of knowing Christ intimately, the Holy Spirit transforms us more and more into His likeness (2 Corinthians 3:18). As we grow in discipleship, our thinking, feeling, and living are progressively changed to look more like Christ's.

Discipleship is an intentional relationship in which a more mature disciple—spiritual mentor, walks alongside another believer—disciple, encouraging him or her to walk in love, to grow toward maturity in Christ, and equipping him or her to teach others as well. I cannot stress this enough: *The process of discipleship is non-effective unless it's personal.*

Multiplication

Discipleship—disciples making disciples, is the correct method of spiritual reproduction. The process of multiplication, at least at the beginning, is slower than the process of addition. For example, a skilled evangelist could help the conversion of 1,000 persons a day. That is a lot! In one year, he could convert 365,000 persons. What a great work! This is wonderful!

I cannot stress this enough: *The process of discipleship is non-effective unless it's personal.*

On the other hand, the work of a skilled spiritual mentor may assist one person per year to become a more mature disciple. The new disciple was thought to do the same as his mentor—to disciple others. This is an extraordinary thing! However, there is no comparison between mentorship and evangelism. There is a vast difference between one person vs. 365,000 people. Keep in mind that at the end of the first year, two people can disciple others. At the end of the second year, there are four more disciple makers. If we do the math, it will take twenty-four years of the ministry of discipleship to match the results of the ministry of evangelism. However, after the twenty-fourth year and onward, the ministry of discipleship takes off exponentially and surpasses the ministry of discipleship. Isn't it amazing? Image what would happen in the world if the church would reset her strategy in such a way that any soul saved through any form of evangelism would immediately go through a proper process of Christian discipleship? Literally, in thirty to forty years, the entire world could be evangelized, and all converts of local churches could be discipled. Think about what the result of this would be. **Christ would have to return**. This is huge! Here is His promise: "This gospel of the kingdom shall be preached in the whole world as a testimony to all the nations, and then the end will come" (Matthew 24:14). Dear reader, if we take the concept of discipleship to heart, the **end** promised by our Lord, could happen in our generation. Is this possible? Yes, it is. The church can speed up the return of Jesus.

Peter urges all of us:

> Since all these things are to be destroyed in this way, what sort of people ought you to be in holy conduct and godliness, looking for and **hastening the coming of the day of God**, because of which the heavens will be destroyed by burning, and the elements will melt with intense heat! (2 Peter 3:11–12)

I know that it is hard to believe, but it is true. Do the math, and you will see it. Let me try to illustrate how quickly exponential sequences grow. Let's consider a simple exercise. Imagine that you are in front of a chessboard. Rice grains are placed upon each square—doubling the number of grains on each subsequent square: one grain on the first square, two grains on the second, four on the third, until the 64th square. May I ask you something? How many grains of rice do you think would be on the chessboard in the end? The total number of grains equals: 18,446,744,073,709,551,615. Unbelievable! This is sufficient to cover the whole territory of India with a meter-thick layer of rice.[41] It is hard to believe, but it is true. The spiritual meaning of this illustration is enormous.

Jesus tells us:

> Truly, truly, I say to you, unless a grain of wheat falls into the earth and dies, it remains alone; but if it dies, it bears much fruit. (John 12:24)

Let's consider another example from finances. Imagine that a wealthy business owner wants to hire you for one year and makes you an offer. The entrepreneur asks you: "Would you rather be paid one million dollars in a lump sum or one penny which doubles every day of a month for a year?" Which options would you be tempted to accept? One million dollars? Or one penny which doubles every day for a year? Well, because of the power of the compounded interest, the second option results in an astronomical amount.

I hope I made the point clear that there is a massive difference between the two ministries. The ministry of evangelism is just addition. The ministry of discipleship is actual multiplication, leading to exponential growth.

The View on Discipleship of a Few Well-Known People

Apostle Paul

The great apostle Paul held a correct view of God's work; he took discipleship seriously. When he arrived in Ephesus, the apostle preached the kingdom of God. Then, because of opposition from the Jews, he took the believers and discipled them in the school of Tyrannus. The impact of his ministry was significant. In two years, "all who lived in Asia heard the word of the Lord, both Jews and Greeks" (Acts 19:10). Wow! Towards the end of his life, Paul instructed his spiritual son—Timothy, to put into practice the ministry of Christian discipleship.

He wrote:

> You, therefore, my son, be strong in the grace that is in Christ Jesus. The things which you have heard from

> me in the presence of many witnesses, entrust these to faithful men who will be able to teach others also. (2 Timothy 2:1–2)

Please observe the exponential multiplication:

– Paul,
– Timothy,
– Faithful men, and others.

Apply this to the illustration with the grain of rice and the chessboard. This is the only way we can explain the fact that in the first three centuries, the church reached with the gospel the entire population of the Roman Empire.

Billy Graham

In an exclusive interview by *Christianity Today* (Vol. III, No. 1, October 13 1985, pg. 5) evangelist, Billy Graham was asked:

> If you were a pastor of a large church in a principal city, what would be your plan of action?" Mr. Graham replied: "I think one of the first things I would do I would be to get a small group of eight or ten or twelve men around me that would meet a few hours a week and pay the price! It would cost them something in time and effort. I would share with them everything I have, over a period of years. Then I would actually have twelve ministers among the laymen who in turn could take eight or ten or twelve more and teach them. I know one or two churches that are doing that, and it is revolutionizing the church. Christ, I think, set the pattern. He didn't spend it with a great crowd. In fact, every time He had a great crowd, it seems to me that there weren't too many results. The great results, it seems to me, came in His personal interview, and in the time He spent with His twelve.[42]

Mr. Graham is echoing the wisdom of Jesus' method—*Christian discipleship*. We all can agree that Billy Graham, even though he was not involved directly in discipleship, had a considerable impact on the Kingdom of God.

Robert Coleman

Robert Coleman, former Professor of Evangelism at Trinity College, once said the following:

> This is our problem of methodology today. Well intended ceremonies, programs, organizations, commissions, and crusades of human ingenuity are trying valiantly to do a job that only can be done by men in the power of the Holy Spirit. **This is not to depreciate these noble efforts, for without them the church could not function as she does.**
> Nevertheless, unless the personal mission of the Master is vitally incorporated into the policy and fabric of all these plans, the Church cannot function as she should.
> When will we realize that evangelism is not done by something, but by someone. It is an expression of **God's love**, and God is a Person. His nature, being personal, is only expressed through personality, first revealed fully in Christ, and now expressed through His Spirit in the lives of those yielded to Him…
> This is the new evangelism we need. It is not better methods, but better men—men who know their Redeemer from something more than hearsay—men who see His vision and feel His passion for the world—men who are willing to be no nothing in order that He might be everything—men who want only for Christ to produce **His life** in and through them according to His own good pleasure.[43]

In fact, what Professor Coleman recommends is nothing more than the method of—*Christian discipleship.*

Difficulties of Christian Discipleship

I am inviting you to put this book down, pick up the Bible, and read Luke 9:57–62. In this passage, there are three aspects which are evident when discussing the difficulties of Christian discipleship. Let's take a look at them.

1. The security of the disciple

A disciple of Christ should not have security in the material possessions offered by this world but in a personal relationship with Jesus.

In Luke 9:57, we read: "A man said to the Lord Jesus: "*I will follow you wherever you go.*" In other words, this man promises: "Anywhere You send me, I will obey Your calling." This sounds pretty impressive. But let's listen carefully how Jesus' answered: "Jesus replied to the man: "Foxes have holes and birds of the air have nests, but the Son of Man has no place to lay His head" (Luke 9:58). Even some holes in the ground represent a stable shelter for the foxes. Several wood branches primitively assembled and cushioned with some dead grass and feathers constitute a stable place for the birds. Does the Lord Jesus demand His disciples to be poor and without a shelter? Does He require Christians not to seek a good education? Is Christ asking us not to pursue a good job? Of course not. However, He requires us not to put our trust in the things of this world, and not to chase desperately after worldly wealth. Matthew writes: "No one can serve two masters; for either he will hate the one and love the other, or he will be devoted to one and despise the other. You cannot serve God and wealth" (Matthew 6:24). Paul also writes: "For it is we who are the circumcision, we who worship by the Spirit of God, who glory in Christ Jesus, and who put no confidence in the flesh" (Philippians 3:3).

2. The inheritance of the disciple

Spreading the Kingdom of God is worth more than the inheritance from our parents

Luke records: "But the man replied, "Lord, first let me go and bury my father" (Luke 9:59). We can say that the noblest obligation we have as children is to take care of our parents when they get old and offer them a decent burial. Is Jesus against such a thing? No, not at all. Then, what is He saying in this passage? We must understand that in the culture of the New Testament, the son that buried his father inherited the most of his father's wealth. We can deduct that this man wanted to get the best of both worlds: follow Christ and get his father's wealth. The answer he received from Jesus appears harsh: "Let the dead bury their own dead, but you go and proclaim the kingdom of God" (Luke 9:60). What Jesus meant was: "Leave your inheritance to those who are also as dead as your father." At first, it seems a hard replay, but now that we understand the context, the Lord Jesus was right. He knows better what is truly in the hearts of people.

3. The highest priority of the disciple

Following Christ implies that the Kingdom of God deserves maximum priority

Moreover, Luke writes: "Still another said, "I will follow you, Lord; but first let me go back and say good-bye to my family" (Luke 9:61). Please observe that this man promises Jesus: "I will follow You, Lord; but..."—which means—"I will follow you sometime in the future, but not immediately." This verse states the man's priority: "...first let me..."—which means that his number one priority right now is something else, not the Kingdom of God.

Similarly, our priorities could be:

- First, let me get married, then I will consider discipleship.
- First, let me finish my studies at the university, then I will focus on God's Kingdom.
- First, allow me to marry my children, then I will have more time for Jesus.
- First, let me grow the business I just started, then I will serve Christ.
- Let me retire first, and then I will follow Jesus and focus on God's Kingdom.
- First let me resolve problem X, Y, and Z, and after I put out these fires, then I will dedicate my life to Christ.

Jesus answered: "No one who puts his hand to the plow and

looks back is fit for service in the kingdom of God" (Luke 9:62). It is clear that the Lord Jesus Christ is categorical when it comes to our loyalty to Him. He wants our whole heart, our full devotion. We cannot serve the world and the Kingdom of God. We cannot serve God and strive to acquire wealth. (See Matthew 6:24).

I hope we can see clearly that the real crisis today is not of energy, or gasoline, or food, or water, or clean air. The real crisis today is of truly consecrated disciples of Christ who genuinely and intimately know Jesus, who are ready to die for Him and for the cause of the Great Commission, who, like the first disciples, are prepared to turn this world upside down (Acts 17:6). Then it is only legitimate to ask ourselves the following heart-probing questions.

If we are sincere with ourselves, the answer to these questions may indicate whether we are indeed disciples of Christ. Let's pray that the contemporary church will take The Great Commission at its face value. Let's hope that it will stop limiting herself to just converting people, but indeed the church will continue with a reliable process of discipleship and spiritual formation of all born-again believers. Of course, only the future would prove if Christians living in the contemporary culture would accept Christ's calling (Luke 9:23), and His demands of discipleship (Luke 9:57–62). My prayer is that they would.

Discussion Questions:

– After reading this chapter has your answer to the questions asked after chapter 1 changed?

– Are you a disciple of Christ? Who is your "Paul"? Who is your "Timothy"?

– Whose *life* are you fighting for? Whose *character* are you reflecting? Whose *name* are you protecting? Whose *kingdom* are you sacrificing for? Are you secretly, building your *little kingdoms*?

– Are you ready to accept Christ's calling and His terms of Christian discipleship? If not, why not? Please elaborate.

– Are you prepared to relinquish everything for the love of Jesus? If not, why not? Please elaborate.

– What are the most significant barriers that prevent you from being His consecrated follower?

Notes

2. Discipleship—The Greatest Need of the Church Today

[34] The Marine Corps motto. Accessed on April 15, 2019. https://www.military.com/marine-corps-birthday/the-marine-corps-motto.html.
[35] A. W. Tozer, *The Old Cross and the New*, Compiled by Anita M. Bailey, *Man: The Dwelling Place of God.* (Camp Hill, Pennsylvania: Christian Publications, 1966), 43–44.
[36] Jim Elliot, *Journal.* Note: This can be found in the October 28, 1949 entry on page 174 (Chapter 4) of the 1978 hardback edition of the Journal and on page 108 (Chapter 11) of the 1958 hardback edition of Shadow of the Almighty. The quote is also used in the prologue of Shadow on page 15. Accessed on October 12, 2018. https://www2.wheaton.edu/bgc/archives/faq/20.htm. As a side note: several years after this entry, on January 8, 1956, Jim Elliot and four other missionaries were martyred in Ecuador.
[37] Walter A. Henrichsen, Disciples are Made, Not Born, (Victor, Cook Communications, Colorado Springs, CO, 1988), 33–34.
[38] Disciple. Accessed on October 11, 2018. https://dictionary.cambridge.org/us/dictionary/english/disciple.
[39] *Mathetes.* Spiros Zodhiates, *The Complete Word Study Dictionary: New Testament*, (AMG International, Chattanooga, TN, 37422, 1993).
[40] *International Standard Bible Encyclopedia*, (1998). PC Study Bible (Version 3.0). Computer Software. USA: Biblesoft.
[41] *Exponential Growth and the Legend of Paal Paysam.* Accessed on April 11, 2019. http://www.singularitysymposium.com/exponential-growth.html.
[42] Robert E. Coleman, *The Master Plan of Evangelism*, (Fleming H. Revell Co., Old Tappan, NJ, 1972), 119–120.
[43] Coleman, 112–114.

CHAPTER 3

Three Kinds of Disciples—Part One

It is enough for the disciple that he become like his teacher, and the slave like his master.

— Matthew 10:25a

Years ago, I prepared a teaching series on discipleship. As I was reading from the Gospel of Mark, something interesting happened. When I got to Mark 2:18: "Why do John's disciples and the disciples of the Pharisees fast, but Your disciples do not fast?" the light came on. Reading it, I realized that during the times of Jesus, there were three kinds of disciples. The categories are spelled out in that verse.

Who were the prominent disciples during the time of Jesus? According to the four gospels, the primary disciples during the life of Jesus and the apostles were:

A. The disciples of the Pharisees
B. The disciples of John the Baptist
C. The disciples of Jesus

Since "there is nothing new under the sun" (cf. Ecclesiastes 1:9), these kinds of disciples who were present in the synagogues during Jesus' ministry, are present in the Christian assemblies today. As I meditated on these things, a thought crossed my mind:

> Wow! We can benefit significantly if we study their characteristics. Each category of "disciples" is based on a specific ideology, therefore knowing their particularities enable us to assess where we are in our spiritual journey.

I knew right away that the Holy Spirit was leading me in this direction. I followed His lead. In the following paragraphs, I want to share with you my findings. Let's look briefly at the three categories of disciples from Jesus' time.

A. The disciples of the Pharisees

Who were these people? Well… they were the most pious Jews living in that era. According to the "Vine's Complete Expository Dictionary of Old and New Testament Words" the word Pharisee, derives from Greek Φαρισαῖος (Strong's Greek Lexicon Number G5330), and from an Aramaic word *peras* (found in Daniel 5:28), signifying "to separate," owing to a different manner of life from that of the general public.

> In their zeal for the Law they almost deified it, and their attitude became merely external, formal, and mechanical. They laid stress, not upon the righteousness of an action, but upon its formal correctness. Consequently, their opposition to Christ was inevitable; His manner of life and teaching was essentially a condemnation of theirs; hence His denunciation of them, e.g., Matthew 6:2, Matthew 6:5, Matthew 6:16; Matthew 15:7 and chapter 23.[44]

From whom did the Pharisees separate? The Bible provides enough light on this topic. The word "Pharisees," appears almost 90 times in the Gospels. These individuals were determined to avoid, or to separate themselves, "from any type of impurity proscribed by the Levitical Law—or, more specifically, their strict interpretation of it."[45] No wonder they were infuriated every time they saw Jesus interacting with the tax collectors and the sinners. Try to imagine how insulted they felt when Jesus said to them: "Truly I say to you that the tax collectors and prostitutes will get into the kingdom of God before you" (Matthew 21:31). I understand why Saul of Tarsus, who was one of them, in his zeal, wanted to exterminate all followers of Christ.

What verse do you think describes more accurately the life of the Pharisees? I would probably choose Matthew 23:26: "You blind Pharisee, first clean the inside of the cup and of the dish, so that the outside of it may become clean also." Jesus applies to them the words prophesied by Isaiah, "Because this people draw near with their words and honor Me with their lip service, but they remove their hearts far from Me, and their reverence for Me consists of tradition learned by rote" (Isaiah 29:13). What an accurate description of the Pharisees and their disciples.

Now, let's look at some specific characteristics of the Pharisees and their disciples.

1. The Pharisees and their disciples formed their traditions.

There are about 613 commandments in the Old Testament. However, during the latter part of the Second Temple period (515 and on), the Pharisees added more restrictions to many of the original commandments.

According to My Jewish Learning.com:

> Traditionally, Jews are required to wash their hands and say a blessing before eating any meal that includes bread or matzah… Some passages in the Talmud indicate that failing to wash hands before a meal is a significant transgression… Upon returning from a Cemetery, this practice (washing) has various reasons attached, among them the need to remove evil spirits associated with burial grounds and a desire to establish a symbolic boundary between the living and the dead.[46]

Mark states:

> For the Pharisees and all the Jews do not eat unless

> they carefully wash their hands, thus observing the traditions of the elders; and when they come from the market place, they do not eat unless they cleanse themselves; and there are many other things which they have received in order to observe, such as the washing of cups and pitchers and copper pots. (Mark 7:3–4)

Christ and His disciples ran into many religious conflicts with the Pharisees. For example, when the disciples did not ceremonially wash their hands before eating bread, the Pharisees were very upset. Mark writes: "The Pharisees and the scribes asked Him, "Why do Your disciples not walk according to the tradition of the elders, but eat their bread with impure hands?" (Mark 7:5). Was Jesus against washing hands, or being clean, or taking good care of the body? Of course not. However, when the religious people, like the Pharisees, place their human-originated traditions above the Word of God, the Lord is undoubtedly displeased. Jesus did not let this pass. He sharply confronted the Pharisees.

Mark writes:

> And He said to them, "Rightly did Isaiah prophesy of you hypocrites, as it is written: 'This people honors Me with their lips, but their heart is far away from Me. But in vain do they worship Me, teaching as doctrines the precepts of men"' Neglecting the commandment of God, you hold to the tradition of men. He was also saying to them, "You are experts at setting aside the commandment of God in order to keep your tradition." (Mark 7:6–9)

Saul of Tarsus learned at the feet of Gamaliel—a very well know Pharisee. After his conversion, he became Paul, the apostle. He knew very well the danger of their traditions. In one of his letters he warned the church in Colossae about this danger: "See to it that no one takes you captive through philosophy and empty deception, according to the tradition of men, according to the elementary principles of the world, rather than according to Christ" (Colossians 2:8).

Furthermore:

> Therefore no one is to act as your judge in regard to food or drink or in respect to a festival or a new moon or a Sabbath day—things which are a mere shadow of what is to come; but the substance belongs to Christ. (Colossians 2:16–17)

2. The Pharisees and their disciples focus on the externals according to their interpretation of the Law

The Pharisees became so absorbed with the outer part of the requirements stipulated in the Pentateuch, that they completely dismissed the more profound and more important requirements of God: *justice* and *mercy* and *faithfulness.* Because of this gross misinterpretation of the Law of Moses, the Lord Jesus rebuked them severely! Matthew writes: "Woe to you, scribes and Pharisees, hypocrites! For you tithe mint and dill and cumin, and have neglected the weightier provisions of the Law: *justice* and *mercy* and *faithfulness*; but these are the things you should have done without neglecting the others" (Matthew 23:23). To convey His point, the Lord reminded them of what Micah said to the people of his generation: "He has told you, O man, what is good; and what does the LORD require of you but to do justice, to love kindness, and to walk humbly with your God?" (Micah 6:8).

3. The Pharisees and their disciples hold high to the letter of the Law, but they do not believe it

The Pharisees and their disciples, who were able to quote the Law very well, required other people to conform to many things, but, (cf. Matthew 23:1–7) they did not believe in the Law nor fulfilled it. This was the main reason why Jesus rebuked them and told them directly, "So you, too, outwardly appear righteous to men, but inwardly you are full of hypocrisy and lawlessness" (Matthew 23:28). No doubt about, these are pretty harsh words. However, let's be assured that Christ did not hate them. To the contrary, He told them these things because He loved them, wanted them to repent and believe in Him. However, we know the history; most of them neither repented nor believed in Him; instead, they condemned Him to die by crucifixion.

4. The Pharisees and their disciples are proud people

Their lack of humility is evident because they sought the "chief seats in the synagogues and places of honor at banquets" (Mark 12:39, Matthew 23:6–7). They wanted to be noticed in public places, so they wore long robes. Moreover, they "like to hear respectful greetings in the marketplaces" (Mark 12:38). The Pharisees and their disciples appear so pious and spiritual. To maintain their image, they were offering long prayers "for appearance's sake" to impress people with their polished spirituality. All of this is leading to a greater condemnation (Mark 12:40).

5. The Pharisees and their disciples have just a form of godliness but are denying its power

Outward religion is very detrimental to the human soul. The apostle Paul warned Timothy about the perilous times in the last days. If that was true in Timothy's generation, how much more it is true today. These kinds of disciples were present among Christians back then, and they are present in our churches today. The Pharisees and their disciples, despite their consistent learning, they never "come to the knowledge of the truth" (2 Timothy 3:7).

Outward religion is very detrimental to the human soul.

Moreover, in his letter to Titus, Paul writes:

> For there are many rebellious men, empty talkers, and deceivers, especially those of the circumcision, who must be silenced because they are upsetting whole families, teaching things they should not teach for the

> sake of sordid gain. (Titus 1:10–11)

With this type of individuals, one cannot just be nice and hope they will get the point. O, no. Paul instructs Titus to "reprove them severely" for them to repent and "be sound in faith" (Titus 1:13).

The five "woes" Jesus told the Pharisees

After surveying the religious state of the Pharisees and their associates, Jesus gave them several severe warning or woes. Let's look briefly at five of the warnings.

1. Woe number one: The Pharisees and their disciples, due to their stubbornness, will not enter into the Kingdom of God

Matthew tells us: "But woe to you, scribes and Pharisees, hypocrites, because you shut off the kingdom of heaven from people; for you do not enter in yourselves, nor do you allow those who are entering to go in" (Matthew 23:13). After a religious tradition is established, its leaders fight hard to keep people under their control. With one occasion, the chief priests and the Pharisees assembled a council to discuss regarding Jesus and His ministry. Their concern was not for the spiritual well-being of people. They were worried about their position of leadership and privileged status in society under the Roman rule. The Pharisees didn't want to lose their comfortable positions of religious leadership.

John writes:

> Therefore the chief priests and the Pharisees convened a council, and were saying, "What are we doing? For this man is performing many signs. If we let Him go on like this, all men will believe in Him, and the Romans will come and take away both our place and our nation." (John 11:47–48)

Jesus, who was about to die for the people, knew their hidden motivation and warned them directly about the danger they were in and the negative influence they had on people.

2. Woe number two: The Pharisees and their disciples will receive a greater condemnation

God loves everybody. David writes: “Praise the LORD! Oh give thanks to the LORD, for He is good; For His lovingkindness is everlasting” (Psalm 106:1). However, God is a just Judge too. When people who know the Law, keep resisting His invitation to repent, they cannot avoid His judgment. The Psalmist writes: “Say among the nations, “The LORD reigns; Indeed, the world is firmly established, it will not be moved; He will judge the peoples with equity”” (Psalm 96:10). Please make no mistake; if people will turn back from their evil ways, and come to Christ to save them, God will judge them accordingly. Jesus said: “He who believes in Him is not judged; he who does not believe has been judged already, because he has not believed in the name of the only begotten Son of God” (John 3:18). There is no sin too great that the blood of Jesus cannot wash away! The greatest sin is not adultery, stealing, homosexuality, or even murder. The greatest sin is the sin of unbelief in the Son of God, the only One capable to save.

After Jesus healed the blind man from birth, He said something of crucial importance: “For judgment, I came into this world, so that those who do not see may see, and that those who see may become blind” (John 9:39). The Pharisees who were around asked Jesus: “We are not blind too, are we?” (John 9:40). The answer Jesus gave them is critical: “If you were blind, you would have no sin; but since you say, “We see,” your sin remains” (John 9:41). Do you see this? They saw a miracle that was never done before—a blind man from birth received his complete sight, meaning that the nervous structure of the brain responsible for the vision function was completely recreated. Despite all of this, they still did not believe. That is the reason why the Pharisees will receive a greater condemnation.

3. Woe number three: The result of their proselytism is twice as bad as the Pharisees themselves

To me, this is the most depressive aspect of all the woe's Jesus told them. Christ pointed to them: "Woe to you, scribes and Pharisees, hypocrites, because you travel around on sea and land to make one proselyte; and when he becomes one, you make him twice as much a son of hell as yourselves" (Matthew 23:15). Imagine that. All that effort. All the expenses in the process of discipleship. And for what? A son of hell. Wow! What a waste of resources.

4. Woe number four. The Pharisees and their disciples practice a formal religion which does not lead to a real transformation of the heart

This is a hard thing to swallow. Imagine a person who is consumed with the outside appearance, but who pays no attention whatsoever at what is going on inside, in his or her heart. That is precisely how the Pharisees conducted their entire lives. There is no liberty or joy in his kind of life.

Jesus addressed them severely:

> Woe to you, scribes and Pharisees, hypocrites! For you clean the outside of the cup and of the dish, but inside they are full of robbery and self-indulgence. You blind Pharisee, first clean the inside of the cup and of the dish, so that the outside of it may become clean also. Woe to you, scribes and Pharisees, hypocrites! For you are like whitewashed tombs which on the outside appear beautiful, but inside they are full of dead men's bones and all uncleanness. So you, too, outwardly appear righteous to men, but inwardly you are full of hypocrisy and lawlessness. (Matthew 23:25–28)

5. Woe number five: Their philanthropic acts and outside religious deeds will not save the Pharisees and their disciples from final damnation

It is hard for us to explain how something like this is even possible. How come outside religious deeds will not save them? Only God knows the hearts of people and their motivation.

Jesus told the Pharisees:

> Woe to you, scribes and Pharisees, hypocrites! For you build the tombs of the prophets and adorn the monuments of the righteous, and say, 'If we had been living in the days of our fathers, we would not have been partners with them in shedding the blood of the prophets." "So you testify against yourselves, that you are sons of those who murdered the prophets. Fill up, then, the measure of the guilt of your fathers." You serpents, you brood of vipers, how will you escape the sentence of hell? (Matthew 23:29–33)

Conclusion

We talked a lot about the Pharisees and their disciples. What have we learned? What is the main lesson here? What is the main conclusion? Most importantly, what did Jesus tell His disciples? What is His warning? The Lord Jesus (cf. Matthew 16:6) expressly told His disciples to "Watch out and beware of the leaven of the Pharisees and Sadducees." At first, the disciples did not know what He was talking about. They thought Jesus is saying that because they forgot to buy bread for the journey. Then Lord reminded them about the "miracle of the five loaves and two fish." Finally, the bulb came on. They realized that Jesus was telling them to watch out and beware "of the teaching of the Pharisees and Sadducees" (Matthew 16:12).

Christ's recommendation is for all of us. I urge you to keep in mind the main characteristics we discussed about in this chapter so we can be able to spot the teaching of the Pharisees and Sadducees from 100 miles away.

Discussion Questions:

– After reading this chapter what concept or idea stood out in your mind?

– Were you surprised that during the time of Jesus there were primarily three kinds of disciples?

– What verse do you think describes most accurately the life of the Pharisees?

– Read Matthew 23. Do you think that Jesus was too harsh with the Pharisees?

– Do you feel that observing a certain tradition is more important that having an intimate relationship with Christ? Please elaborate.

– What is your opinion about discipleship in general? Do you think that your local church is doing a pretty good job in promoting discipleship? Please elaborate.

Notes

3. Three Kinds of Disciples—Part One

[44] W.E. Vine, *Vine's Complete Expository Dictionary of Old and New Testament Words*, (Nashville, TN, Thomas Nelson Publishers, 1996), 470.
[45] *Pharisees*. Accessed on June 24, 2019. https://www.biblestudytools.com/dictionaries/bakers-evangelical-dictionary/pharisees.html.
[46] *Ritual Hand Washing Before Meals*, myjewishlearning.com. https://www.myjewishlearning.com/article/hand-washing/. Accessed on July 1, 2019).

CHAPTER 4

Three Kinds of Disciples—Part Two

The Law and the Prophets were proclaimed until John; since that time the gospel of the kingdom of God has been preached, and everyone is forcing his way into it.
— Luke 16:16

As I shared previously, while I was preparing a teaching series on discipleship, I realized that during the times of Jesus, there were three kinds of disciples:

A. The disciples of the Pharisees
B. The disciples of John the Baptist
C. The disciples of Jesus

These kinds of disciples who were present in the synagogues during Jesus' ministry are present among Christians today. I am strongly suggesting studying their characteristics so we know how to evaluate our spiritual walk.

In the previous chapter, we discussed the Pharisees and their disciples. In this section, we are going to learn about the disciples of John the Baptist.

B. The disciples of John the Baptist

Anybody who reads the gospels will discover this unique Bible hero—John the Baptist. Luke introduces him in the first chapter of his gospel. Before the birth of Jesus, there was a family of devout people, "a priest named Zacharias, of the division of Abijah; and he had a wife from the daughters of Aaron, and her name was Elizabeth" (Luke 1:5). They were advanced in years and had no children. In that culture, unlike ours, to be childless was a disgrace among people. It appears that they had been praying for a baby for a long time, but so far, nothing had happened. However, when God's timing comes, nothing can prevent His plans. When Zechariah performed his priestly service in the Temple, an angel appeared and told him that God heard their prayers and granted their request for a child. Not only that, but this child was going be the greatest prophet of the Old Testament—the forerunner before Christ, operating in the spirit and power of Elijah (cf. Luke 1:17). With John the Baptist, the legacy of the old covenant prophets would end, and a new era of the work of the Holy Spirit in the lives and hearts of people would be ushered in. The angel quoted Malachi 4:5, the last words of the Old Testament.

Luke writes:

> But the angel said to him, "Do not be afraid, Zacharias, for your petition has been heard, and your wife Elizabeth will bear you a son, and you will give him the name John. You will have joy and gladness, and many will rejoice at his birth. For he will be great in the sight of the Lord; and he will drink no wine or liquor, and he will be filled with the Holy Spirit while yet in his mother's womb. And he will turn many of the sons of Israel back to the Lord their God. It is he who will go as a forerunner before Him in the spirit and power of Elijah, TO TURN THE HEARTS OF THE FATHERS BACK TO THE CHILDREN, and the disobedient to the attitude of the righteous, so as to make ready a people prepared for the Lord." (Luke 1:13–17)

Even though this man got so many details about his future son, his human logic got the best of him. So as any rational male who knew his own natural state, blurted out, "I am an old man and my wife is advanced in years" and, having huge doubts about

God's promise, asked the angel, "How will I know this for certain?" (Luke 1:18). Zechariah learned very quickly that it is not a good idea to argue with God's messenger. Now the angel disclosed his identity, "I am Gabriel, who stands in the presence of God, and I have been sent to speak to you and to bring you this good news" (Luke 1:19). As a sign, Gabriel told him, "And behold, you shall be silent and unable to speak until the day when these things take place, because you did not believe my words, which will be fulfilled in their proper time" (Luke 1:20). Why? "For nothing will be impossible with God" (Luke 1:37).

Lo and behold, after Zechariah finished his priestly duties at Jerusalem, he went back home, and the rest is history.

Luke tells us what happened:

> After these days Elizabeth his wife became pregnant, and she kept herself in seclusion for five months, saying, "This is the way the Lord has dealt with me in the days when He looked with favor upon me, to take away my disgrace among men." (Luke 1:24–25)

The story of John the Baptist is essential because Elizabeth's pregnancy is connected to Mary's—the mother of Jesus. Luke told us that just about the sixth month of Elizabeth's pregnancy; Mary conceived Jesus by the Power of the Holy Spirit. (See Luke 1:24–27).

From "*God remember*" to "*God is gracious*"

God is faithful to all His promises. Not a single word which comes from God will ever fall to the ground. Nine months after these days, Elizabeth held in her arms a baby boy. People expected them to name him—Zechariah, after his father. But the parents had to obey the instructions of God, and to everybody's surprise, they named the boy—John. (See Luke 1:59–64).

Names are important in the Bible. They have special meanings and, many times, communicate deeper things of God. According to "Behind the Name," Zekharyah, menas "YAHWEH remembers". It comes from "zakhar" meaning "to remember" and "yah" referring to the Hebrew God.[47] On the other hand, according to the same source, John is the English form of Iohannes, from Latin and Ioannes, from Greek, derives from the Hebrew name "Yochanan" meaning "YAHWEH is gracious", from the roots "yo" referring to the Hebrew God and "chanan" meaning "to be gracious".[48] Amazing, isn't it? From "God remember" to "God is gracious." In His own economy of time and space, God remembered all His promises scattered all over the Old Testament writings, about sending His own grace incarnated in the Person of His only begotten Son—Jesus.

We must keep in mind that descendants of Aaron (cf. 1 Chronicles 24) have been divided, by Kind David, into 24 divisions or orders of priests. These divisions would rotate throughout the year serving two weeks annually. In addition to this, all of them had to help during major festivals. What is very interesting to me is that God knew exactly when the division of Abijah would serve in the Temple. This took place precisely six months before the incarnation of His only begotten Son. Aren't these little details interesting? I am fascinated by this!

From the *"old priesthood"* to the *"new priesthood"*

It wasn't uncommon during the Old Testament times for priests to minister also as prophets. Jeremiah, Ezekiel, and Zachariah, were part of priestly families. One aspect important to remember is that Zechariah was a descendant of Aaron, the High Priest. This fact places John in the important category of the Old Covenant priesthood. This has a huge spiritual significance! Once John the Baptist died, spiritually speaking, the Old Testament priesthood "died" or "ceased" to exist. In God's economy with the coming of His Son, a new priesthood—according to the order of Melchizedek replaced the old priesthood—according to the order of Aaron. These aspects are explained in the book of Hebrews. (See Hebrews 5:1, 6, 10, 6:20, 7:1, 17).

The Ministry of John the Baptist

To better understand the characteristics of the disciples of John the Baptist, we must know the crucial components of John's ministry.

1. John the Baptist prepared the way for the Lord Jesus and His messianic ministry

The essence of John's message was *repentance*. Matthew tells us: "Now in those days John the Baptist came, preaching in the wilderness of Judea, saying, "Repent, for the kingdom of heaven is at hand"" (Matthew 3:1–2). The gospel writer explains that this was the fulfillment of the words of Isiah, "The voice of one crying in the wilderness, "Make ready the way of the Lord, make His paths straight!"", spoken more than 700 years before Christ. **Repentance refers to man's responsibility before God.** It is directed towards people. In a nutshell, this was John's mission. God sent him to fulfill several prophecies from the Old Testament, such us: Isaiah 40:1–5, Malachi 3:1, and 4:5–6.

In case you are curious, the exact words of Isaiah are:

> Comfort, O comfort My people," says your God. "Speak kindly to Jerusalem; and call out to her, that her warfare has ended, that her iniquity has been removed, That she has received of the LORD'S hand Double for all her sins." A voice is calling, "Clear the way for the LORD in the wilderness; Make smooth in the desert a highway for our God. Let every valley be lifted up, and every mountain and hill be made low; and let the rough ground become a plain, and the rugged terrain a broad valley; then the glory of the LORD will be revealed, And all flesh will see it together; for the mouth of the LORD has spoken. (Isaiah 40:1–5)

Wow! What a powerful promise! Beautiful and comforting words were coming from a loving God and Father! Jesus Himself confirms that John fulfilled the prophetic words delivered by Malachi in 3:1. "This is the one about whom it is written, "Behold, I sent My messenger ahead of you, who will prepare your way before You"" (Matthew 11:1).

2. John the Baptist introduces the act of water baptism

Everybody agrees that it was John the Baptist, who used water baptism as the central sacrament of his ministry. This is the reason why he is called the Baptist, not that he was a Baptist. The Baptist branch of Christianity was formed in the early 1600. According to Wikipedia, "Historians trace the earliest "Baptist" church to 1609 in Amsterdam, Dutch Republic with English Separatist John Smyth as its pastor."[49]During his ministry, John the Baptist was very cautious not to attract people towards himself, but to point them to the Lamb of God (John 1:36). Matthew writes: "As for me, I baptize you with water for repentance, but He who is coming after me is mightier than I, and I am not fit to remove His sandals; He will baptize you with the Holy Spirit and fire" (Matthew 3:11).

3. John the Baptist preached clearly about the necessity of the baptism with the Holy Spirit

As the forerunner of Christ, John the Baptist explicitly told his followers the huge difference between his ministry and Christ's: "I baptize you with water for repentance" vs. "He will baptize you with the Holy Spirit and fire." This detail has a tremendous importance in the life of the Church; therefore, all gospels include it:

> As for me, I baptize you with water for repentance, but He who is coming after me is mightier than I, and I am not fit to remove His sandals; He will baptize you with the Holy Spirit and fire. (Matthew 3:11)
>
> I baptized you with water; but He will baptize you with the Holy Spirit. (Mark 1:8)

John answered and said to them all, "As for me, I baptize you with water; but One is coming who is mightier than I, and I am not fit to untie the thong of His sandals; He will baptize you with the Holy Spirit and fire." (Luke 3:16)

John answered them saying:

> I baptize in water, but among you stands One whom you do not know... I did not recognize Him, but He who sent me to baptize in water said to me, 'He upon whom you see the Spirit descending and remaining upon Him, this is the One who baptizes in the Holy Spirit.'" (John 1:26, 33)

Let's never forget this detail.

4. John the Baptist proclaimed the supremacy of Christ and His ministry

The ministry of John the Baptist spread like wildfire throughout Judea and attracted multitudes of people to the Jordan River where he was baptizing people. This triggered a lot of concern with the religious leaders of that day. A lot of scrutiny took place. In the Gospel of John, we read:

> This is the testimony of John, when the Jews sent to him priests and Levites from Jerusalem to ask him, "Who are you?" And he confessed and did not deny, but confessed, "I am not the Christ." They asked him, "What then? Are you Elijah?" And he said, "I am not." "Are you the Prophet?" And he answered, "No." Then they said to him, "Who are you, so that we may give an answer to those who sent us? What do you say about yourself?" He said, "I am a voice of one crying in the wilderness, "Make straight the way of the Lord," as Isaiah the prophet said." (John 1:19–23)

John was just a voice in the wilderness. He did not want to take any credit. He told everybody that the real "Deal"—Christ, will come shortly to start His unique and incredible ministry. Jesus is the One who stated: "The Law and the Prophets were proclaimed until John; since that time the gospel of the kingdom of God has been preached, and everyone is forcing his way into it" (Luke 16:16). In other words, the work and the ministry of John the Baptist were just preparatory for the ministry Christ, and His work of salvation, reconciliation, and regeneration, as some of the prophets foretold. I like the way Peter explain this paradox.

He writes:

> As to this salvation, the prophets who prophesied of the grace that would come to you made careful searches and inquiries, seeking to know what person or time the Spirit of Christ within them was indicating as He predicted the sufferings of Christ and the glories to follow. It was revealed to them that they were not serving themselves, but you, in these things which now have been announced to you through those who preached the gospel to you by the Holy Spirit sent from heaven—things into which angels long to look. (1 Peter 1:10–12)

God never intended the work and ministry of John the Baptist to become a movement and his teaching a doctrine in itself. The Lord didn't envision John's disciples continuing; instead, they will would become disciples of Christ, according to the Great Commission. I am pretty sure that John the Baptist did not want his legacy to continue. As soon as the real deal was in town, the prophet's desire was to decrease so Christ could increase.

The gospel of John, tells us:

> You yourselves are my witnesses that I said, "I am not the Christ," but, "I have been sent ahead of Him." He who has the bride is the bridegroom; but the friend of the bridegroom, who stands and hears him, rejoices greatly because of the bridegroom's voice. So this joy of mine has been made full. "He must increase, but I must decrease." (John 3:28–30)

Beautiful, isn't it?

5. John the Baptist has some doubts about Jesus

John was six months older than his cousin-Jesus. His ministry probably started no more than six months before Jesus began His ministry. Shortly after the baptism of Jesus, John the Baptist was arrested and beheaded at the commandment of Herod Antipas. While in prison awaiting his death, John inquired about Jesus. He sent some of his disciples to ask Jesus directly if He is the One. Matthew writes: "Are You the Expected One, or shall we look for someone else?" (Matthew 11:3).

Even though towards the end of his life, John the Baptist, had some doubts regarding Jesus, his mission was an extraordinary one. No wonder his disciples continue to exist abroad even today. Of course, they don't identify themselves as the disciples of John the Baptist, but they resemble many of his characteristics.

The disciples of John the Baptist

After the ascension of Christ, on the day of the Pentecost, the Holy Spirit fell on the one-hundred-twenty disciples gathered in the upper room. All of them were filled with the Spirit of God. This marks the birth of the New Testament church. Let's fast forward a couple of decades. The Church is expanding. The apostle Paul took the gospel to Asia Minor. During his second missionary journey, approximately 52 AD, Paul reached Ephesus—an important city on the western coast of Asia Minor (modern Turkey) and preached the gospel there. This time Paul remained there just a short time. He left his ministry associates, Aquila and Pricilla, to continue the work in that town.

To our surprise, the disciples of John the Baptist were already in Ephesus. As we can see the influence and the ministry of John spread around and traveled outside the borders of Judea. According to some sources, the straight-line distance between Jerusalem and Ephesus is 991 Km or 613.3 miles. The travel time to reach the city is approximately 37 hours and 44 minutes. Assuming that the Lord was crucified and rose again in 33 AD that means that after 20 years there were disciples of John the Baptist in Ephesus. In this city, Aquila and Pricilla met Apollo, a Jew born in Alexandria, "an eloquent man... mighty in the Scriptures" (Acts 18:24). Luke tells us that, "This man had been instructed in the way of the Lord; and being fervent in spirit, he was speaking and teaching accurately the things concerning Jesus, being acquainted only with the baptism of John" (Acts 18:25). Aquila and Pricilla listened carefully to Apollos' preaching. They noticed something is missing in his message. As any good Christian leader would do, "they took him aside and explained to him the way of God more accurately" (Acts 18:26). Possibly, they explained to Apollos specifics of Christ's teaching, miracles, death, resurrection, and His ascension at the right hand of the Father, and, most importantly, told him what happened at Pentecost. Perhaps they taught him that every believer is required to be, not only baptized in water, as John taught (Matthew 3:11), but to be baptized with the Holy Spirit as Jesus told His disciples (Acts 1:8). As a result of their brief discipleship, Apollos, became a great Christian apologetic, who later helped Paul's ministry in Corinth.

Luke writes:

> And when he wanted to go across to Achaia, the brethren encouraged him and wrote to the disciples to welcome him; and when he had arrived, he greatly helped those who had believed through grace, for he powerfully refuted the Jews in public, demonstrating by the Scriptures that Jesus was the Christ. (Acts 18:27–28)

What struck me when I studied this subject was the fact that it is possible for a well-educated person to be fervent in spirit, to teach accurately the things concerning Jesus, and still miss important details regarding the work of grace and the ministry of the Holy Spirit. Please observe that Doctor Luke, who usually pays close attention to details about people, wrote that Apollo was fervent in spirit, but he didn't say that he was filled with the Holy Spirit. He was most likely a type A personality and very well educated from the School of Alexandria. Again, a person with a strong personality, plus a very good education, can make a powerful preacher. But this does not mean he is yet filled with the Holy Spirit.

In 53–58 AD, Paul went on his third missionary trip. This time, his team, included Gaius and Aristarchus (Acts 19:29). They arrived in Ephesus, where they spent more than two years. This happened while Apollos was already in Corinth. As Paul and his traveling companions from Macedonia entered this great city, they found some disciples (Acts 19:1). It is unclear if Paul had an inner knowledge regarding the spiritual state of these disciples. Most likely, he found out from Aquila and Pricilla about the experience they had with Apollos. Paul asked them directly: "Did you receive the Holy Spirit when you believed?" And they said to him, "No, we have not even heard whether there is a Holy Spirit" (Acts 19:2). Obviously, these disciples did not receive the Holy Spirit when they believed. The Bible tells us that they have not even heard about this kind of baptism. People don't know what they don't know. Therefore, it is crucial not to be ignorant regarding the whole truth of the gospel. Meriam-Webster dictionary defines the verb "to know": to perceive directly, to have direct cognition of, to have understanding of, to be acquainted or familiar with, to have experience of."[50] On the other hand, the noun "ignorance" can be defined as: "the state or fact of being ignorant, lack of knowledge, education, or awareness."[51] Finally, the noun "truth" means: the body of real things, events, and facts, a transcendent fundamental or spiritual reality, fidelity to an original or to a standard, sincerity in action, character, and utterance."[52] Knowing the truth leads to freedom and victory.

At this point, Paul asked "into what" were they baptized. They said they were baptized into John's baptism. Then, Paul explained that the baptism of John was for repentance, but John told people to believe in the One Who was coming after him—Jesus Christ. They were very receptive, and after hearing Paul's explanation they all, about twelve men, were baptized in the name of the Lord Jesus.

This passage indicates two things:

(1) The disciples of John, not only had a doctrinal problem regarding the baptism in water,
(2) They had a huge spiritual problem—the acute need to be baptized into the Holy Spirit.

The climax of this experience, as recorded by Luke, is that: "when Paul had laid his hands upon them, the Holy Spirit came on them, and they began speaking with tongues and prophesying" (Acts 19:6).

Ten to twelve years later, the great apostle wrote the epistle to the Ephesians. In Ephesians 1:13 we read: "In Him, you also, after listening to the message of truth, the gospel of your salvation—

having also believed, you were sealed in Him with the Holy Spirit of promise." I am sure this is based on the experience explained in Acts 19. This passage is a very interesting one. When this verse is interpreted outside of its historical context, it can lead to an erroneous understanding. One of the most known and frequently made errors is: "People are baptized into the Holy Spirit in the moment they believed." The short analysis we performed above clearly shows that this is simply not true. Believers must be discipled appropriately in this area. The paradox is that in our days many Christians, based on Ephesians 1:13, erroneously believe that they have been baptized into the Holy Spirit when they believed. But the sad reality is that they have not been baptized and have no proof to argue otherwise. (See Acts 19:1–7).

Let me share with you an experience from more than thirty years ago. I became a Christian in 1976. I had not been raised in a Christian family, so a lot of things, especially aspects regarding the baptism into the Holy Spirit, spiritual gifts, and the Spirit's manifestations in the church were unclear to me. Naturally, given my personality, after a brief period, I began investigating this subject. I started by asking my best Christian friend and even my pastor all kinds of questions. Most of those questions were related to the Holy Spirit, such as speaking in other languages, prophesying, supernatural healing, casting out demons, and alike. My best friend assured me:

The paradox is that in our days many Christians, based on Ephesians 1:13, erroneously believe that they have been baptized into the Holy Spirit when they believed. But the sad reality is that they have not been baptized and have no proof to argue otherwise. (See Acts 19:1–7).

> Valy, do not be too concerned about those matters because you had received the Holy Spirit when you believed. This is written in Ephesians 1:13.

My pastor explained to me:

> Valy, the gifts of the Holy Spirit are no longer needed today because now we have the biblical canon—the Bible in its entirety. These manifestations were necessary during the first century to prove their apostleship and speaking in other tongues was required for people to hear the Gospel message in their languages and dialects. But, now, this is no longer necessary.

I was more confused than before. What they told me did not help me at all. Their explanation was in contradiction to what I read in my Bible about the events which took place at Pentecost.

Peter stated, very clearly:

> Peter said to them, "Repent, and each of you be baptized in the name of Jesus Christ for the forgiveness of your sins; and you will receive the gift of the Holy Spirit. <u>For the promise is for you and your children and for all who are far off, as many as the Lord our God will call to Himself</u>." (Acts 2:38–39)

At some point, I said to my friend:

> Let's attend some prayer meetings held by believers who believe the Holy Spirit is working today as He was two thousand years ago. I have heard that they are speaking in tongues and have visions. I would like to see with my own eyes and hear with my ears if these things are for real. And if it is not valid, there is nothing to worry about in the future. What do we have to lose? I want to get this thing out of my mind.

He agreed. We went to some of those prayer meetings. Indeed, they spoke in other languages and prophesied. This thing intrigued me even more! I said to my friend: "If the Holy Spirit still works today as in the first century, I also want to be baptized with the Holy Spirit." My friend replied: "You already have all you need. I will never hear you speaking in other languages!" This was like a "prophecy" on his part! After I finished my military service, I went back to those prayer meetings. After a while of fervent prayers, I received the Holy Spirit. How did I know that? Simple. I spoke in other tongues. My friend, on the other hand, had moved from Bucharest and, for several decades, I have not seen him. How interesting! He never heard me speak in other languages exactly as he "self-prophesied"!

Now let's look at a few characteristics specific to the disciples of John.

1. The disciples of John the Baptist are well intended and sincere people. However, they lack a complete understanding regarding the work of Christ and the Holy Spirit send by God. (See Acts 19:1–7)

People can be sincere and at the same time, sincerely wrong. Despite their sincerity, they rely too much on their efforts, instead of on the power of the Holy Spirit. John the Baptist told the people, "I baptize in water, but among you stands One whom you do not know" (John 1:26).

2. The disciples of John the Baptist need to be baptized with the Holy Spirit and transformed in the inner person. (See Acts 19:6)

The disciples of John the Baptist are either ignorant or willingly reject the revelation coming from God. The good news is that when they are open, they can experience the presence of the Holy Spirit in their lives the way the disciples in Ephesus experienced. Luke writes: "And when Paul had laid his hands upon them, the Holy Spirit came on them, and they began speaking with tongues and prophesying" (Acts 19:6). There is power in believing the whole gospel message.

3. The disciples of John the Baptist need to be accurately trained in the way of God by mature spiritual mentors. (See Acts 18:25)

We have seen already that Apollos, even though he was fervent in spirit and very knowledgeable in the Scriptures, needed to be taught more accurately in the way of God. Thank the Lord for mature, godly mentors like Aquila and Pricilla, who were paying close attention to Apollos' message. When they realized that Apollos had some "holes" in his understanding of the whole gospel of Christ, they properly mentored this fine man of God. (See Acts 18:26). Many of us would ignore it; not Aquila and Pricilla.

I know from personal experience that it is hard to disciple people who are so ingrained in their interpretation of the Bible. Often, it is even harder if they are smart people and well educated. It is easier to disciple a person who has no knowledge about the Bible than to disciple those who think they know the Scriptures very well.

4. The disciples of John the Baptist, eventually, should separate from those who persist in disobedience and hardness of heart. (See Acts 19:9)

Dr. Luke continues his story from Ephesus. Paul entered the synagogue and preached the gospel of Christ for three months. However, not everybody shared his enthusiasm for the kingdom of God. Some of them "were becoming hardened and disobedient." Not only that, they started "speaking evil of the Way before the people." Paul had enough, "he withdrew from them and took away the disciples, reasoning daily in the school of Tyrannus" (Luke 19:9).

5. The disciples of John the Baptist need to experience the Holy Spirit and the manifestation of the gifts of the Spirit in their lives

You may wonder what happened to me after I was filled with the Holy Spirit. Well, when the leadership of my church found out about my experience, they decided to exclude me from that church. You could not imagine how heartbreaking it was for me. But God guided my steps and placed me into a spirit-filled church. Looking back now, I can declare that "all things work together for good to those who love God, to those who are called according to His purpose," (Romans 8:28). I have seen so many miracles, and I grew so much in faith. It was worth all the pain and rejection.

Luke records that after Paul moved away from the synagogue, God started performing extraordinary miracles by the hands of Paul.

He writes:

> God was performing extraordinary miracles by the hands of Paul, so that handkerchiefs or aprons were even carried from his body to the sick, and the diseases left them and the evil spirits went out. (Acts 19:11-12)

I can boldly testify that the presence of the Holy Spirit and His gifts were so real in my life. Because of God's power, it was easier to resist the pressure and persecution I endured back in the days in Romania. Otherwise, I am sure it would have been a lot tougher to endure such hardships.

Discussion Questions:

– After reading this chapter, which characteristics specific to the disciples of John you noticed in the local church?

– What aspect impressed you the most regarding the ministry of John the Baptist? Please elaborate.

– If Paul would visit your small group and ask you: "Did you receive the Holy Spirit when you believed?" (Acts 19:2), what would your answer be?

– What is your opinion about the Person and the Power of the Holy Spirit? Please elaborate.

– What is your exposure to the work of the Holy Spirit? How about the manifestation of the gifts of the Spirit?

Notes

4. Three Kinds of Disciples—Part Two

[47] *Zechariah, Behind the Name*, https://www.behindthename.com/name/john. Accessed on July 12, 2019. See also: http://www.abarim-publications.com/Meaning/Zechariah.html#.XSjRcOhKg2w.
[48] *John, Behind the Name*, https://www.behindthename.com/name/john. Aaccessed on July 12, 2019. See also: http://www.abarim-publications.com/Meaning/John.html#.XSjQ8uhKg2w.
[49] *Baptists*. Accessed on July 12, 2019. https://en.wikipedia.org/wiki/Baptists.
[50] *Know*. Accessed on July 15, 2019. https://www.merriam-webster.com/dictionary/know.
[51] *Ignorance*. Accessed on July 15, 2019. https://www.merriam-webster.com/dictionary/ignorance.
[52] Truth. Accessed on July 15, 2019. https://www.merriam-webster.com/dictionary/truth.

CHAPTER 5

Three Kinds of Disciples—Part Three

By this, all men will know that you are My disciples if you have love for one another.
— John 13:35

In the middle of preparing a teaching series on discipleship I realized that during the times of Jesus there were three kinds of disciples:

A. The disciples of the Pharisees
B. The disciples of John the Baptist
C. The disciples of Jesus

Previously we looked at the disciples of the Pharisees and the disciples of John the Baptist. Now let's look at the disciples of Jesus.

A simple definition of a disciple

We analyzed Luke 9:23, concept by concept. Based on this verse we came up with a simple working definition of a disciple:

> A true disciple is a born-again believer who willingly and consistently follows Jesus. He or she accepts the cross and seeks to put off the old self daily. Motivated by love and devotion for Christ, the disciple happily

> accepts the hardship of life with its sufferings and losses of all kinds. If necessary, the disciple literally sacrifices his or her life for Jesus.

Of course, there are other definitions out there:

> A disciple of Christ is one who: 1. believes His doctrine, 2. rests on His sacrifice, 3. imbibes His spirit, and 4. imitates His example (Matthew 10:24; Luke 14:26 Luke 14:27 Luke 14:33; John 6:69).[53]

> Being a true disciple of Christ means learning from God and putting His Word into action."[54] A disciple is simply someone who believes in Jesus and seeks to follow Him in his or her daily life.[55]

> A disciple is a learner and a follower of the Lord Jesus. He is one who has made Jesus his Example and seeks to conform his life to his Master's in every possible way.[56]

> A disciple is a person who learns to live the life his teacher lives. And gradually he teaches others to live the life he lives.[57]

> A disciple is a person who: is following Christ (*head*); is being changed by Christ (*heart*): is committed to the mission of Christ (*hands*).[58]

And the list can continue…

C. The disciples of Jesus

The Christian life is a journey with Christ. Throughout this journey, everybody receives various calls. The way we respond to these calls makes a difference in this life—the impact we may make on the earth, as well as in the life to come—the rewards we may receive in heaven.

The three major calls Christ addresses are:

1. Calling to Salvation
2. Calling to Sanctification
3. Calling to Service

Let's briefly look into these callings.

1. Calling to Salvation

A genuine disciple of Jesus is a born-again believer

People cannot see nor understand the kingdom of God unless they are born again. Receiving Christ by faith gives people the right to become a child of God (cf. John 1:12, 13, 3:3, 6). Christian discipleship is directly linked to people who have been saved.

> A true disciple is a born-again believer who willingly and consistently follows Jesus. He or she accepts the cross and seeks to put off the old self daily. Motivated by love and devotion for Christ, the disciple happily accepts the hardship of life with its sufferings and losses of all kinds. If necessary, the disciple literally sacrifices his or her life for Jesus.

Nicodemus, a known Jewish religious leader, had an interview with Jesus. He was perplexed when Christ told him about the need to be born again to enter into the kingdom of God. Even though he was a teacher of Israel, this was a radical concept for him: "How can a man be born when he is old? He cannot enter a second time into his mother's womb and be born, can he?" (John 3:4). Nicodemus, as all of us at one point in life, tried to make sense of the words of Jesus in natural terms. But to be born again is a supernatural thing, it is not what a human being can do. Spiritual rebirth is a God-thing, something that only the Holy Spirit can do.

2. Calling to Sanctification

Under the calling to sanctification, there are various important calls:

2.1: The call to discipleship
2.2: The call to intimacy with Christ
2.3: The call to transformation
2.4: The call to emotional honesty
2.5: The call to spiritual maturity

2.1 The call to discipleship

Discipleship is the New Testament's vehicle for the progressive sanctification in the lives of born-again believers. This may shock some of you, but a born-again believer does not automatically become a disciple of Christ. It is important to understand that disciples are made, not born. After people are born again, they belong to God's family, but they are not disciples yet. After a while, believers are presented with the invitation to embrace the cross (see Matthew 10:38 39, Luke 9:23 24). For some people, this happens shortly after they are born again. For others, the call to discipleship may take place many years down the road. It all depends on each individual's intentional response to the Holy Spirit.

The calling to salvation is addressed to sinners. The calling to discipleship is addressed to saints. Salvation is a gift—it costs people nothing (cf. Ephesians 2:8-9). Discipleship requires the cross—it costs Christians everything (cf. Luke 9:23-24). Salvation opens the door to eternal life. Discipleship opens the door to heavenly rewards (cf. 1 Corinthians 3:11-15, Daniel 12:3). I hope you can see the difference.

2.2 The call to intimacy with Jesus

A genuine disciple of Jesus cultivates his or her intimacy with Christ. When Jesus ministered on earth, He called His disciples to be with Him (cf. Mark 3:13-15). Intimacy with God does not happen overnight: **it requires intentionality on our part.** An important characteristic of Christ's disciples is that they progressively cultivate their intimacy with God the Father, the Son, and the Holy Spirit (cf. John 17:3). This is the very essence of Christianity. Jesus tells us: "And this is life eternal, that they might know thee the only true God, and Jesus Christ, whom thou hast sent" (John 17:3). Discipleship is a journey of intimate knowledge of Christ. For more on this topic, I highly recommend reading the chapter called "The Power of Intimacy with Jesus," from my book titled *Fullness of Christ*.[59]

I like the chorus of Alexander Pappas's worship song, *More of You*:

I wanna know Your love Your love
I need more of You less of me
I wanna know more of Your heart
Make me who You want me to be
God this is my prayer
Make me more aware of You
I wanna know You
I wanna know You
Jesus, Jesus
I need more of You
More of You less of me.

Christianity is not another religion in competition with other religions. The reality is that Christianity is a relationship with the Father, Son, and the Holy Spirit. Discipleship is about true relationship. Jesus does not want His disciples to follow Him grudgingly, but rather out of love and devotion for Him. Everything that Christians are doing for God and people from exercising spiritual gifts, acts of faith, ministry to the poor, to martyrdom, (cf. 1 Corinthians 13:1 3), should be out of love. If our discipleship does not spring forth from our intimacy with Jesus, it profits us nothing.

2.3 The call to transformation

Discipleship is about mind-renewal (cf. Romans 12:2), supernatural transformation (cf. 2 Corinthians 3:18), and the fruit of the Spirit (Galatians 5: 22-23). When we spend quality time in the Word of God (cf. John 8:3-32), the living Word renews our mind. The author of Hebrews states that: "For the word of God is living and active and sharper than any two-edged sword, and piercing as far as the division of soul and spirit, of both joints and marrow, and able to judge the thoughts and intentions of the heart" (Hebrews 4;12). When we spend quality time in the Bible, God speaks to us, He influences and changes our character. When we follow Christ closely, our inner person is supernaturally transformed into His likeness, and, when we yield to God, the Spirit produces in us His fruit. Mind renewal, the transformation of the inner person, and spiritual fruitfulness are not of human origin: **they are supernatural.**

Discipleship is about transformation, not mere information. The Spirit of God is the One who regenerated us at salvation. The Holy Spirit also is the One who supernaturally transforms us during our earthly journey and prepares us for eternity.

2.4 The call to emotional honesty

Many Christians do not pay attention to the way they feel, rather they stuff their emotions and deny what is going on inside their soul. Lack of emotional awareness causes believers to remain emotionally immature. But, as Peter Scazzero asserts—"It is not possible to be spiritually mature while remaining emotionally immature."[60] Therefore, the path to spiritual growth includes emotional honesty, it implies assuming responsibility for our emotions, it requires resolving all negative emotional experiences related to the old self (cf. Ephesians 4:20-32). Emotional honesty is crucial in the process of sanctification of every disciple.

The Holy Spirit desires access to all the rooms of our heart, including the special room where we store our hurts, disappointments, bitterness, rejections, betrayals, traumas, and so on. We must know that the Spirit of God enters in those areas by invitation only. With these truths in mind, we can say that disciples are:

– Intentional about healing from past emotional wounds (Ephesians 4:31).
– Committed to a lifestyle of forgiveness (Ephesians 4:32).

– Handling anger healthily and biblically (Ephesians 4:26–27).
– Pursuers of true peace with all men (Romans 12:18, Hebrews 12:14).

And the list could continue.

2.5 The call to spiritual maturity

Discipleship is about spiritual growth and maturity (cf. 1 Peter 2:1–3, Hebrews 5:11–14, 6:1–3, Ephesians 4:11–16). Spiritual growth is a process. Nobody was biologically born as an adult. Similarly, we were born again as spiritual infants. All parents want their children to grow and develop properly and become well-adjusted and well-educated adults. The Father does not desire that any of us remain infants until we die or Christ returns. As disciples of Christ, we must be committed to growing into spiritual adulthood. For more on the topic of spiritual growth I highly recommend reading the chapter called "Spiritual Growth in Christ," from my book *Fullness of Christ.*

Peter exhorts new born-again believers to "grow in respect to salvation" (1 Peter 2:1–3). The author of Hebrews encourages Christians to "press on to maturity." This does not come naturally for Christians. It necessitates leaving (cf. Hebrews 6:1 3) the elementary teaching of Christ—*milk diet*, and moving to the deeper things of God—*solid food.*

We belong to Christ. Jesus is our spiritual Head, and God desires His children (cf. Ephesians 4:11–16) to reach the fullness of Christ. However, "Even though the fullness of Christ is what the Father desires for all of us, it will not happen automatically."[61] So let's be intentional about all these aspects. The bottom line is genuine disciples progressively mature toward the fullness of Christ.

3. Calling to Service

Christ's most important calling is to spiritual multiplication. Spiritual multiplication is the heart of the Great Commission. A genuine disciple, upon maturing, multiplies according to the same model of Christian discipleship designed by Jesus and modeled by His apostles (cf. Matthew 28:19–20, 2 Timothy 2:2).

The result of every local church (cf. 2 Timothy 2:2) should be disciples making disciples who are making disciples. Jesus showed us how to disciple others. This is one of the reasons the gospels were written. The apostles implemented Christ's model. This is one of the reasons why Dr. Luke wrote the book of Acts. In one sense, we are living in Acts 29. Now it is our turn to follow in the footsteps of the spiritual founders of the Church and continue the Great Commission by making disciples. That is why the epistles were written. Discipleship is still in effect until Jesus' return. The beauty of this is that we are not alone on this journey. Jesus promised to be with us from the beginning to the end. "And lo, I am with you always, even to the end of the age" (Matthew 28:20). Christ's presence is part of the Great Commission.

Characteristics of Christ's Disciples

Now let's look at several key Scriptures and map a few important aspects regarding Christ's Disciples. Of all the gospel writers, Dr. Luke wrote the most about discipleship. Here are some of the key characteristics of Jesus' disciples:

1. Christ—the highest devotion

A disciple displays the highest devotion and loyalty to Christ, above parents, siblings, and even his or her own life. Luke writes: "If anyone comes to Me, and does not hate his own father and mother and wife and children and brothers and sisters, yes, and even his own life, he cannot be My disciple" (Luke 14:26). Is Christ saying that we are supposed to "hate" our parents? Of course not. We are supposed to honor and respect them (cf. Ephesians 6:1-3). Are we supposed to neglect our children? Not at all. We are supposed to bring them up in the instruction of the Lord (cf. Ephesians 6:4). However, Jesus wants the highest loyalty. Our relationship with Him comes first, then our family, our jobs, and everything else.

2. The cross

Christ's disciples know their cross, and without any reservation, carry it daily and faithfully. According to Luke: "Whoever does not carry his own cross and come after Me cannot be My disciple" (Luke 14:27). Discipleship is costly. A disciple (cf. Luke 14:28–30) is a person who calculated the cost of discipleship and accepted it so God's will can be done in his or her life. The cross is the place where our will intersects with the will of God. For more about the cross, I highly recommend reading the chapter called "The Power of the Cross," from my book *Fullness of Christ.* The cross is the crossroads where we are denying the will of the flesh and are accepting the will of God. (See diagram 4.) This is a daily process and a daily procedure. Every day is a new day when we start afresh with the decision to surrender our will before God and take up our cross.

Diagram 4

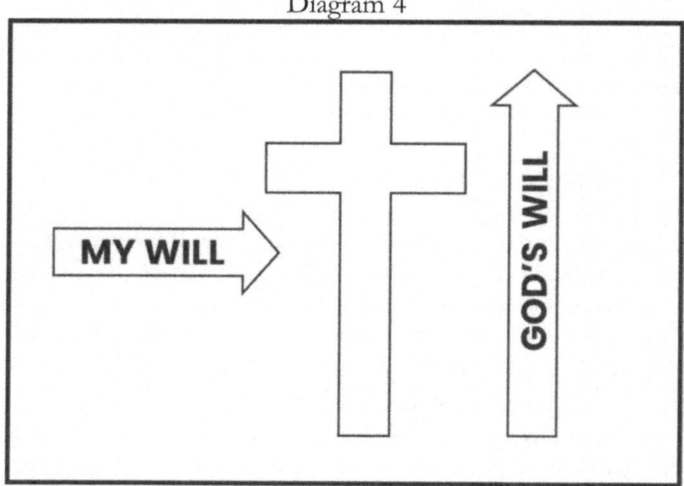

3. Spiritual warfare

Christ's disciples understand that they are in a spiritual battle. In Luke 14:3, 32, the author uses the imagery of a battle. Like it or not, as soon as we accepted the lordship of Christ, we became Satan's enemies. As disciples, we are in a continuous war with the domain of darkness. We must agree to wage this war until the return of the Captain—Jesus. We are either attacking the domain of darkness causing it massive losses, or we are under attack experiencing losses and casualties. Making peace with the domain of darkness is a disastrous option. I like the way Walter E. Henrichsen interprets Luke 14:31, 32:

> If you are unwilling to pay the cost," says the Lord, "then send your ambassador and sue for peace." As a Christian, you can go to the devil and say, "Look, Satan, I am already a Christian and I am on my way to heaven; but I want to make a deal with you. If you leave me alone, I will leave you alone. I will not be a true disciple of Jesus Christ. I will not threaten your hold over the lives of men or invade your kingdom. return, you don't bother me. Let me live in comfort and quiet." And the devil will say, "Friend, you've got yourself a deal." But remember, Satan is a liar and the father of lies. You have no guarantee that he will not double-cross you. The cost you will pay for not being a disciple is infinitely greater than the cost you will pay for being one"[62]

At one point in His ministry, Jesus surveyed His disciples' view of Him. He asked: "But who do you say that I am?" (Matthew 16:13). Jesus was not having an identity crisis; He was not looking for the assurance of His men. The question was for them, for their benefit. He considered it was time for the disciples to get a deeper revelation from God. Peter answered: "You are the Christ, the Son of the living God" (Matthew 16:16). This revelation was directly from God. Then, Christ declared that "upon this rock"—Christ, the Son of the living God," I will build My church, and the gates of Hades will not overpower it" (Matthew 16:18). What does that mean? I believe it means that the church is in a continuous opposition with Satan until Christ's return.

Jesus' disciples, know very well that the "struggle is not against flesh and blood, but against the rulers, against the powers, against the world forces of this darkness, against the spiritual forces of wickedness in the heavenly places" (Ephesians 6:12). As disciples, having this spiritual perspective in mind, we are committed to wearing the spiritual armor of God "so that we will be able to resist in the evil day, and having done everything, to stand firm" (Ephesians 6:11, 13).

A defeated church is an oxymoron and negative advertising for God's kingdom: "Come to us so you will be defeated too."

4. God vs., mammon

Disciples of Jesus consider all their possessions as belonging to God. Luke writes: "So then, none of you can be My disciple who does not give up all his own possessions" (Luke 14:33). There is no question about, this is a sobering statement. Still, God made sure it is in the Bible.

God created us to be creatures of passion. Therefore, discipleship is an issue of the heart. If we treasure God's kingdom, we are going to sacrifice for it; if we treasure the earthly possessions, we are going to sacrifice for them. We cannot be Christ's disciples with a divided heart. We must follow Jesus without earthly entanglements.

First Timothy 6:10, states: "For the love of money is a root of all sorts of evil". In the Romanian language, there is this idiom: "Banul este ochiul dracului" "Money is the devil's eye." In the Sermon on the Mount, Jesus uses the word: mammon, referring to wealth. Mammon—a Chaldee or Syriac word meaning "wealth" or "riches" (Luke 16:9–11); also, by personification, the god of riches (Matt. 6:24; Luke 16:9–11).[63]

The reality is that we cannot have two masters and be able to please them both. Jesus, says: "No one can serve two masters; for either he will hate the one and love the other, or he will be devoted to one and despise the other. You cannot serve God and wealth" (Matthew 6:24). If Christians think they can be devoted to Christ and to mammon at the same time, they are already deceived by Satan.

Does all this mean that God wants His children to be poor, sleep in cardboard boxes or under bridges, and beg for food, clothing, and other necessities of life? Absolutely not! God loves His children. The Father knows that we need all these things. Christ is talking about having the correct priorities. The sad reality is that many of us Christians are as anxious about these things as our non-Christian neighbors (see Matthew 6:31–32). Christ wants us to "seek first His kingdom and His righteousness, and all these things will be added to you" (Matthew 6:33).

5. Love God and others

Christ's disciples love God and others as themselves. This is a foundational principle: "We love, because He first loved us" (1 John 4:19). Moreover, John 14:15, states: "If you love Me, you will keep My commandments." **The right motivation for obedience is love.** This is what the Lord expects of us. Please notice that the emphasis is not on the *commandments* but on the *relationship*: "If you love Me." This is an important distinction. If sincere love, respect, and reverence are missing from our relationship with Christ, the "stuff" that we are doing is no longer discipleship; it is just a religion. Maybe you've heard or read this statement: *Rules without a relationship lead to rebellion.* God does not want us to serve Him without first having a good relationship with Him. Serving Him out of obligation looks similar to children who grudgingly do chores for their parents without any love or respect. That type of relationship with God is called legalism which sooner or later will lead to rebellion.

The flip side of John 14:15 is John 14:21: "He who has My commandments and keeps them is the one who loves Me; and he who loves Me will be loved by My Father, and I will love him and will disclose Myself to him." At first glance, this seems to be a circular argument, but it is not. Jesus tells us that true love for Him is demonstrated in our sincere obedience to Him. True obedience is not just hearing about His commandments but keeping all His commandments. In other words, we cannot go around saying, "Oh, how I love Jesus!" and not move a finger to keep all His commandments. This is an oxymoron.

In his first epistle, John reiterates the idea of keeping Christ's commandments: "For this is the love of God, that we keep His commandments; and His commandments are not burdensome" (1 John 5:3). I think you observe the same order: "love of God" and "keep His commandments." The reality is that keeping all His commandments with the right motivation is not a burden; it gives us joy and a sense of great fulfillment. Keeping all God's commandments is not what we *have* to do, as maturing disciples of Christ it is what we *want* and get to do. The bottom line is that Christ's disciples diligently seek first the kingdom of God. They are passionate about the work of the ministry. The disciples of Jesus, motivated by their love and devotion to God, minister to the people who do not know Christ.

God's love is the true fuel for our passion. To be passionate for the kingdom of God and seeking the kingdom of God means involvement in the work of the kingdom, giving ourselves to Him, sacrificing our time, talents, and treasure for the Great Commission. It does not mean just talking about the kingdom or just thinking about it. Our service in the kingdom is not to earn God's love; we are loved, therefore we work for Him. True discipleship is about loving God and loving others as ourselves.

When we were born-again, God poured agape love into our hearts. Paul writes: "because the love of God has been poured out within our hearts through the Holy Spirit who was given to us" (Romans 5:5). For more about the meaning of love I highly recommend reading the chapter called "A More Excellent Way," from my book *Fullness of Christ*. Agape love is the essence of God's nature (cf. 1 John 4:8). The true sign that we belong to the family of God is the ability to love with His kind of love. John writes: "By this all men will know that you are My disciples, if you have love for one another" (John 13:35). Attending a local church regularly, being part of a Christian denomination, being baptized in water, having your name on a church-roll, can be good things, but none of these are true indicators that we are part of God's family. Agape love is the true badge of discipleship. This sign cannot be imitated, either we have it or not.

This is how John argues his case:

> If someone says, "I love God," and hates his brother, he is a liar; for the one who does not love his brother whom he has seen, cannot love God whom he has not seen. And this commandment we have from Him, that the one who loves God should love his brother also. (1 John 4:20–21)

Christ summarized the entire Old Testament in two commandments: Love God and love your neighbor (see Mark 12:29–31).

6. Power in prayer

A true disciple is a fighter in prayer. Prayer is the breath of the soul.[64] The human body can survive without food for several days, without water for a few days, but without oxygen, it would die in less than seven minutes. No wonder Paul exhorts Christians to pray without ceasing (cf. 1 Thessalonians 5:17).

Pastor Glenn McDonald writes:

> Prayer is not about fulfilling our wish lists. Prayer is about joining our hearts with the heart of God. As we come into the presence of the Father, He asks us to do what Jesus did. *He asks us to die.* Unless we don't release our vice-like grip on our dreams, our desires, our affections and our ambitions—the entirety of the way we organize our lives apart from God's desires for us—the will of the Father, Son, and Holy Spirit cannot be fulfilled within our lives.[65]

The disciples of Jesus understood the importance of prayer and asked the Lord to teach them to pray. "One day, Jesus was praying in a certain place. When the prayer was over, one of His disciples said to Him, "Lord, teach us to pray just as John also taught his disciples" (Luke 11:1b).

The Apostle Paul also understood the importance of the intercessory prayer. In his letter to Romans, he writes: "Now I urge you, brethren, by our Lord Jesus Christ and by the love of the Spirit, to strive together with me in your prayers to God for me" (Romans 15:30).

Oswald Chambers (1874-1917), a renowned pastor and teacher from Scotland, known for his powerful devotional book *My Utmost for His Highest*, wrote: "Prayer does not equip us for greater works—prayer is the greater work."[66]

Moreover, E.M. Bounds, (1835-1913), a Methodist pastor, considered by many to be an expert in the art of prayer, wrote:

> What the Church needs to-day is not more machinery or better, not new organizations or more and novel methods, but men whom the Holy Ghost can use—men of prayer, men mighty in prayer. The Holy Ghost

> does not flow through methods but through men. He does not come on machinery but on men. He does not anoint plans, but men—men of prayer.[67]

George Müller (1805-1898), was a Christian evangelist who coordinated the orphanages in Bristol, England, and during his lifetime he cared for more than 10,000 orphans. He was able to do this ministry because of prayer. Müller prayed for five of his friends. After several months one of them was saved. Ten years later, two others came to Jesus. It took twenty-five years before his fourth friend was saved. So far four out of his five close friends were saved. Müller could have said: "O, well, I guess this is it. My fifth friend is not on God's list." He didn't give up. He persevered in prayer until death for the last man on his list. His faith was rewarded. Shortly after his death, his last friend came to faith in Christ.

George Müller wrote:

> It is not enough for the believer to begin to pray, nor to pray correctly; nor is it enough to continue for a time to pray. We must patiently, believingly continue in prayer until we obtain an answer.[68]

Let me share one of my experiences regarding the power of prayer. I am the first one who was saved from my family. I became a Christian in 1976. At the age of 17, I start preaching the Gospel. I tried to share the good news with my parents, but they would not receive my message. After a few years, I asked God specifically regarding my parents. The Holy Spirit told me not to lose hope for them, instead to be persistent in prayer for my parents, because after a while my Mom will be saved, and after a long while, during some suffering, my Dad will be saved too. This gave me wings to continue praying for the salvation of my parents. I knew in my heart that God is always faithful, and He will keep His promises. I prayed and prayed for my mother that she would receive Jesus as her personal Savior. After twelve years my Mom was saved. I continued praying for my father for twelve more years. After twenty-four years, my dad had near-fatal cerebral congestion. He was in a coma for about three days. It was during that period the Holy Spirit worked in his heart. Upon his recovery, Dad expressed his desire to receive Christ as his personal Savior. Shortly after he was discharged from the hospital he was baptized in water. Glory to God who answers prayers!

7. Spreading the Good News

A disciple is committed to spreading the good news. God could have sent the angels to preach the gospels, but He didn't. Christ entrusted us to spread the good news. The bottom line is that the Gospel of Christ must be proclaimed. Jesus told His disciples: "This gospel of the kingdom shall be preached in the whole world as a testimony to all the nations, and then the end will come" (Matthew 24:14).

On the other hand, Paul writes: "But what does it say? "THE WORD IS NEAR YOU, IN YOUR MOUTH AND IN YOUR HEART"—that is, the word of faith which we are preaching" (Romans 10:8). This implies that we are responsible to preach the Word. Moreover, in his first letter to the Corinthians, Paul writes:

> Now I make known to you, brethren, the gospel which I preached to you, which also you received, in which also you stand, by which also you are saved, if you hold fast the word which I preached to you, unless you believed in vain. (1 Corinthians 15:1, 2)

If the Gospel of Jesus is not preached by His disciples, then who will bring the good news to the unsaved world? How can other people be saved if we are unwilling to share Christ with our neighbors, coworkers, and even strangers? Christ's disciples cannot keep their mouth shut. In Romans we read:

> How then will they call on Him in whom they have not believed? How will they believe in Him whom they have not heard? And how will they hear without a preacher? How will they preach unless they are sent? Just as it is written, "HOW BEAUTIFUL ARE THE FEET OF THOSE WHO BRING GOOD NEWS OF GOOD THINGS!" (Romans 10:14, 15)

Every disciple of Jesus has a powerful message—Christ, and

Christ crucified.

Paul writes:

> For indeed Jews ask for signs and Greeks search for wisdom; but we preach Christ crucified, to Jews a stumbling block and to Gentiles foolishness, but to those who are the called, both Jews and Greeks, Christ the power of God and the wisdom of God. (1 Corinthians 1:22–24)

Christ's disciples (cf. 2 Corinthians 4:5), are not preaching themselves, but Christ. The most efficient way of preaching the gospel is by combining words with the right actions. The Christian message is important, but it needs to be supported by a genuine Christian lifestyle.

To ensure his favorite disciple will never forget his main responsibility—to preach the gospel, Paul, before his martyrdom, charged Timothy with these words:

> I solemnly charge you in the presence of God and of Christ Jesus, who is to judge the living and the dead, and by His appearing and His kingdom: preach the word; be ready in season and out of season; reprove, rebuke, exhort, with great patience and instruction. (2 Timothy 4:1, 2)

We are Christ's disciples and He charged us to preach the gospel. Mark writes: "And He said to them, "Go into all the world and preach the gospel to all creation"" (Mark 16:15). Are we really taking Jesus' charge to heart? Are we committed to preaching the gospel to all creation? I certainly hope so.

8. Genuine humility

An authentic disciple is humble and faithful to the work entrusted to him or her by the Lord. Humility is the key, the only key in life for any spiritual progress. Humility is the confidence placed in the right place—God. Pride is confidence in ourselves or other things. If our confidence is not in God, we live in pride. Both

Peter and James stated that "God is opposed to the proud, but gives grace to the humble" (1 Peter 5:5, James 4:6).

Therefore, as disciples of Christ, we should ask ourselves: In *whom* or in *what* do I trust now? An authentic disciple trusts only in God, not in his or her resources. Paul writes: "for we are the true circumcision, who worship in the Spirit of God and glory in Christ Jesus and put no confidence in the flesh" (Philippians 3:3). In and of ourselves we have nothing to offer. If you are a good communicator—God gave you that ability. If you have a good memory—the Great Specialist placed more RAM in your "computer." If you can manage great wealth—The Owner of all the riches (cf. Haggai 2:8) blessed you with these skills.

No matter who we think we are, or what abilities we believe we possess, we are just stewards of the resources God has entrusted to us. Paul writes:

> Let a man regard us in this manner, as servants of Christ and stewards of the mysteries of God. In this case, moreover, it is required of stewards that one be found trustworthy. (1 Corinthians 4:1–2)

Everything that we have is a gift from God. Understanding this principle is fundamental to the disciple of Christ. As soon as we begin to praise ourselves, to compare ourselves with others, or we start criticizing, or envying others who are better than we are, we slipped already on the slippery slope of pride. If everything we have is a gift from God, boasting in our abilities or achievements is a clear indicator that we are deceived. Paul warns believers: "For who regards you as superior? What do you have that you did not receive? And if you did receive it, why do you boast as if you had not received it?" (1 Corinthians 4:7).

9. Spiritual disciplines

An authentic disciple has learned and practices spiritual disciplines. *Disciple* and *discipline* come from the same Latin root word—*discipulus*. A disciple of Christ is a disciplined person. Dr. Anderson writes: "Discipleship requires mental discipline. People who will not assume responsibility for their thoughts cannot be discipled."[69] I agree. A disciple has learned and practices the inward spiritual disciplines of prayer, fasting, meditation, and the outward spiritual disciplines of simplicity, solitude, submission, and service.[70]

In his first letter to the Corinthians believer, Paul, uses the image of sports competitions, mainly the Olympics, which were very familiar to Greeks and Romans, to exhort them to exercise spiritual discipline in their lives:

> Do you not know that those who run in a race all run, but only one receives the prize? Run in such a way that you may win. Everyone who competes in the games exercises self-control in all things. They then do it to receive a perishable wreath, but we an imperishable. Therefore I run in such a way, as not without aim; I box in such a way, as not beating the air; but I discipline my body and make it my slave, so that, after I have preached to others, I myself will not be disqualified. (1 Corinthians 9:24-27)

Regarding spiritual discipline and its connection with Christian discipleship, Henri Nouwen writes:

> Discipline is the other side of discipleship. Discipleship without discipline is like waiting to run in the marathon without ever practicing. Discipline without discipleship is like always practicing for the marathon but never participating. It is important, however, to realize that discipline in the spiritual life is not the same as discipline in sports. Discipline in sports is the concentrated effort to master the body so that it can obey the mind better. Discipline in the spiritual life is the concentrated effort to create the space and time where God can become our master and where we can respond freely to God's guidance. Thus, discipline is the creation of boundaries that keep time and space open for God. Solitude requires discipline; worship requires discipline, caring for others requires discipline. They all ask

> us to set apart a time and a place where God's gracious presence can be acknowledged and responded to.[71]

Paul encourages his favorite disciple—Timothy, and implicitly us, with these words: "Fight the good fight of faith; take hold of the eternal life to which you were called, and you made the good confession in the presence of many witnesses" (1 Timothy 6:12).

10. True Worshipers

A genuine disciple of Jesus is a true worshiper in Spirit and in truth. Christ traveled through Samaria and shared the gospel message with a woman by the well of Jacob. The Samaritan woman brought up the subject of worship. According to her understanding worship was linked to a place (for example: a specific mountain—*Mount Gerizim*, or a specific city—*Jerusalem*). Evidently, she was confused regarding true worship. Jesus told her directly that God is looking for a special kind of worshipers—worshipers in spirit and truth.

John writes:

> But an hour is coming, and now is, when the true worshipers will worship the Father in spirit and truth; for such people the Father seeks to be His worshipers. God is spirit, and those who worship Him must worship in spirit and truth. (John 4:23–24)

The reality is that many believers are confused too regarding worship. What is worship? Is worship a soft song we sing in church on Sunday morning? Is worship a long and emotional prayer? Does worship mean spending time in the middle of God's creation? Do we worship when we stay in silence before the Lord for several minutes or hours? Is worship when we go on mission trips or donate a considerable amount of money to a charity? All these aspects are good things, and we are encouraged to excel in good works. These may be various expressions of worship, but none of those aspects, in themselves, touch the heart of worship.

According to the Online Etymology Dictionary, the word "worship" means: "condition of being worthy, dignity, glory, distinction, honor, renown." Worship means: "reverence paid to a supernatural or divine being." This word was first recorded around 1300.[72] In other words, when we worship God, in essence, we declare His worth. If we don't declare God's worth, He is not losing even an ounce of His worth. If we worship God, we don't add another ounce to His worth. He is worthy; therefore, we worship Him and declare His infinite worth.

If we keep this truth at the heart of our worship, then, all the activities I listed previously could become expressions of our worship of God. When we sit in the local church focusing on God's worth and we sing along with the worship team—we worship God. In the morning when I pray, or I listen to a good hymn while acknowledging that God is worthy of my praise—I worship God. When I see a flower blooming, a bird chirping, marvel at a waterfall, or admire the horizon from a mountaintop—I worship God. When I hold a day-old baby in my arms and am in awe of the miracle of birth, silently praising the Creator—I am worshiping God. When I go overseas to a third-world country and see people being saved hearing a simple gospel message—I worship God.

But Paul goes even deeper into the meaning of worship. In his letter to Romans, after he finished writing his systematic theology, Paul encourages us: "Therefore I urge you, brethren, by the mercies of God, to present your bodies a living and holy sacrifice, acceptable to God, which is your spiritual service of worship" (Romans 12:1). What is Paul saying here? He is saying that the only way we can truly declare God's worth is by offering our very lives to Him as a holy sacrifice. Nothing else will do but this. This is our true worship. Period.

Christ's Ultimate Intention

Let me end this chapter by sharing with you a great experience I had many years ago on a mission trip abroad. I was in a church, ready to start a spiritual formation seminar. As I stood in front of the congregation, I heard myself saying aloud the following statement:

> The ultimate intention of the church is a mature disciple who knows God intimately and personally

> (John 17:3), who accepted the discipleship call and carries the cross daily (Luke 9:23, Galatians 2:20), whose mind and character is continuously renewed and transformed by the Spirit and the Word of God (Romans 12:2, 2 Corinthians 3:18, Galatians 5:22-23), who grows and matures into the fullness of Christ (Ephesians 4:11-16, Hebrews 5:11-14, 6:1-3), and who, ultimately, multiplies disciples according to the Christ's and the apostles' discipleship model (Matthew 28:19-20, 2 Timothy 2:2).

It is one thing to read the notes based on your study before starting the seminar; it is a different experience when you hear yourself for the first time saying those things. When I finished speaking, I wrote those words in my journal including the corresponding Bible verses. I decided that after getting back to the States I would put these concepts into a nice bookmark. And that was exactly what I did. When I forget the meaning of discipleship, I pull out the bookmark from my Bible and read it. All the fogginess dissipates, and clarity on discipleship is restored. May I give you my bookmark? Visit **www.urfm.org** for details how to obtain one.

Discussion Questions:

– After some reflection and meditation on the topic of discipleship, in which area did the Holy Spirit convict you the most? Please share.

– Under the calling to sanctification, there are five important calls. Which one challenged you the most and why? Feel to share with your small group leader or with a spiritual mentor.

– After reading and studying the characteristics of Christ's disciples, which characteristics spoke to your heart the most? Please elaborate.

– Do you agree that the ultimate intention of the church is a mature disciple who, in return, multiplies disciples? If not, why not? Please elaborate and share with a trusted friend.

– Are you currently working with a spiritual mentor? How is your experience so far? Please elaborate.

Notes

5. Three Kinds of Disciples—Part Three

53 *Disciple*. Accessed on August 19, 2019. http://eastonsbibledictionary.org/1041-Disciple.php.

54 Billy Graham, *How to Be a True Disciple of Christ*. Accessed on August 19, 2019. https://www.christianpost.com/news/billy-graham-how-to-be-a-true-disciple-of-christ.html.

55 Billy Graham, *How Can I Be a True Disciple of Christ?* Accessed on August 19, 2019. https://billygraham.org/story/how-can-i-be-a-true-disciple-of-christ-billy-grahams-answer/.

56 Zac Poonen, *Practical Discipleship*. Accessed on August 19, 2019. https://www.cfcindia.com/books/practical-discipleship.

57 Juan Carlos Ortiz, Disciple, *A Handbook for New Believers*, (Orlando, FL: Creation House, Books about Sprit-Led Living, 1995), 105.

58 Jim Putman & Bobby Harrington with Robert Coleman, *DiscipleShift. Five Steps That Help Your Church to Make Disciples who Make Disciples*, (Zondervan, Grand Rapids, MI, 2013), 51.

59 Valy Vaduva, *Fullness of Christ*. https://smile.amazon.com/Fullness-Christ-Expressing-Character-through/dp/1930529341/ref=sr_1_10?keywords=fullness+of+christ&qid=1569433224&sr=8-10.

60 Peter Scazzero, *Emotionally Healthy Spirituality*, (Zondervan, Grand Rapids, MI, 2017), 19.

61 Valy Vaduva, *Fullness of Christ*, (Livonia, MI: Upper Room Fellowship Ministry, 2018), 202.

62 Walter A. Henrichsen, *Disciples are Made not Born,* (Victor, Cook Communications, Colorado Springs, CO, 1988), 39.

63 *Mammon*. Accessed on September 25, 2019. http://eastonsbibledictionary.org/2396-Mammon.php.

64 *Prayer: The Soul's Breath*. Accessed on September 24, 2019. https://www1.cbn.com/prayer/prayer-the-souls-breath.

65 Glenn MacDonald, *The Disciple Making Church*. (FaithWalk Publishing, Grand Haven, MI, 2004), 197.

66 Oswald Chambers, *The Key of the Greater Work*. Accessed on September 25, 2019. https://utmost.org/the-key-of-the-greater-work/,

67 E.M. Bounds, *Power Through Prayer*. Christian Classics Ethereal Library (CCEL). Accessed on September 24, 2019. https://www.ccel.org/ccel/bounds/power.http://www.prayerfoundation.org/booktexts/z_embounds_powerthroughprayer_01.htm.

68 George Muller, *How To Pray Aright*. Accessed on September 24, 2019. https://www.georgemuller.org/quotes/category/persistence.

69 Neil T. Anderson, *Victory over the Darkness*, (Ventura, CA: Regal Books, 2000), 222.

70 Richard Foster, *Celebrating of Discipline*. (Harper Collins Publishers, Inc. San Francisca, CA, 1978).

71 Henri Nouwen, *Creating Space for God*. Accessed on September 24, 2019. https://henrinouwen.org/meditation/creating-space-god/.

---

[72]*Worship*. Accessed on September 24, 2019. https://www.etymonline.com/word/worship.

CHAPTER 6

Lack of Spiritual Maturity

For though by this time you ought to be teachers, you have need again for someone to teach you the elementary principles of the oracles of God, and you have come to need milk and not solid food.

— Hebrews 5:12

There is a lack of spiritual maturity in the North American church today. Nobody argues this anymore. Many Christian leaders agree that believers don't display the Life and the Character of Christ in and through them, even after many years of attending church services. Believers in North America have beautiful church buildings, many Bible translations, seminary-educated leaders, and access to a lot of religious literature. However, despite all these wonderful resources, believers lack spiritual maturity and transformation leading to the *fullness of Christ.* Almost ten years ago Glenn McDonald, former Senior Pastor of Zionsville Presbyterian Church in suburban Indianapolis, considered that churches focused too much on the ABC (attendance, building, and cash) model, thus exhibiting at least two characteristics that prove to be „*disciple-making liabilities.*" First, the tendency to look for programmatic solutions and opportunities. However, programs cannot and will not be acceptable substitutes for vision. God's vision for His church is disciple making not ABC or more programs. Second, reliance on working hard and moving forward without really looking at the damage done to the case of Christ stated in Matthew

28:19–20.
McDonald writes:

> Classically, North American congregations have relied on a single individual to generate church-wide progress in bringing people to maturity in Christ. That person is the pastor. For roughly 300 years, Protestant pastors have been charged with the spiritual development of everyone within the church's reach—a mission to be accomplished through preaching, teaching, worship leadership, counseling, direction of appropriate boards and committees, home visitation, correspondence, administration, janitorial duties, praying at civic functions, and whatever other "*hats*" might be required apparel at a particular church. The ultimate issue therefore becomes: "How can we expose a maximum number of people to the work of our pastor, so that he or she can work a maximum amount of spiritual magic?"[73]

This is an impossible task. I hope my readers see this too. Such a thing did not work, does not work, and it is not going to work. Church leadership must return to the biblical principles of empowering the entire Body of Christ to grow, mature, and serve as stated by Paul in Ephesians:

> And He gave some as apostles, and some as prophets, and some as evangelists, and some as pastors and teachers, for the equipping of the saints for the work of service, to the building up of the body of Christ; until we all attain to the unity of the faith, and of the knowledge of the Son of God, to a mature man, to the measure of the stature which belongs to the fullness of Christ. As a result, we are no longer to be children, tossed here and there by waves and carried about by every wind of doctrine, by the trickery of men, by craftiness in deceitful scheming; but speaking the truth in love, we are to grow up in all aspects into Him who is the head, even Christ, from whom the whole body, being fitted and held together by what every joint

> supplies, according to the proper working of each individual part, causes the growth of the body for the building up of itself in love. (Ephesians 4:11–16)

I agree with Paul that in God's mind the entire Body of Christ has to be fitted together with every joint and every necessary body part that in the end this living spiritual organism (not organization) builds up itself in love, as is stated in verse sixteen.

Evangelism without disciple-making

Most churches focus on evangelism but forget almost entirely about Christ's objective to bring church attendants to the measure of *mature man*. Regarding this aspect, Bill Hull writes: "The church has tried to get world evangelization without disciple making."[74] Even though some churches win some converts, they fall short of God's ***ultimate intention***—"to grow up in all *aspects* into Him" (Ephesians 4:15). According to *Westminster Dictionary of Theological Terms,* "A convert is someone who changes from one faith to another." People can change their faith, but only God, through the Holy Spirit by Scriptures, can change the hearts. Just by attending a specific church of a particular denomination does not make me a disciple of Jesus Christ. In his forward to Henrichsen's book, *Disciples are Made not Born*, the late Howard G. Hendricks, distinguished Professor at Dallas Theological Seminary writes: "*'Make disciples'* is the mandate of the Master (Matthew 28:19-20). We may ignore it, but we cannot evade it."[75] I fully agree with this statement; it very nicely drives home the point of discipleship.

Christianity without the cross

It appears that Christians are not mindful of how the cross is central to their identity as Christ's followers. D. A. Carson writes: "The cross, then, is dismissed and derided by everyone. But still, Paul insists, "*we preach Christ crucified*" (1 Cor. 1:23). The message of the cross may be nonsense to those who are perishing, "a stumbling block to Jews and foolishness to Gentiles" (1 Cor. 1:23), "but to those whom God has called, both Jews and Greeks, Christ the power of God and the wisdom of God" (1 Cor. 1:24). This is an astonishing claim!" Let's not forget also what Rohr writes about the importance of the cross: "The doctrine of the cross is the great interpretative key that makes many things clear, at least for Christians, but perhaps also for history. . . . *'Crux probat omnia'* . . . 'the cross proves everything.'"[76] Carson concludes that we might "recognize that a cross-centered ministry is characterized by the Spirit's power and is vindicated in transformed lives."[77] However, for many Christians today, the call to deny self, take up their cross, and follow Christ appear to be non-important and non-essential for their spirituality. This is very distressing! Dietrich Bonheoffer writes: "Discipleship means adherence to the person of Jesus, and therefore submission to the law of Christ which is the law of the cross . . . When Christ calls a man, he bids him to come and die."[78]

A *"cross"* without suffering

Christians often fail to appropriate the life of the cross on a day-to-day basis. This could be caused by a lack of clear understanding about biblical teaching about *suffering*, which is the way of the cross. Bonheoffer writes: "Suffering and rejection sum up the whole cross of Jesus. To die on the cross means to die despised and rejected of men . . . Jesus must therefore make it clear beyond all doubt that the "*must*" of suffering applies to his disciples no less than to Himself . . . The cross is laid on every Christian."[79] I think that it is important to go back to the teaching of Jesus and the apostles and see afresh that the Bible does not exclude suffering in the lives of God's children.

"Discipleship means adherence to the person of Jesus, and therefore submission to the law of Christ which is the law of the cross . . . When Christ calls a man, he bids him to come and die."

Cheap discipleship

Believers today assume incorrectly that the cost of discipleship outweighs the benefits of discipleship lifestyle. George Barna writes: "Discipleship is not a program. It is not a ministry. It is a life-long commitment to a lifestyle."[80] We should never forget that, "The cost you will pay for not being a disciple is infinitely greater than the cost you will pay for being one."[81]

Spiritual opposition

Many who proclaim to follow Christ are not aware of the dynamics of the spiritual forces who oppose their spiritual progress. On one hand there is the opposition between the flesh and the spirit. Paul writes: "For the flesh sets its desire against the Spirit, and the Spirit against the flesh; for these are in opposition to one another, so that you may not do the things that you please" (Galatians 5:17). On the other hand, there is the struggle against the forces of darkness. The Bible tells us: "For our struggle is not against flesh and blood, but against the rulers, against the powers, against the world forces of this darkness, against the spiritual forces of wickedness in the heavenly places" (Eph. 6:12). Jim Peterson writers, "Since Satan rules over the ungodly, it should come as no surprise that we will suffer at his hands through his people. Satan works. He takes initiative. He has people at his disposal who will do his bidding. He has demonic forces under his command. And we can expect to be on the receiving end of his schemes."[82] It is clear that because of immaturity; many cannot appropriate their God-given victory. Paul explains, "Now I say, as long as the heir is a child, he does not differ at all from a slave although he is owner of everything" (Galatians 4:1). Only when believers go through proper discipleship, they begin knowing by experience who they are in Christ, become adequately equipped to deny self (Lk. 9:23), hate the world (1 John 2:15), submit to God (James 4:7(a), and resist the devil (James 4:7(b), 1 Peter 5:7).

Contentment with spiritual immaturity

Another important aspect is that many Christians don't see the need for spiritual maturity, but instead feel content in a spiritually immature state (when measured by the biblical standard of Christian discipleship).

Jim Peterson writes:

> To be spiritual is to be dependent on the Spirit. This dependence should characterize our normal, everyday relationship with Him . . . Maturity comes in time, out of a spiritual life that is nourished by an increasing knowledge of Christ through experience with Him.[83]

I think that this aspect is extremely important and requires further explaining. Let's explore some important reasons why spiritual maturity is either ignored or resisted.

First, there is a **lack of knowledge.** It is possible that many do not know the meaning of *Christian* and *Christianity*. Believers from almost any denomination take the word '*Christian*' with superficiality. It is possible that many don't even know that to be a Christian means to be a follower of Christ, (Gr. *mathetes*)—a disciple of Jesus. According to Professor Dallas Willard, the word "*disciple*" occurs 269 times in the New Testament. In contrast, the word "*Christian*" is found three times. Willard writes: "The New Testament is a book about disciples, by disciples, and for disciples of Jesus Christ."[84] A disciple is a person who wants to be modeled and transformed by the Word of God thorough the power of the Holy Spirit from inside out so she (or he), in character, heart, and will, looks more like Jesus Christ. George Barna writes: "Not one of the adults we interviewed said that their goal in life was to be a committed follower of Jesus Christ or to make disciples."[85] What a tragedy! As Willard writes: "The last command Jesus gave the church before he ascended to heaven was the **Great Commission**, the call for Christians to "make disciples of all the nations." But Christians have responded by making "Christians," not "disciples." This has been the church's **Great Omission**."[86] Wow! It hurts my heart! But more than this, it hurts the heart of our Abba God.

Secondly, there is **a superficial understanding regarding discipleship:** It appears that the majority of Christians consider discipleship as an unnecessary task. The common rejection is expressed like this: "*Since I am already saved, why should I waste my time with discipleship. I have recited the 'sinner's prayer' and I am on my way to heaven. Therefore, for that matter, I don't need discipleship or spiritual growth.*" George Barna writes: "Most born-again adults have a very narrow view of what they are striving to become as Christians, what spiritual maturity might look like in their lives, and what it would take for them to maximize their potential as followers of Christ. The dilemma is not that believers deny the importance of spiritual growth or have failed to consider the challenges it raises, but that they seem to have settled for a very limited understanding of the Christian faith and their potential in Christ."[87] I hope that you see this difficulty too when it comes to the subject of discipleship and spiritual maturity. It is very hard to ask believers to become disciples (Luke 9:23-24) when most churches don't insist on discipleship (Mathew 28:19-20) as being part of what their normal Christian life.

Thirdly, there is a **superficial understanding regarding spiritual growth and maturity.** The Scriptures clearly state that God desires His children to be different than the mainstream culture and to shine in this world. (See Matthew 5:14 and Philippians 2:15). But this requires our full engagement with the Spirit in the *process* of *spiritual growth.* (See 2 Corinthians 3:18, Romans 12:1–2). Willard writes: "Spiritual formation, without regard to any specifically religious context or tradition, is the process by which the human spirit or will is given a definite *form* or character. Make no mistake; it is a process that happens to everyone." The real question is what type of character is it going to be? Willard continues, "Christian spiritual formation is the redemptive process of forming the inner human world so that it takes on the character of the inner being of Christ himself."[88] This is exactly what God wants all of His children to experience to the fullest measure possible. (See 2 Corinthians 3:18 and Ephesians 4:11–16).

Fourth, there is **a lack of understanding about God's *ultimate intention*:** Most Christians do not have a clear understanding about Christ's objective with and for them. According to DeVern Fromke, God's *ultimate intention* is for Christ to have a Body. Fromke writes: "The Father is realizing that which His heart has yearned for throughout the ages—a vast family of sons conformed to the image of His only Begotten. His is a family who will bring to Him paternal honor, glory and satisfaction. The Lord Jesus, the Son, is receiving what the Father has purposed for Him—a many-membered Body which will be for the expression of Himself throughout the universe. The Spirit is receiving a glorious temple built of living stones which will be for His eternal habitation."[89] This causes several misconceptions among believers. Some of these misconceptions are:

1. A man-centered (self-referenced) point of view instead of God-centered (Christ-referenced) point of view.
2. A superficial understanding about salvation and what it means. Many believe that God had just to repair what happened at the fall. Others believe that it is all about "*me.*" This is the–*the poor man* in need of salvation–type of mentality. Still others have almost no knowledge regarding the *Plan of God* "before of foundation of the world" (Eph. 1:4) to bring "many sons into glory" (Heb.2:10). I hope that you see clearly that the two views are on a collision course with each other.

Fifth, many have **a distorted identity.** Sad to say, but many Christians do not know who they are in Christ. Neil T. Anderson writes: "Understanding your identity in Christ is essential for living the Christian life. People cannot consistently behave in ways that are inconsistent with the way they perceive themselves."[90] Views like these are predominant in many churches: I am just a *sinner* saved by grace. The focus is on *sin* not on *grace.* Or, *I* can do everything I *want* because I am *saved.* The focus is on *I* and *want* not on the *saved* and the privilege and responsibility that comes from that status.

Sixth, there is **a lack of vision about God's glorious and eternal plan**. Tragically, only a few know that they are a new creations in Christ (2 Corinthians 5:17), seated with Christ in heavenly places (Ephesians 2:6), called to be disciples of Jesus (Luke 9:23), and ambassadors for Christ (2 Corinthians 5:21), appointed to be men and women of God ruling in life through Christ (Romans 5:17). Without the eyes of the heart being '*enlightened*' by the Holy Spirit, Christians will not and cannot know 'what is the hope of His calling, what are the riches of the glory of His inheritance in the saints' (Ephesians 1:18). Therefore, having a distorted and a limited vision, Christians have no motivation to grow spiritually and tend just to cling to a religion and, sadly, many live pathetic lives. The only hope many who call themselves Christians have, is to go to heaven when they die. Barna writes:

"The chief barrier to effective discipleship is not that people do not have the ability to become spiritually mature, but they lack the passion, perspective, priorities, and perseverance to develop their spiritual lives."[91] I think that this is just depressing. No wonder Paul prayed so fervently for the church in Ephesus.

Here is Paul's prayer:

> I pray that the eyes of your heart may be enlightened, so that you will know what is the hope of His calling, what are the riches of the glory of His inheritance in the saints, and what is the surpassing greatness of His power toward us who believe. These are in accordance with the working of the strength of His might which He brought about in Christ, when He raised Him from the dead and seated Him at His right hand in the heavenly places, far above all rule and authority and power and dominion, and every name that is named, not only in this age but also in the one to come. And He put all things in subjection under His feet and gave Him as head over all things to the church, which is His body, the fullness of Him who fills all in all. (Ephesians 1:17–23).

I am not sure about you, but as for me I subscribe to Paul's prayer one hundred percent. Amen?

Discussion Questions:

– After reading this chapter, what concept, statistic, or idea, challenged you the most? Please share with a trusted friend.

– Please re-read Pastor Glenn McDonald's statement from page 86, 87. What do you think about his assessment? It is, at least, partially true of your local church?

– Valy presented six major reasons why Christians are content with spiritual immaturity. Which argument challenged you the most?

– What do you think of George Barna affirmation about "lack passion, perspective, priorities, and perseverance to develop their spiritual lives."? Please elaborate and share with your small group.

Notes

6. Lack of spiritual maturity

73 McDonald, 7.
74 Bill Hull, *The Disciple-Making Pastor: The Key to Building Healthy Christians in Today's Church*, (Grand Rapids, MI: Fleming H. Revell, 1988), 23.
75 Walter A. Henrichsen, *Disciples are Made not Born*, (Colorado Springs, CO: Victor, 1974), Forward section.
76 Richard Rohr, *Things Hidden (Scripture as Spirituality)*, (Cincinnati, OH: St. Anthony Messenger Press, 2008), 185.
77 D. A. Carson, *The Cross and Christian Ministry*, (Grand Rapids, MI: Baker Books, 2004), 22, 40.
78 Dietrich Bonheoffer, *The Cost of Discipleship,* (New York, NY: Simon & Schuster, 1959), 89.
79 Bonheoffer, 87, 89.
80 Barna, 19.
81 Walter A. Henrichsen, *Disciples are Made not Born*, (Colorado Springs, CO: Victor, 1974),39.
82 Jim Peterson, *Lifestyle Discipleship: The Challenge of Following Jesus in Today's World*, (Colorado Springs, CO: Navpress, 1994), 132, 133.
83 Peterson, 1994, 65.
84 Willard, 3.
85 Barna, 6.
86 Willard, (2006), front cover flap.
87 Barna, 40, 42.
88 Willard, 104, 105.
89 DeVern F. Fromke, *The Ultimate Intention*, (Shoals, IN: Sure Foundation, 1963), 179.
90 Neil T. Anderson, *Victory over the Darkness*, (Ventura, CA: Regal Books, 2000), 47.
91 Barna, 54.

CHAPTER 7

Spiritual Growth—The Badge of a Genuine Disciple

My Father is glorified by this, that you bear much fruit, and so prove to be My disciples.
— John 15:8

Elena and I got married when we were twenty years old. God blessed us with four healthy children, two girls and two boys. My wife was and still is such a good and caring mother. She made sure the kids ate and slept properly for their ages. The pediatrician checked their weight and height on a regular basis. We paid close attention to their diet, emotional and mental development. Now, all our children are married and have children of their own. They are good parents and closely monitor the well-being of our grandchildren to make sure they develop properly and proportionally for their respective ages. My wife loves all the grandkids. Even though she is tempted to say: "O, how I wish they would stay babies forever, so I can hold them, and delight in them!" she wants all of them to develop and grow in all aspects of their existence: physical, emotional, intellectual, mental, and so on.

I understood, from some medical articles, that in some cases kids do not meet the expected standards of development and growth. When children don't gain weight as expected, the pediatricians call this "failure to thrive." In most cases this condition is caused by eating issues and illnesses. Dr. Rupal Gupta, a pediatrician from Kansas City, Missouri, explains that, "In general, kids who fail to thrive don't receive or cannot take in, keep, or use the calories that would help them grow and gain enough weight."[92] Among the most recognized causes for the improper physical development of children are: not enough food offered, the child eat insufficiently, digestive system issues, food intolerances, and metabolic problems.

I have not seen any parents who would not do anything in their power to make sure their children grow and mature properly. How much more our heavenly Father desires all of us to thrive, to grow spiritually and mature in such a way that our character looks progressively more like Christ's.

The foundation of spiritual growth

In this chapter, I am providing you some elements which over the years of involvement in spiritual formation, proved to be crucial in my own life. I can genuinely say that the very foundation of spiritual growth and maturity rests on these two important building blocks: 1. *The finished work of the cross*, and 2. *The Zoe life of God.*

1. The finished work of the cross

Having a correct understanding of our co-crucifixion with Christ as written in Galatians 2:20 is foundational for our spiritual growth. Paul writes: "I have been crucified with Christ, and I no longer live, but Christ lives in me. The life I live in the body, I live by faith in the Son of God, who loved me and gave himself for me." When we correctly appropriate the cross in our lives, it opens the spiritual portal for Christ to live in us.

2. The Zoe life of God

God gave Christ's life for us, in order to give Christ's life to us, in order that Christ might live His life through us. Our spiritual formation depends on our correct understanding of the forces which are trying to prevent us from walking in the abundant life promised by our Good Shepard—Jesus. John writes: "The thief comes only to steal and kill and destroy; I have come that they may have life, and have it to the full" (John 10:10).

Spiritual growth and maturity

We must realize that spiritual growth and maturity is not going to happen overnight; it is a lifelong process; it takes time, testing, and trials. Based on John 21:15–17, the disciples are passing through various stages of growth: a. Lambs, b. Young sheep and c. Mature sheep. This means that nobody jumps out from the baptismal water and becomes a spiritual parent instantly. According to 1 John 2:12–14, disciples are moving across three levels of spiritual formation:

– Children in Christ
– Youth in faith
– Mature in Christ or Spiritual Parents

If we study the letter to the Ephesians carefully, we can clearly understand God's intentions for His church across the entire history. Starting with the first century up to the contemporary church, the Father desires to have a family of sons and daughters who resemble the image of His Son—Jesus. The author of Hebrews writes: "For it was fitting for Him, for whom are all things, and through whom are all things, in bringing many sons to glory, to perfect the author of their salvation through sufferings" (Hebrews 2:10).

Paul also writes:

> And we know that God causes all things to work together for good of those who love God, to those who are called according to His purpose. For those whom He foreknew, He also predestined to become conformed to the image of His Son, so that He would be the firstborn among many brethren; and these whom He predestined, He also called; and these whom He called, He also justified; and these whom He justified, He also glorified. (Romans 8:28–30)

We could easily use multiple pages to unpack these verses and would still not get to the bottom of the wisdom contained in them. Without unpacking this famous passage, let me give you just a simple sketch of this great passage:

1. The foreknowledge of God
2. God's predestination[93]
3. God's calling
4. Justification
5. Glorification

Now let's look closely at the passage from Ephesians 4:11–16:

And He gave some as apostles, and some as prophets, and some as evangelists, and some as pastors and teachers, for the equipping of the saints for the work of service, to the building up of the body of Christ; until we all attain to the unity of the faith, and of the knowledge of the Son of God, to a mature man, to the measure of the stature which belongs to the fullness of Christ. As a result, we are no longer to be children, tossed here and there by waves and carried about by every wind of doctrine, by the trickery of men, by craftiness in deceitful scheming; but speaking the truth in love, we are to grow up in all aspects into Him who is the head, even Christ, from whom the whole body, being fitted and held together by what every joint supplies, according to the proper working of each individual part, causes the growth of the body for the building up of itself in love (Ephesians 4:11–16).

Please observe that, in this short paragraph, the apostle Paul mentions at least five phrases that suggest spiritual growth:

– Building up of the body of Christ
– Mature man
– Fullness of Christ
– Grow up
– Growth of the body

Therefore, it should be clear to us that priority number one of any local church should be the spiritual growth of all believers, accomplished through Christian discipleship.

Furthermore, in 1 Corinthians 13:11, the apostle Paul writes: "When I was a child, I used to speak like a child, think like a child, reason like a child; when I became a man, I did away with childish things." I challenge you to look at this verse in the light of the Christian's growth.

Paul is saying that:

– The speech
– The thinking process
– The reasoning style

of a child are fundamentally different from:

– The speech
– The thinking process
– The reasoning style

of a mature person.

The distinction is so profoundly different, that the apostle Paul declares: "when I became a man, I did away with childish things." Once again, we observe the idea of g-r-o-w-t-h even in the Love Chapter.

The Power of the Seed

I am so impressed by the prophetic words of Isaiah. Some people call this book, "The Gospel, according to Isaiah."

In chapter 55, the prophet writes:

> For as the rain and the snow come down from heaven, And do not return there without watering the earth And making it bear and sprout, And furnishing seed to the sower and bread to the eater; So will My word be which goes forth from My mouth; It will not return to Me empty, Without accomplishing what I desire, And without succeeding in the matter for which I sent it. (Isaiah 55:10–11).

There is power in the Word of God! There is no question

about it. We cannot live without the Word of God. Christ Himself declares: "It is written, 'Man shall not live on bread alone, but on every Word that proceeds out of the mouth of God'" (Matthew 4:4). Let's look in Isaiah 55:10–11. Do you see the connection between what the prophet Isaiah and Jesus are saying? "So will My word be which goes forth from My mouth" (Isaiah), and "Word that proceeds out of the mouth of God" (Matthew). The Word of God is living and active. God's Word doesn't get dull or old; His Word speaks to us today, right now. This is essential to remember! When we read the Bible, we are not just reading black letters on white pages, as it is with any other book. When we read the Bible, we are in communion with the Living Word of God. When we open the Bible, God opens His mouth and speaks to us. The author of Hebrews writes: "For the word of God is living and active and sharper than any two-edged sword, and piercing as far as the division of soul and spirit, of both joints and marrow, and able to judge the thoughts and intentions of the heart (Hebrews 4:11). There is no other manuscript or piece of writing out there capable of such deep penetration into the human spirit, soul, heart, mind, and emotions. When we read the Bible, the Word of God is reading us. There is power in the Seed of the Word.

In the Gospel of Mark, Jesus tells us:

> And He was saying, The kingdom of God is like a man who casts seed upon the soil; and he goes to bed at night and gets up by day, and the seed sprouts and grows—how, he himself does not know. The soil produces crops by itself … But when the crop permits, he immediately puts in the sickle, because the harvest has come (Mark 4:26–29).

When I read this passage, the statement: **The soil produces crops by itself**, captured my attention. Wow! It was like I have seen this sentence for the first time. What does it mean? Why/how does the soil produces crops by itself? The real power is in the seed. However, the quality of the ground can harness that power, or it can block its ability. The seed needs a proper soil in which to grow. If the seed falls into the ground, and it incorporates the seed: "the seed sprouts and grows." The metaphor of the seed and the soil is powerful! Likewise, there is power in the seed of the Word, but it needs the soil of a human heart in which to germinate, to sprout and grow, and produce fruit.

In the gospel of Matthew, chapter 13, Jesus told His audience a different parable, known as: "The Parable of the Sower."

> Behold, the sower went out to sow; and as he sowed, some seeds fell beside the road, and the birds came and ate them up. Others fell on the rocky places, where they did not have much soil; and immediately they sprang up, because they had no depth of soil. But when the sun had risen, they were scorched; and because they had no root, they withered away. Others fell among the thorns, and the thorns came up and choked them out. And others fell on the good soil and yielded a crop, some a hundredfold, some sixty, and some thirty. He who has ears, let him hear (Matthew 13:3–9).

The sower spreads around the seeds having inside the same quality and power. What made the difference in the outcome is not the quality of the seed, but the quality of the soil. According to this parable, the seeds fell on all four types of soil:

– First place is beside the road. Because of the proximity to the road, the birds ate up the seeds.
– The second one is a hard place. In rocky terrain, there is not enough fertile soil permitting the plant to deepen its roots. Therefore, the plants sprang up quickly, and quickly they withered.
– The third place is among the thorns. We can easily imagine that these little plants did not have any chances to survive because the thorns choked them out.
– The good soil represents that last place. This soil incorporates the seed and facilitates the environment for it to sprout and grow. Ultimately this soil yielded various degrees of harvest: "some a hundredfold, some sixty, and some thirty" (cf. Matthew 13:8).

The good news is that we don't have to scratch our heads to

understand what this parable means. The Lord Jesus interprets it, so the disciples get a proper understating of its meaning. It is evident that the seed is the gospel message speaking about the kingdom of God. The soil represents the hearts of people.

Here are a few important aspects:

1. The birds mentioned in the first place represent evil spirits who quickly pluck away the word from people's hearts. When the human heart is void of the Word of God, there is no growth and no harvest.
2. The rocky places represent superficiality. People don't take the Word of God seriously and, as a result, there is no firm root to sustain them during life's afflictions and possible persecutions. So, when the hard times come, these people fall away from the faith.
3. The thorny places represent those people who think that they can have the best of both worlds: God's kingdom and this world. Jesus desires loyalty to Him and the kingdom of God. Matthew writes that people cannot serve two masters: God and wealth (cf. Matthew 6:24). Because their hearts are divided, these people cannot be fruitful for Christ.
4. The good soil speaks of the people who hear the Word and understand it. They facilitate the development of a good root system of the Word in their hearts. The result of this is a plenteous harvest: "some hundredfold, some sixty, and some thirty" (cf. Matthew 13:23).

Growing up, I remember when my dad bought a small nectarine tree and planted it in our backyard. The first year I asked him: "Dad, do you think that this tree is going to bring any nectarines this year?" Dad explained that the tree needs more time to mature before it can bring forth any fruits. The second year I asked him the same question, and I got a similar response. The third year my dad spotted some flowers in that young nectarine tree. He said: "This year we have a better chance to eat some nectarines from it. Of course, assuming that the tree keeps its flowers, and after the fruits are formed, they reach maturity and ripen." I got excited! I told my dad: "I can't wait to taste the fruits of this tree."

I also remember one fall when my mom placed tomato seeds in dark soil in a wooden box. She watered the soil regularly and kept the box inside the house throughout the winter. Surprisingly, the next spring, little green plants started coming out from the dark ground. My mom kept on watering these tiny plants, and they kept on growing. When it was warm enough outside, she transferred the tomato plants in the vegetable garden. Guess what? In a few months, we were able to eat delicious tomato salad. It all started with some small seeds buried in dark soil. There is power in the seed.

Spiritual growth takes place because there is power in the Seed of the Word.

It is crucial to understand that spiritual growth is gradual. According to Mark 4:26–29, reaching the state of fruitfulness, requires three stages of growth:

– The blade
– The head
– The mature grain

God is interested in mature sons and daughters, who bring a harvest for Christ's glory.

Let me share something from my spiritual journey. More than two decades ago, God planted deep into my heart the "seed" of the ministry of spiritual growth and maturity. It was a small seed with tremendous potential. The Holy Spirit used two specific "seeds" from the Word of God. The first one is in John 15:8: "My Father is glorified by this, that you bear much fruit, and so prove to be My disciples." The second one is found in 2 Peter 1:4–11:

> For by these He has granted to us His precious and magnificent promises, so that by them you may become partakers of the divine nature, having escaped the corruption that is in the world by lust. Now for this very reason also, applying all diligence, in your faith supply moral excellence, and in your moral excellence, knowledge, and in your knowledge, self-control, and in your self-control, perseverance, and in your perseverance, godliness, and in your godliness, brotherly kindness, and in your brotherly kindness,

> love. For if these qualities are yours and are increasing, they render you neither useless nor unfruitful in the true knowledge of our Lord Jesus Christ. For he who lacks these qualities is blind or short-sighted, having forgotten his purification from his former sins. Therefore, brethren, be all the more diligent to make certain about His calling and choosing you; for as long as you practice these things, you will never stumble; for in this way the entrance into the eternal kingdom of our Lord and Savior Jesus Christ will be abundantly supplied to you.

By the guidance of the Holy Spirit, I was able to connect the dots. John 15:8 communicates that our fruit glorifies our Father. Second Peter 1:8 explains that to be fruitful, we need to cultivate certain qualities, such as faith, moral excellence, knowledge, self-control, perseverance, godliness, brotherly kindness, and love. Peter said: "For if these qualities are yours and are increasing, they render you neither useless nor unfruitful." At this point, the light bulb came on so bright! After this understanding, I was completely sold out to this vision. When keeping these things in the right perspective, the Great Commission made so much sense. There is no substitute for making disciples, no program, no religion, no law, nothing. Fruitfulness glorifies the Father. Fruitfulness is the real badge of proof of our genuine discipleship. It displays our humble obedience and reliance on the Holy Spirit to bring His fruitfulness to our service. This is what Jesus tells us: "My Father is glorified by this, that you bear much fruit, and so prove to be My disciples" (John 15:8). There is not much space for debate in this verse—*fruitfulness* and *discipleship* go hand in hand.

> The only vehicle for spiritual growth and multiplication is discipleship.

If we put all these things in perspective, the grand conclusion is clear: **Spiritual growth takes place because there is power in the Seed of the Word.**

The quality of the soil is also important. If the heart is good soil, it produces a harvest: "some a hundredfold, some sixty, and some thirty" (Matthew 13:8). This entire process, from the preparation of the soil to casting the seed into the ground, and regularly watering it, is called discipleship. Paul explains: "I planted,

Apollos watered, but God was causing the growth" (1 Corinthians 3:6). Paul understood the process of discipleship very well. The Lord Jesus Christ is the chief model in discipleship. Paul, also, did his best to model what a mentor-mentee relationship looks like. He dared to write: "Be imitators of me, just as I also am of Christ" (1 Corinthians 11:1). When Paul sensed that his time was near, he admonished his son in the faith—Timothy, to give his highest attention to the process of discipleship. He writes: "The things which you have heard from me in the presence of many witnesses, entrust these to faithful men who will be able to teach others also: (2 Timothy 2:2).

In other words, the greatest apostle is saying: The only vehicle for spiritual growth and multiplication is discipleship.

May God bless every one of us to follow in the footsteps of Jesus, and, as Paul did, we too, may leave clear marks for others to follow the Great Master—Christ, thus fulfilling the Great Commission.

Discussion Questions:

– What is your opinion on Spiritual Formation? Do you think that it is important for Christians to grow spiritually? Please elaborate.

– Where are you in your own spiritual journey regarding spiritual growth? Please share with a trusted friend or, if you have one, with your spiritual mentor.

– In what areas do you consider yourself more mature? In which areas are you lacking spiritual growth? Please share with your small group.

– What constitutes your spiritual diet? What are you actively doing to "eat" the right spiritual diet for your stage of spiritual growth? Please elaborate and share with a trusted friend or with your spiritual mentor.

Notes

7. Spiritual Growth—The Badge of Genuine Discipleship

[92] Gupta, R. Christine, MD, *Failure to Thrive*, Kidshealth, November 2014.Accessed on June 25, 2019. https://kidshealth.org/en/parents/failure-thrive.html.

[93] The term "predestination" used here by this author has nothing to do with the views held in Calvinism "that God appointed the eternal destiny of some to salvation by grace, while leaving the remainder to receive eternal damnation for all their sins, even their original sin." Accessed on June 19, 2019. https://en.wikipedia.org/wiki/Predestination_in_Calvinism.
This author is saying that because God is omniscient, He sees the end from the beginning. Based on His foreknowledge, as Paul states so very well: "He predestined us to adoption as sons through Jesus Christ to Himself, according to the kind intention of His will, to the praise of the glory of His grace, which He freely bestowed on us in the Beloved" (Ephesians 1:5–6). Let's continue to wonder and not try to box God in any of our theological boxes.

CHAPTER 8

The Perils of Spiritual Immaturity—Part One

Therefore leaving the elementary teaching about the Christ, let us press on to maturity, not laying again a foundation of repentance from dead works and of faith toward God.
— Hebrews 6:1

In the mid-90s I was drawn by the Holy Spirit into the field of spiritual growth and maturity. At that time, I had a tiny "office" in the basement of our home. After work and after completing necessary chores I would crawl into that office. Many times, I spent hours at a time digging into the Scriptures to learn more about this marvelous field. So, the thoughts and ideas I am going to share next have been springing up from Ephesians 4:11–16, a passage that has become very important to me over the years. I normally use this portion of Scripture to explain the importance of spiritual growth and maturity. However, during a mission trip to India and Italy a few years back, I felt strongly led to start teaching and writing about the dangers of spiritual immaturity. While in those foreign lands, it was a brand-new message for me too. I had never preached from this passage in this manner before. The message came freely from the depths of my heart without any prior preparation. Even before reading this chapter, I suggest you pause and pray for a few minutes:

> Father God, please open my eyes to see You, open my ears to hear the voice of the Spirit, open my heart and fill it with the love of Jesus, open my mind to

> comprehend the Scriptures, and empower me with the will to surrender my life one hundred percent to Your divine purposes. I pray in the wonderful name of Jesus Christ. Amen!

I have been praying for you, my readers, so I expect a deep understanding to come from above into your souls.

In Ephesians 4:11–16, Paul talks about the five-fold ministry of the church. I like to call it the "*hand*" of God. It contains the following "*fingers*":

– Apostles
– Prophets
– Evangelists
– Pastors
– Teachers

This s*pecial hand* is given for the overall edification of the Body of Christ. All these s*pecial fingers* are called for a specific three-prong objective:

– For the equipping of the saints
– For the work of service
– To the building up of the body of Christ

This objective was not finished during the apostolic generation of the Church in the first centuries. It continues today. I firmly believe that this great objective must be accomplished before the return of Christ. In this passage, Paul is saying that in the process of accomplishing this great tri-fold objective, three major aspects must be kept in focus:

– Attaining to the unity of the faith, and of the knowledge of the Son of God
– Reaching the stature of a mature man
– Attaining the fullness of Christ (see Ephesians 4:13)

It is my understanding that attaining the fullness of Christ is God's ultimate intention for His Church. I shared this in the past, but it is worth repeating:

> The *ultimate intention* of the church is a mature disciple who knows God intimately and personally (cf. John 17:3), who accepted the discipleship call and carries the cross daily (cf. Luke 9:23; Galatians 2:20), whose mind and character are continuously renewed and transformed by the Spirit and the Word of God (cf. Romans 12:2; 2 Corinthians 3:18; Galatians 5:22–23), who grows and matures into the fullness of Christ (cf. Ephesians 4:11-16, Hebrew 5:11–14, 6:1-3), and who, ultimately, multiplies disciples according to Christ's and the apostles' discipleship model (cf. Matthew 28:19–20; 2 Timothy 2:2).[94]

This was the case for the first century Church and it is still in effect for the Church of the last days prior to His glorious return.

That is why I am passionate about writing on the topic of the *dangers of spiritual immaturity*. I am strongly convinced that these aspects are both extremely important and extremely urgent! If believers continue to remain in the state of spiritual immaturity, they are in danger of forfeiting God's purpose for their lives. Luke writes: "But the Pharisees and the lawyers rejected God's purpose for themselves, not having been baptized by John" (Luke 7:30). In other words, we can say: "But some Christians rejected God's purpose by not taking heed to their spiritual growth and maturity, therefore they forfeited the ultimate intention of God for them." In this portion of Scripture (Ephesians 4:11–16) Paul is not talking about salvation. Expounding upon this passage, I am not talking about salvation either. I am talking about the great danger of not reaching the full potential our loving Father desires for each of us as His beloved children.

It is sad to see that many Christians today are content with the *status quo*. So many church-goers falsely believe that spiritual maturity is done on some sort of *automatic pilot*. They think that just going through the motions will eventually result in growth, spiritual development, and maturity. This is exactly what the enemy of our souls would like us to think. But that doesn't lead to maturity. In fact, Jesus warned us in the parable of the Sower: "The seed which fell among the thorns, these are the ones who have heard, and as they go on their way they are choked with worries and riches and pleasures of this life, and bring no fruit to maturity" (Luke 8:14). Even though the fullness of Christ is what the Father desires for all of us, it will not happen automatically. Belonging to a local church does not make the cut either. Spiritual growth and maturity are the result of spiritual transformation led by the Holy Spirit. As a result, God displays the life and character of Christ through the believer. Discipleship is factored in by our *intentions* and *decisions* and it is translated out by our *faith in action.* It will not happen by itself. I believe that this is exactly what the Holy Spirit is speaking to churches today: "Believers, if you have an ear to hear, the will of the Father is to once again bring the cross of Christ to the forefront of the Church."

As the Holy Ghost impressed upon my heart, I perceived that there are five main dangers of spiritual immaturity.

1. Carnality

Carnality is a very great danger of immaturity. In his first epistle to the Corinthians Paul writes: "And I, brethren, could not speak to you as to spiritual men, but as to men of flesh, as to infants in Christ. I gave you milk to drink, not solid food; for you were not yet able to receive it. Indeed, even now you are not yet able, for you are still fleshly. For since there is jealousy and strife among you, are you not fleshly, and are you not walking like mere men?" (1 Corinthians 3:1–3). In the endnotes section,[95] please see various renderings of these verses from various Bible translations. First Corinthians 3:1–3, is a very interesting passage of Scripture. Paul is using various words to describe the spiritually immature state of the believers in Corinth. These words are:

- Men of flesh
- Infants in Christ
- Milk drinkers
- Fleshly
- Jealousy
- Strife
- Mere men

What does Paul mean by the expression *men of flesh*? Simply put, *men of flesh* means people who are controlled by their human nature instead of by the Holy Spirit. According to *Vine's Complete Expository Dictionary of the Old and New Testament Words* the Greek word used here is σαρκικός—*sarkikos.* It corresponds to Strong's #4559. It derives from *sarx* which means *flesh.*

Sarkikos signifies:

(a): "having the nature of flesh," having its seat in the animal nature, or excited by it, as in 1 Peter 2:11. "Fleshly" or as the equivalent of "human," with the added idea of weakness. It also communicates the idea of un-spirituality, of human wisdom, "fleshly," as in 2 Corinthians 1:12.

Sarkikos also signifies:

(b): "pertaining to the flesh" (i.e., the body), as in Romans 15:27 and 1 Corinthians 9:11.[96]

Furthermore, the Greek word σάρκινος—*sarkinos—fleshly* corresponds to Strong's #4560.

Sarkinos denotes:

> "*Of the flesh, fleshly*" as in 2 Corinthians 3:3 KJV: "but in fleshy tables of the heart." "The adjectives "*fleshly*," "*carnal*" are contrasted with spiritual qualities in Romans 7:14; 1 Corinthians 3:1, 3, 4; 2 Corinthians 1:12; Colossians 2:18. Speaking broadly, the *carnal* denotes the sinful element in man's nature, by reason of descent from Adam. On the other hand, the *spiritual* is that which comes by the regenerating operation of the Holy Spirit.[97]

The word *carnal* here σάρκινοῖς—sarkinois, is not the same word which used in 1 Corinthians 2:14 which is translated "natural" *ψυχικός*—psuchikos. "That" refers to one who is un-renewed, and who is wholly under the influence of his sensual or animal nature and is nowhere applied to Christians.[98]

"The carnal state is a state of continual sinning and failure."[99] "Carnal Christians are persons under the influence of fleshly appetites; coveting and living for the things of this life."[100]

Unfortunately, the majority of believers in Corinth were in a carnal state.

According to *Gill's Exposition of the Entire Bible*:

> The carnal state Christians, are not as unregenerate men are; but had carnal conceptions of things, were in carnal frames of soul, and walked in a carnal conversation with each other; though they were not in the flesh, in a state of nature, yet the flesh was in them, and not only lusted against the Spirit, but was very predominant in them, and carried them captive, so that they are denominated from it.[101]

Andrew Murray, in *The Master's Indwelling*, writes: "In these carnal Corinthians there was a little of God's Spirit, but the flesh predominated; the Spirit had not the rule of their whole life."[102] Pastor, J. B. Hall, in the *"Carnal Christian"* sermon, posted in sermoncentral.com, explains:

> The carnal Christian then, much like the lost person, serves to oppose the work of God in a church. He has his own agenda and is completely insensitive and unresponsive to the spiritual work God is trying to accomplish in His church.[103]

During my online research, when I typed the question: "What is a carnal Christian?" I got this answer:

> The key thing to understand is that while a Christian can be, for a time, carnal, a true Christian will not remain carnal for a lifetime.[104]

I like Andrew Murray's perspective on this subject:

> We shall say to Him, "*It must be changed. Have mercy upon us.*" But, ah! that prayer and that change cannot come until we have begun to see that there is a carnal root ruling in believers; they are living more after the flesh than the Spirit; they are yet carnal Christians.[105]

This angle is even more interesting! According to Andrew Murray it is impossible for Christians to grow from the carnal state into the spiritual state. He considers it deception.

He writes:

> There are Christians who think that they must grow out of the carnal state into the spiritual state. You never can.[106]

Then what is the solution we may ask? He continues:

> What could help those carnal Corinthians? To give them milk could not help them, for milk was a proof they were in the wrong state. To give them meat would not help them, for they were unfit to eat it. What they needed was the knife of the surgeon. Paul says that the carnal life must be cut out. "*They that are Christ's have crucified the flesh*" (Galatians 5:24). When a man understands what that means, and accepts it in the faith of what Christ can do, then one step can bring him from carnal to spiritual. One simple act of faith in the power of Christ's death, one act of surrender to the fellowship of Christ's death as the Holy Spirit can make it ours, will make it ours, will bring deliverance from the power of your efforts.[107]

Furthermore, Andrew Murray writes:

> So, in the spiritual life, you may go to teacher after teacher, and say, "*Tell me about the spiritual life, the baptism of the Spirit, and holiness,*" and yet you may remain just where you were. Many of us would love to have sin taken away. Who loves to have a hasty temper? Who loves to have a proud disposition? Who loves to have a worldly heart? No one. We go to Christ to take it away, and He does not do it; and we ask, "Why will He not do it? I have prayed very earnestly." It is because you wanted Him to take away the ugly fruits while the poisonous root was to stay in you. You did not ask Him that the flesh should be

> nailed to His cross, and that you should henceforth give up self entirely to the power of His Spirit.[108]

The key is in trusting the Spirit and surrendering it to God. Murray adds:

> It is the Holy Spirit alone who by His indwelling can make a spiritual man. Come then and cast yourself at God's feet, with this one thought, "Lord, I give myself an empty vessel to be filled with Thy Spirit."[109]

The good news is that prayers like this are receiving a quick answer from the Father.

Suggested prayer:

> O, dear Father, I come before You with my empty vessel cleansed by the Blood of the Holy Lamb. My God will fulfill His promise! I claim from Him the filling of the Holy Spirit to make me, instead of a carnal, a spiritual Christian.[110]

All these things sound so good on paper, don't they? But when the rubber meets the road, things appear to be different. The question is: Is there a true spiritual life? Is such a thing possible for ordinary people like you and me? If it is: *How can you and I enter into such life?* Well, I am glad you asked! Let me see if I can explain it in plain terms.

– First of all, God is asking for it and He promises this type of life. The Bible teaches, "Therefore you are to be perfect, as your heavenly Father is perfect" (Matt. 5:48). Jesus is telling us, "I came that they may have life, and have it abundantly" (John 10:10b).

– Secondly, based on these two passages, it is clear that living this kind of life is impossible when believers are trying to live independently of God. Only Christ, through the Holy Spirit, operating in us can live that kind of life. After all it is His life.

So, what must we do? A few things are of a vital importance:

– We must be *filled with the Spirit* (Ephesians 5:18)
– We must be *led by the Spirit* (Romans 8:14)
– We must *walk by the Spirit* (Galatians 5:25)

If we don't see these aspects clearly, we must repent. In other words, we must change our minds about carnality of any kind and see it as incompatibility with God's nature of which we are partakers (2 Peter 1:4). It must be settled once and for all that for a genuine believer in Christ, these outbreaks of carnality should be an exception, not the rule.

– Third, the believer must be convicted of the bankruptcy of his or her flesh. We must see that there is something terribly wrong with our carnal state as believers, and we must agonize before God to deliver us from it. Paul writes: "Wretched man that I am! Who will set me free from the body of this death?" (Romans 7:24). Without this deep conviction we can never become truly spiritual men. Transition from the carnal state to the spiritual state is one step away. At this point, we see Galatians 2:20 with a different set of eyes. We declare, "it is no longer I who live, but Christ lives in me." There must be a legal breakup with the flesh. And rest assured that the cross is what has done (past tense) that. This is the place where Christ desires His brothers and sisters to live and operate, by Him and through Him. And this requires total surrender (Romans 12:1)—not just a one-time deal, but daily surrender, daily picking up and carrying the cross.

Spiritual life and abundant life are a walk. It is a dynamic life, not a static one. Only in the position of total surrender can the Word of God renew the mind of the believer. Only with the *renewal of the mind* (cf. Romans 12:2) and *transformation of character* (cf. 2 Corinthians 3:18) can the believer increasingly display the life and character of Christ, and thus be less and less carnal. This process, as others may explain it, is known as *progressive sanctification.*

If the Holy Spirit has convicted you about your own spiritual state, I highly encourage you to declare before God three positive things:

– Father God, I desire to eat solid food. Please cause me to grow.
– Dear Lord, I am so disappointed how carnal I am because I am still clinging to the flesh. I realize now "that nothing good dwells in me, that is, in my flesh" (Romans 7:18). Take Your "knife" and cut it off.
– Dear Holy Spirit, assist me and guide me in the process of spiritual growth and maturity.

Now that you have made these powerful declarations, let's pray this heartfelt prayer:

> O, Abba Father, I know that You love me. I present before You my empty vessel cleansed by the pure Blood of Your Son, Jesus. Take Your "knife" and cut off everything that is fleshy in me. You promised to give the Holy Spirit to all who ask for Him. I claim the filling of the Holy Spirit to make me a spiritual Christian instead of a carnal one. I pray in the wonderful name of Christ.

2. Instability

Probably one of the most visible dangers of spiritual immaturity is *instability*. Paul writes: "As a result, we are no longer to be children, tossed here and there by waves and carried about by every wind of doctrine, by the trickery of men, by craftiness in deceitful scheming" (Ephesians 4:14). According to *Merriam Webster Dictionary*, "to toss," means to "to throw (something) with a quick, light motion, to move or lift quickly or suddenly, to move (something) back and forth or up and down."[111]

Paul is using four words to warn believers about the danger of spiritual immaturity:

– Trickery
– Craftiness
– Deceitful
– Scheming

The word *trickery* in this verse refers to the opposite of being honest, truthful, frank, and open. The word *craftiness*, according to *Merriam Webster Dictionary*, is the skill of achieving one's ends through indirect, subtle, or underhanded means.[112] *Deceitful* means to do something based on or using dishonest methods to acquire something of value. The fourth word used by Paul is *scheming,* which means being clever at attaining one's ends by indirect and often deceptive means. Paul is not using this combination of words to impress the believers in Ephesus with his elevated Greek vocabulary. Under the inspiration of the Holy Spirit, Paul wanted to emphasize the danger of instability when believers remain at the childlike state. In other words, if we don't want to be carried about by every wind of doctrine, we must "grow in grace, and in the knowledge of our Lord and Savior Jesus Christ" (2 Peter 3:18).

Immature believers do not have a stable theological stand. If a preacher says something, he or she is moved in that direction. If a different teacher comes and preaches something else, he or she is thrown in that direction. Without spiritual maturity, believers are in danger of being carried away by the *trickery of men.* Deceitful men win over people who are carried about with ease. These men have some sort of false *charisma* to gain the sympathy of their audience. Bottom line—immaturity, a childlike state, is dangerous because of instability.

If this describes you, please acknowledge this danger in your life. I am asking you to declare three positive things:

– God, I need stability.
– Lord Jesus, I have decided to grow.
– Holy Spirit, please make me stable and consistent in my faith and my walk with You.

After making these important declarations I encourage you to kneel before God and pray this prayer:

> Father God, I want to be stable. I have decided to embrace the process of spiritual growth and maturity. Dear Lord Jesus, I realize that growing and maturing in Your grace and knowledge is the only way I can ensure stability in my life. Dear Holy Spirit, please work in me, transform me, and mature me according to God's plans and purposes. My only desire is to

> display the Life and the Character of Christ in and through me. I pray in the name of Jesus. Amen.

3. Repulsion towards Solid Food

Spiritually speaking, *milk* stands for the "elementary teaching about Christ." According to Hebrews 6:1-2, *the milk-diet*, includes: teachings about "repentance from dead works," percepts regarding "faith towards God," instructions related to the Church Sacraments, "resurrection of the dead and eternal judgment." Milk is good! No question about it. But milk is the primary food for babies, not for adults. As any good parent, our Father does not want His children to continue indefinitely on the milk-diet. God desires us to "grow in respect to salvation" as Peter puts it so well in 1 Peter 2:1–3. For this to happen, we must "press on to maturity" (Hebrews 6:1), which requires a willful decision. Pressing on is not an easy task; it implies overcoming resistance; it requires stick-to-it-ness. Moreover, pressing on requires advancing, heading toward, making headway, and progressing. As you can see, all these words are suggesting something dynamic, not static.

Solid food stands for advanced teaching regarding the righteousness of God and spiritual discernment. According to 2 Peter 3:18, solid food refers to mature teaching about the grace and knowledge of Christ. According to Paul's prayers in Ephesians 1:15–23 and 3:14–21, solid food means enlightened understanding about our identity in Christ and a deep comprehension of agape love and its spiritual dimensions. Based on Paul's teaching in Romans 8:14 and Galatians 5:16–26, solid food represents a correct understanding of what it really means to be led by the Holy Spirit. Moreover, solid food implies a deep knowledge of what it means to be transformed into Christlikeness (2 Corinthians 3:18; 1 Corinthians 5:2–3).

Immature believers have a *natural* tendency to dislike solid food. Repulsion is a feeling of strong dislike or disgust towards something. D. A. Carson writes:

> But there are Christians who are international-class projectile vomiters, spiritually speaking, after years and years of life. They simply cannot digest what Paul calls "solid food." You must give them milk, for they are

> not ready for anything more. And if you try to give them anything other than milk, they upchuck and make a mess of everyone and everything around them. At some point the number of years they have been Christians leads you to expect some mature behavior from them, but they prove disappointing. They are infants still and display their wretched immaturity even the way that they complain if you give them more than milk. Not for them solid knowledge of Scripture; not for them mature theological reflection; not for them growing and perceptive Christian thought. They want nothing more than another round of choruses and a "simple message"—something that won't challenge them to think, to examine their lives, to make choices, and to grow in their knowledge and adoration of the living God. So the Corinthians, then, are wretchedly immature believers.[113]

In my travels around the world teaching about spiritual growth and maturity I heard so many excuses (even from Christian leaders) regarding spiritual growth. Let me share just a few of them:

- It is so hard! Even the Bible tells us that too much teaching is weary to the body (cf. Ecclesiastes 12:12).
- I do not want to acquire too much knowledge because then God will expect much from me (cf. Luke 12:48).
- I don't have to study the Bible before I preach or make myself a plan or a sermon sketch because the Holy Spirit will give me the exact words I have to speak (cf. Mark 13:11).
- It is written not to have too many teachers (cf. James 3:1).

If you look at the Bible references I provided, all of these Scriptures are taken out of context, proving further the danger of spiritual immaturity. Obviously, a biological baby cannot be transitioned overnight from *milk* to *solid food.* It would be foolishness to have such an unrealistic expectation. It is a gradual process. He or she must be weaned first. The taste buds of a baby must be cultivated to *like* solid food. In the same way our spiritual "taste buds" must be cultivated to desire solid food over a period of time. But by no means should the weaning period take forty years; perhaps three or four, but not more than that. Charles R. Swindoll writes:

> You see, in order for a Christian to handle solid food, he has to have a grown, mature digestive system. He needs teeth. He needs to have an appetite that is cultivated over a period of time for deep things, for the solid things of God. Spiritual babies must grow up. Some of the most difficult people to live within the church of Jesus Christ are those who have grown old in the Lord but haven't grown up in Him.[114]

The more we delay our exposure to solid food, the longer it takes to like it. It requires a willful decision to move from milk to solid food, otherwise we will remain "dull of hearing." The author of Hebrews puts it this way: "But solid food is for the mature, who because of practice have their senses trained to discern good and evil" (Hebrews 5:14). Do you see the pattern? Practice leads to training of the senses, which leads to spiritual discernment.

You probably noticed this already, but it is not easy to measure spiritual maturity. Many believers erroneously assume that as time passes, they will automatically mature spiritually. Unlike physical maturity that is primarily a function of time, spiritual maturity is not. The time factor is obvious when it comes to physical maturity. We can easily differentiate between a three-year-old boy and a thirty-year-old man. In the spiritual realm growth and maturity are not a function of time but rather a function of our spiritual diet. For example, there could be some Christians out there who have been attending the local church for thirty years and still be at the level of toddler, acting like a three-year-old Christian. With proper discipleship, it is possible for a Christian who received Christ three years ago to be spiritually mature, displaying the life and character of Christ. (See Galatians 5:22–23; John 15:8).

Spiritual immaturity affects our speech, thinking, and decision-making. Paul writes: "When I was a child, I used to speak like a child, think like a child, reason like a child" (1 Corinthians 13:11a). Therefore, it is imperative to engage in the process of spiritual growth and maturity immediately so we can do away with childish things. Paul continues, "when I became a man, I did away with childish things" (1 Corinthians 13:11b).

The opposite of immaturity, of course, is spiritual maturity. Maturity is the high calling of every child of God and it is primarily evidenced by one's priorities. Do we continue to pursue the "*things*" of this world and "*success*" according to the flesh, or seek the supreme goal of God set before us—*intimacy with Christ*? Paul writes: "I press on toward the goal for the prize of the upward call of God in Christ Jesus" (Philippians 3:14). If the great apostle Paul felt the need to "press on," how much more you and I have to do it. Paul admonishes Christians engaged in the process of perfection with these words: "Let us therefore, as many as are perfect, have this attitude; and if in anything you have a different attitude, God will reveal that also to you" (Philippians 3:15). Christian maturity does not mean sinless perfection. It does not mean that those who are mature are a higher class than individuals who cannot humble themselves to live in unity with other people. By no means!

The Greek word *perfection* (Gr. τέλειος, teleios)[115] used by Paul in Philippians 3:15 means "full age, adulthood, full-grown, of persons, meaning full-grown in mind and understanding (cf. 1 Corinthians 14:20); in knowledge of the truth (cf. 1 Corinthians 2:6; Philippians 3:15, Hebrews 5:14); in Christian faith and virtue (cf. Ephesians 4:13)."[116] Paul explains, "However, let us keep living by that same standard to which we have attained" (Philippians 3:16). As Peter Meiderlin[117] once said: "In essentials unity, in non-essentials liberty, in all things charity."[118]

Spiritual maturity is not a competition between who can recite more theological facts. Rather, spiritual maturity is evidenced by love—agape love. The Bible teaches us, "But the goal of our instruction is love from a pure heart and a good conscience and a sincere faith" (1 Timothy 1:5). Genuine spiritual maturity is characterized by displaying a genuine and mature agape love, which is the very nature of God.

Believe me, it was not pleasant to write this section, and I am sure it was not pleasant for you to read it either. Please, do yourself a great favor, declare before God three positive things:

– God, I am hungry for solid food.
– Holy Spirit, I desire to eat like a mature Christian.
– Dear Lord Jesus, I am in pursuit of spiritual growth. My

> deep desire is to be a mature Christian. I invite You to display the life and character of Christ in me.

Now that you have declared these important statements please seal them in a prayer like this:

> Dear God, please plant a deep desire for Your Word in me. Please develop my taste buds for solid food. O, Lord Jesus, please carry me in Your arms and take me to green pastures so I can grow more and more into the grace and knowledge of You. So help me God. Amen!

Discussion Questions:

– After reading and re-reading this chapter what concept or idea stood out the most? Please explain why! Share your own insights with a trusted friend or your spiritual mentor.

– Read carefully and meditatively 1 Corinthians 3:1–3. How would you interpret this passage? How did you hear other pastors, teachers, or authors interpret it? Do you agree with any of these interpretations? Please share with your small group.

– What is your overall impression about the section called: "Carnality"? Which concept is new to you? Share your insights with a close friend.

– What is your overall impression about the section called: "Repulsion towards Solid Food"? Share your own insights with a trusted friend or with your spiritual mentor.

Notes

8. The Perils of Spiritual Immaturity–Part One

[94] Valy Vaduva, *Advanced Discipleship Training (ADT)—Registration Manual,* (Livonia, MI: Upper Room Fellowship Ministry, 2010), 7.

[95] Parallel Verses from various Bible Translations:

New International Version: Brothers and sisters, I could not address you as people who live by the Spirit but as people who are still worldly—mere infants in Christ.

New Living Translation: Dear brothers and sisters, when I was with you I couldn't talk to you as I would to spiritual people. I had to talk as though you belonged to this world or as though you were infants in the Christian life.

English Standard Version: But I, brothers, could not address you as spiritual people, but as people of the flesh, as infants in Christ.

New American Standard Bible: And I, brethren, could not speak to you as to spiritual men, but as to men of flesh, as to infants in Christ.

King James Bible: And I, brethren, could not speak unto you as unto spiritual, but as unto carnal, even as unto babes in Christ.

Holman Christian Standard Bible: Brothers, I was not able to speak to you as spiritual people but as people of the flesh, as babies in Christ.

International Standard Version: Brothers, I couldn't talk to you as spiritual people but as worldly people, as mere infants in the Messiah.

NET Bible: So, brothers and sisters, I could not speak to you as spiritual people, but instead as people of the flesh, as infants in Christ.

Aramaic Bible in Plain English: And I, my brethren, have not been able to speak with you as with spiritual ones but as with the carnal and as to babies in The Messiah.

GOD's WORD® Translation: Brothers and sisters, I couldn't talk to you as spiritual people but as people still influenced by your corrupt nature. You were infants in your faith in Christ.

Jubilee Bible 2000: And I, brothers, could not speak unto you as unto spiritual, but as unto carnal, even as unto babes in Christ.

King James 2000 Bible: And I, brethren, could not speak unto you as unto spiritual, but as unto carnal, even as unto babes in Christ.

American King James Version: And I, brothers, could not speak to you as to spiritual, but as to carnal, even as to babes in Christ.

American Standard Version: And I, brethren, could not speak unto you as unto spiritual, but as unto carnal, as unto babes in Christ.

Douay-Rheims Bible: And I, brethren, could not speak to you as unto spiritual, but as unto carnal. As unto little ones in Christ.

Darby Bible Translation: And *I*, brethren, have not been able to speak to you as to spiritual, but as to fleshly; as to babes in Christ.

English Revised Version: And I, brethren, could not speak unto you as unto spiritual, but as unto carnal, as unto babes in Christ.

Webster's Bible Translation: And I, brethren, could not speak to you as to spiritual, but as to carnal, even as to babes in Christ.

Weymouth New Testament: And as for myself, brethren, I found it impossible to speak to you as spiritual men. It had to be as to worldlings—mere babes in Christ.

World English Bible: Brothers, I couldn't speak to you as to spiritual, but as to fleshly, as to babies in Christ.

Young's Literal Translation: And I, brethren, was not able to speak to you as to spiritual, but as to fleshly—as to babes in Christ.
96 *Sarkikos*. Accessed on June 10, 2014.
http://www.studylight.org/dictionary/ved/view.cgi?n=411.
97 Vine, 243.
98 Sarkinois. Accessed on May 30, 2014.
http://www.studylight.org/commentaries/bnb/view.cgi?bk=45&ch=3.
99 Andrew Murray, *The Master's Indwelling*, 4. Accessed on June 12, 2014.
http://www.ccel.org/ccel/murray/indwelling.html.
100 *Carnal Christians*, Adam Clarke Commentary on 1 Corinthians 3:1-3, Accessed on May 30, 2014.
http://www.studylight.org/commentaries/acc/view.cgi?book=1co&chapter=003.
101 *Carnal state Christians, Gill's Exposition of the Entire Bible*. Accessed on May 30. 2014. http://www.biblestudytools.com/commentaries/gills-exposition-of-the-bible/1-corinthians-3-1.html.
102 Murray, 5.
103 J B Hall, *Carnal Christian*, 5, May 30, 2008. Accessed on June 10, 2014.
http://www.sermoncentral.com/sermons/carnal-christian-j-b-hall-sermon-on-growth-in-christ-120681.asp?Page=1.
104 *What is a carnal Christian?* Accessed on May 30, 2014.
http://www.gotquestions.org/carnal-Christian.html.
105 Murray, 6.
106 Ibid, 8.
107 Ibid, 9.
108 Ibid, 9.
109 Ibid, 10.
110 Ibid, 10.
111 *To toss*. Accessed on April 23, 2014. http://www.merriam-webster.com/dictionary/tossed.
112 *Craftiness*. Accessed on May 29, 2014, http://www.merriam-webster.com/thesaurus/craftiness.
113 Carson, 72.
114 Charles R. Swindoll, *The Tale of the Tardy Oxcart*, (Nashville, TN, Word Publishing, 1998), 80.
115 τέλειος, (*teleios*): Short Definition: perfect, full-grown, perfect, (a) complete in all its parts, (b) full grown, of full age, (c) specially of the completeness of Christian character. Accessed on August 11, 2014. http://biblehub.com/greek/5046.htm.
116 *Perfection* (τέλειος, teleios). Spiros Zodiathes, 1372.
117 Rupertus Meldenius, aka Peter Meiderlin (b. 1582- d. 1651) Lutheran theologian. Accessed on August 11, 2014.
http://en.wikipedia.org/wiki/Peter_Meiderlin.
118 Latin phrase: "In necessariis unitas, in dubiis libertas, in omnibus caritas."

CHAPTER 9

The Perils of Spiritual Immaturity–Part Two

Therefore, putting aside all malice and all deceit and hypocrisy and envy and all slander, like newborn babies, long for the pure milk of the word, so that by it you may grow in respect to salvation, if you have tasted the kindness of the Lord.
— 1 Peter 2:1–3

What a tragedy, to be a child of God and yet still be ignorant about your spiritual identity. If Christians only see themselves as **sinners saved by grace**, they have a view that is extremely detrimental to their core identity. Immature believers cannot comprehend who they are in Christ. They don't understand that they are already righteous in God's sight. As God's children, we have access to all that God has. Due to immaturity we are ignorant of all His riches and, practically speaking, live like pauper even though we are co-owners with Christ.

4. Spiritual Identity Ignorance

Let me try to illustrate this point. While slaves in Egypt, God promised the Jews a country flowing with milk and honey—the Promised Land. God told Moses:

> So I have come down to deliver them from the power of the Egyptians, and to bring them up from that land to a good and spacious land, to a land flowing with milk and honey, to the place of the Canaanite and the Hittite and the Amorite and the Perizzite and the Hivite and the Jebusite. (Exodus 3:8)

At least 600,000 adult male Jews received this promise from God. This was a glorious offer. As we all know, God cannot lie (cf. Hebrews 6:18). Still, because of their unbelief, which, according to Hebrew 3:17–19, leads to disobedience, only two of them actually entered the "land flowing with milk and honey." This represents only 0.00033% of the Jews who received the promise. I think that this is heartbreaking for the heavenly Father.

Spiritual immaturity is not only dangerous, it is costly too. Paul writes: "Now I say, as long as the heir is a *child* (Gr. νήπιος, népios[119]), he does not differ at all from a *slave*[120] although he is owner of everything" (Galatians 4:1). The person who lacks maturity cannot speak spiritual thoughts using spiritual words because he or she is unlearned and unenlightened (1 Corinthians 2:13–14). Therefore, he or she cannot handle the spiritual inheritance of God. As a result, the Father cannot entrust him or her with anything of importance.

As God's children, we have been seated with "Him in the heavenly places in Christ Jesus" (Ephesians 2:6). By spiritual birth, this is our rightful position. However, without developing "wings" through spiritual maturity we cannot fly like eagles; instead, we keep gobbling the same words, like turkeys going around and around the same old barn. To receive and handle spiritual responsibilities, God's children are required to grow and mature in "the grace and knowledge of Christ" (2 Peter 3:18). For us to leave the spiritual poverty of the old "barn," we need to grow wings like eagles and fly higher in the sky.

The author of Hebrew writes so boldly about this: "For everyone who partakes only of milk is not accustomed to the word of righteousness, for he is an infant" (Hebrews 5:13). Therefore, when it comes to spiritual identity, the doctrine of the believer's righteousness is crucial. Righteousness[121] is the state of moral perfection required by God to enter heaven. Dikaiosuné, which means righteousness, "is the conformity to the claims of higher authority and stands in opposition to anomia (Strong Number 458), lawlessness"[122] According to *Merriam-Webster Dictionary*, to be righteous means: "Acting in accord with divine or moral law: free from guilt or sin."[123] Synonyms to righteousness are: fairness, goodness, honor, justness, rectitude, respectability, uprightness, virtue.[124]

The entire Old Testament Law, including the Ten Commandments plus the "moral" Law which, according to some Old Testament experts, amounts to approximately 613 laws, represents the moral character of God. The "Law is holy, and the commandment is holy and righteous and good" (Romans 7:12). But when it comes to conferring us righteousness, because of the flesh, the Law is impotent (Romans 8:4). The New Testament teaching is clear that "by the works of the Law no flesh will be justified" (Galatians 2:16).

To make sure I am not taking things out of the context, I would like, to very, very briefly, say a few things about the Law:

- First, the role of the Law was to show how horrible sin is. Paul explains, "that through the commandment (Law) sin would become utterly sinful" (Romans 7:13).
- Second, the Law was to be a tutor for us, to direct us to Christ. The Bible tells us, "Therefore the Law has become our tutor to lead us to Christ, so that we may be justified by faith" (Galatians 3:24).

The Scripture makes it clear that when Christ came, there was no longer a need to remain under this "tutor." "But now that faith has come, we are no longer under a tutor" (Galatians 3:25). When it comes to the subject of righteousness, Paul sets the record straight. He teaches that we "may be found in Him, not having a righteousness of my own derived from the Law, but that which is through faith in Christ, the righteousness which comes from God on the basis of faith" (Philippians 3:9). According to the New Testament, the foundation for our righteousness as New Covenant believers is based solely on the finished work of Christ on Calvary's Cross—His death, resurrection, and His ascension.

A New Testament believer is considered righteous by faith in Jesus Christ (see Romans 4 and 5). In a deeper sense, righteousness is more than being right with God. Paul, in 2 Corinthians 5:21, spells it out very clearly: "He (God) made Him (Christ) who knew no sin to be sin on our behalf, so that **we might become the righteousness of God in Him.**" According to this verse, as God's children we have a righteousness as valuable and precious as Christ's own righteousness. Why? Because He is our righteousness. Since Christ Himself dwells in our hearts by faith (cf. Philippians 1:20–21, Romans 8:10, 1 Corinthians 1:30, Galatians 2:20, Ephesians 3:17, Colossians 3:4), He is the basis for our righteousness. In his prophetic writings, Jeremiah speaks about Messiah as "a righteous Branch" (Jeremiah. 23:5), and that He will be called, "The LORD our righteousness" (Jeremiah 23:6). This was prophesied several hundred years before the crucifixion of Christ! No wonder Paul writes so confidently that Jesus Christ is our righteousness. "But by His doing you are in Christ Jesus, who became to us wisdom from God, and **righteousness** and sanctification, and redemption" (1 Corinthians 1:30). When it comes to righteousness, 1 Corinthians 1:30 is one of my all-time favorite verses. The basis of our salvation and the only hope for righteousness stands firm on Christ alone:

- Christ's blood on Calvary (see: Roman. 3:24, 4:25, 5:9, 8:3–4, 1 Corinthians 15:3, Galatians 2:20, Ephesians 1:7, Hebrews 9:14, 1 Peter 1:18–19, 1 John 4:10)
- His resurrected life in our hearts (see: Romans 4:25, 5:9-10; 8: 10–11, Galatians 2:20, Colossians 3:1–3)

Paul is the expert in the doctrine of righteousness. He argues and demonstrates this important topic from multiple angles. The first part of Romans is dedicated to receiving righteousness by faith. He writes: "For in it (the gospel) the righteousness of God is revealed from faith to faith; as it is written, 'But the righteous man shall live by faith'" (Romans 1:17). Then in Romans 3:21–22, we read, "But now apart from the Law the righteousness of God has been manifested, being witnessed by the Law and the Prophets, even the righteousness of God through faith in Jesus Christ for all those who believe; for there is no distinction."

It is so important to understand that Paul does not say anywhere in the New Testament that righteousness is obtained by observing the Old Testament Law. He writes: "Because by the works of the Law no flesh will be justified in His sight" (Romans 3:20). Even the righteousness Abraham received, he received by faith. Paul writes: "For what does the Scripture say? Abraham believed God, and it was credited to him as righteousness… But to the one who does not work, but believes in Him who justifies the ungodly, his faith is credited as righteousness" (Romans 4:3, 5). Otherwise, it would be based on merit, and the promise would be invalidated: "For if those who are of the Law are heirs, faith is made void and the promise is nullified" (Romans 4:14).

Some may ask: Brother Valy, are you suggesting that since we have Christ's righteousness then it does not matter how we live our lives? May it never be! This is a big misunderstanding. Paul was misunderstood as well. Remember how he responded to this kind of question: "What shall we say then? Are we to continue in sin so that grace may increase?" (Romans 6:1). He answered his own rhetorical question, "May it never be! How shall we who died to sin still live in it?" (Romans 6:2). **To be righteous at the inner core of our beings and continue in sin is incompatible.** It is like going against our very nature.

Let me try to illustrate it for you. A lion is a carnivore. It is in his nature to eat meat. A cow is an herbivore. It is in her nature to eat grass. For a lion to eat grass would be against his very nature. For a cow to eat meat would be against her very nature. For a Christian to continue in sin would be incompatible with his or her very nature—a saint and partaker of God's own nature (2 Peter 1:4).

Does all this mean that God is not interested in moral behavior or in character development just because we have Christ's righteousness? Of course not. This is a deception coming from the pit of hell. God is very much interested in our behavior, but He does not grant us His righteousness based on our good behavior. This would mean re-instituting the Old Testament Law.

So how did God get around this? In Christ, God killed us and then resurrected us in Him, thus making us as righteous as Christ. God placed us in Christ and when Christ died on the cross we died with Him (cf. Romans 6:3–4); when He was raised from the dead, we were raised with Him (Colossians 2:12); when He ascended to the right hand of the Father we were (past tense) also seated with Him at the right hand of the Father in Christ (Ephesians 1:12, 2:6). Pretty awesome!

Now, because of the position we have in Christ, and the fact that He is in us (Colossians 1:27), sin no longer has dominion over us so we can freely live for God. It appears simple, but it is not simplistic. The Bible teaches us, "Present yourselves to God as those alive from the dead, and your members as instruments of righteousness to God" (Romans 6:13). Since we are not under law but under grace (cf. Romans 6:14), we continue to be saved by Christ's life. Paul writes: "For if while we were enemies we were reconciled to God through the death of His Son, much more, having been reconciled, we shall be saved by His life" (Romans 5:10). The secret of living a victorious and fulfilled life is **Christ's life**. Because we are indwelt by Christ, we can present ourselves and all our members to God in obedience and, as a result, we enjoy a practical righteousness. The Bible tells us: "Do you not know that when you present yourselves to someone as slaves for obedience, you are slaves of the one whom you obey, either of sin resulting in death, or of obedience resulting in righteousness?" (Romans 6:16). Now, because of the special position that we have **in Christ**, we became slaves of righteousness (cf. Romans 6:18).

Is God interested in holiness? Of course He is! His standards of holiness have not changed, not even by one micron[125]. More than that, God is looking for genuine holiness. How can Christians attain it? Only in one way—by presenting ourselves and our members as slaves to righteousness. This will result in sanctification. This is the only way Christians arrive at genuine holiness. Make a note of this and keep it handy. Yes, Christians are required to be holy people (cf. Matthew 22:11–12). But make sure this is read it in the context of Ephesians 2:10 and Revelation 19:7–8. Does this mean that salvation is by faith and sanctification by works? Of course not! This is the enemy's trap to cause us to act independently from God. This is living and walking after the flesh. Paul strongly rebukes this way of thinking and acting. He writes: "Are you so foolish? Having begun by the Spirit, are you now being perfected by the flesh?" (Galatians 3:3).

Now, some may ask: Brother Valy, I am confused! Do you mean that I can cross my arms over my chest and do nothing? I am being perfected by some sort of automatic pilot?

No, not at all! The Bible teaches us that we have an active role in the process of practical sanctification. "So then, my beloved, just as you have always obeyed, not as in my presence only, but now much more in my absence, work out your salvation with fear and trembling" (Philippians 2:12). Please make sure when we read this verse, we pay attention that Paul is not saying: **work *for* our salvation**. But he is saying: **work *out* our salvation**. Big difference.

Some may say: Well… that sounds like "work" to me. It may sound like that, but it isn't. In God's economy, the power source and motivation make all the difference. The following verse explains it: "For it is God who is at work in you, both **to will** and **to work** for His good pleasure" (Philippians 2:13). In the end, what counts is Christ's life being manifested in and through us. Paul writes: "When Christ, who is our life, is revealed, then you also will be revealed with Him in glory" (Colossians 3:4). That is why knowing who we are in Christ is the very key to spiritual victory.

When it comes to the topic of spiritual identity, we must be honest with ourselves, otherwise it will cost us dearly. With a much fuller understanding now, let's declare before God three positive things:

– God, I am so ignorant of who I really am.
– Dear Lord Jesus, I want to grow into my rightful position as a mature son (huios) and thrive in God's household.
– Holy Spirit, please reveal to me my spiritual identity.

Now let's bow before God in prayer with these words:

> Father God, I thank you for placing me in Christ, so when He died on the cross, I died with Him. I believe that when You raised Jesus from the dead, You also justified me and made me righteous in Him. I have no words to thank You for the glorious position of being seated with Christ at Your right hand in heaven. This is my identity; this is my destiny; this is my new life now. I am the righteousness of God in Christ. I pray in the wonderful name of Jesus, who is my life, my everything. Amen.

5. Inability to Make a Meaningful Contribution to the Spiritual Body of Christ

Paul writes:

> But speaking the truth in love, we are to grow up in all aspects into Him who is the head, even Christ, from whom the whole body, being **fitted** and **held** together by what **every joint** supplies, according to the proper working of each individual part, causes the growth of the body for the building up of itself in love. (Ephesians 4:15–16)

It is vitally important to understand that God is looking at both the spiritual growth and maturity of the individual members and the growth of the entire body.

– First: "We are to grow up in all aspects into Him."
– Second: "The whole body… according to the proper working of each individual part, causes the growth of the body."

Do you see this spiritual dynamic? I hope you do! The conclusion is clear. Immaturity in individual members of the Church causes stagnation of the spiritual growth of the entire body. And this is, probably, the greatest danger of spiritual immaturity.

I believe that there are five extremely important aspects that derive from Ephesians 4:16:

1. The whole body, being fitted together
2. The whole body, being held together
3. By what every joint supplies
4. Every individual part must contribute to the work of spiritual growth and maturity of the entire body
5. The body—the Church—is to be built on love

Allow me to say a few things about each of these five aspects.

1. The whole body, being fitted together

This sounds good on paper, but the question is: what can accomplish the fitting together of the Body of Christ?

I think you'll agree that it is love that joins the Body together. In his letter to the Colossians, Paul indicates that compassion, kindness, humility, gentleness, patience, and forgiveness are all important for the overall spiritual and emotional health of the local church. Then he writes: "Beyond all these things put on love, which is the perfect bond of unity" (Colossians 3:14). You see? **Love is the perfect bond of unity**.

We can only arrive at this deep point of understanding through a personal experience of the death and resurrection of Christ. The Bible teaches us:

> For the love of Christ controls *and* urges *and* impels us, because we are of the opinion *and* conviction that [*if*] One died for all, then all died; And He died for all, so that all those who live might live no longer to *and* for themselves, but to *and* for Him Who died and was raised again for their sake. (2 Corinthians 5:14–15 AMP)

Only when we understand our identification in Christ's death and resurrection can we live for Him and not for ourselves. **There is no other cure for our self-centeredness than the cross of Christ.**

If we are to "grow up in all aspects into Him," we must practice speaking the truth in love. In other words, in our fellowship with one another, we must exercise enough transparency and acceptance to speak the truth, not in hurtful ways, but in love. John writes so tenderly, "Little children, let us not love with word or with tongue, but **in deed and truth**" (1 John 3:18). At the opening of his second letter John writes: "Grace, mercy and peace will be with us, from God the Father and from Jesus Christ, the Son of the Father, **in truth and love**" (2 John 1:3). Similarly, in the third letter, John writes: "The elder to the beloved Gaius, whom I **love in truth**" (3 John 3:1). **Agape love cannot exist without truth; and truth cannot exist without agape love**.

Timothy Keller, in a Facebook post he published on March 3,

2015, said:

> Love without truth is sentimentality; it supports and affirms us but keeps us in denial about our flaws. Truth without love is harshness; it gives us information but in such a way that we cannot really hear it.[126]

These two go hand in hand and contribute to our spiritual growth.

2. *The whole body, being held together*

This speaks of a deep organic unity! But the question is: what keeps (or holds) the Body of Christ together?

I believe that the only thing that can accomplish this is the truth. The truth is the only force that keeps the Christian Church together. Only the Person of Truth—*Christ Himself*—holds us together. Here is a powerful Scripture: "He is before all things, and in Him all things hold together" (Colossians 1:17). **Christ**, in a sense, **is the belt of truth that wraps around us**. Paul writes: "stand therefore, having your loins girded about with truth, and having on the breastplate of righteousness" (Ephesians 6:14). "Having your loins girded about with truth," means "to encircle with a belt or band" and "to prepare (oneself) for action."

In the Old Testament it is written:

> These words, which I am commanding you today, shall be on your heart. You shall teach them diligently to your sons and shall talk of them when you sit in your house and when you walk by the way and when you lie down and when you rise up. You shall **bind them** as a sign on your hand and they shall be as frontals on your forehead. (Deuteronomy 6:6–8)

Commenting on this verse, John Wesley writes: "Thou shalt bind them—Thou shalt give all diligence, and use all means to keep them in thy remembrance, as men often bind something upon their hands, or put it before their eyes to prevent forgetfulness of a thing which they much desire to remember."[127] In other words, we should behold the Lord Jesus and be always mindful of His words. The wise king of the Old Testament writes: "Bind them on your fingers; Write them on the tablet of your heart" (Proverbs 7:3).

3. *By what every joint supplies*

We all agree that Christ has only one Church. He is coming for a single Bride, not for 41,000[128] or more little brides. The Body of Christ is not a member by itself but many members in unity! Still, practically speaking, God's people live in much disunity. Paul understood the principle of organic unity very well. He writes: "For the body is not one member, but many" (1 Corinthians 12:14).

I challenge you to keep in mind the following principle: "What makes the physical body powerful is not the individual members separated from each other but rather the joints coming together in unity." The same is true in the spiritual arena. When believers are tightly bound with God and each other by obeying His commands, they can fight to advance His kingdom instead of quarrelling with each other. The Bible states: "How could one chase a thousand, and two put ten thousand to flight" (Deuteronomy 32:30a).

Allow me to illustrate. Let us look at the shoulder. The human shoulder is made up of three bones: the clavicle (collarbone), the scapula (shoulder blade), and the humerus (upper arm bone), as well as associated muscles, ligaments, and tendons. If any of these three bones were separate from each other, they could do nothing. What makes the shoulder powerful is the fact that all these parts between the bones of the shoulder come together to make up the shoulder joints.

Let me give you another example: the elbow. The human elbow joint is the synovial hinge joint between the humerus in the upper arm and the radius and ulna in the forearm which allows the hand to be moved towards and away from the body. It is obvious that these components (the humerus in the upper arm, and the radius and ulna) by themselves cannot perform (if separated from each other) what the elbow (as a joint) can do.

Should I go further? Should I explain how the hip operates? The hip joint, scientifically referred to as the acetabulofemoral joint, is the joint between the femur and acetabulum of the pelvis. Its primary function is to support the weight of the body in both static (standing) and dynamic (walking or running) postures. The hip joints are the most important part in retaining balance. The pelvic inclination angle, which is the single most important element of human body posture, is adjusted at the hips. It is the coming together of the femur and acetabulum that forms this important joint. These elements by themselves can do nothing, but together the hip joint helps the whole body when standing or running. Isn't this amazing? We could go on with these examples from the human body.

If these are true for the human body, it is the same for the spiritual Body—*the Church.* Paul writes: "For even as the body is one and yet has many members, and all the members of the body, though they are many, are one body, so also is Christ" (1 Corinthians 12:12). Think about a body that is decapitated! Can that body perform anything? Of course not! It does not function. It is dead. In the same way the spiritual body, *the Church,* cannot function. **The Church is dead without her perfect union with Christ**. That is why the Lord Jesus clearly tells His disciples, "Abide in Me, and I in you. As the branch cannot bear fruit of itself unless it abides in the vine, so neither can you unless you abide in Me" (John 15:5). I hope we get this concept sooner rather than later.

4. *Every individual part must contribute to the work of spiritual growth and maturity of the entire body*

Now we reached the point where the rubber meets the road. In the same way that the three bones, the clavicle, the scapula, and the humerus, come together to form the joint of the shoulders, so it must be done in the body of Christ. The prophet Isaiah foretold about the coming of the Child who will be given to us. He stated "that the government will rest on His shoulders" (Isaiah 9:6). I don't think it would be stretching to say that Christ's "shoulders" on this earth are us—the Church, coming in unity to serve God's purposes. I like this connection! I hope you do too!

The Pareto principle[129], the law of the vital few, also known as the 20/80 Rule, states that, for many events, roughly 80% of the effects come from 20% of the causes. This principle seems to affect churches as well. If we are sincere, we must attest to these facts:

- 20% of Christians complete 80% of the ministries of the local Church.
- 80% of financial contributions are donated by 20% of supporters.

Interesting, isn't it? "According to researchers Scott Thumma and Warren Bird, most churches—mega-sized and small, black and white—are actually run by 20 percent of the congregation. The other 80 percent, they say, tend to act like spectators: they are minimally involved and attend infrequently or not at all."[130] This is staggering! However, God does not want the 20/80 Rule to be in effect in His Church. God wants the 100/100 Rule to be in effect inside Christ's Body. The Bible tells us: "From whom the whole body, being fitted and held together by what every joint supplies, according to the proper working of each individual part, causes the growth of the body for the building up of itself in *love*" (Ephesians 4:16). In other words, there should be no idleness in the body of Christ. No individual member should be "unemployed," but all should be involved in something good for God and others. Paul writes: "Now you are Christ's body, and individually members of it" (1 Corinthians 12:27). This has been written to discourage any forms of division inside the Body of Christ, "so that there may be no division in the body, but *that* the members may have the same care for one another" (1 Corinthians 12:25).

5. *The Body—the Church—is to be built on love*

This, in a sense, is a climax in Paul's writings. He writes: "in whom the whole building, being fitted together, is growing into a holy temple in the Lord, in whom you also are being built together into a dwelling of God in the Spirit" (Ephesians 2:21–22). "According to the proper working of each individual part, causes the growth of the body for the building up of itself in love" (Ephesian 4:16b). I believe with all my heart that if every Christian would be conscientious of this principle—*the body of Christ is built on love*—it would bring tremendous revival. This would be a love revolution with every church member declaring: **Not me but Him. Not us but the Kingdom of God!**

No matter what, God is going to be consistent with His own nature (*agape love)* and all His principles.

Paul warns us:

> Now if any man builds on the foundation with gold, silver, precious stones, wood, hay, straw, each man's work will become evident; for the day will show it because it is *to be* revealed with fire, and the fire itself will test the quality of each man's work. (1 Corinthians 3:12–13).

The more I look into the vast theme of spiritual growth and maturity, the more I am convinced that as the individual members of any local church experience spiritual growth, **spiritual joints** are being formed by the Holy Spirit within the Universal Body. The Body of Christ gets to a point of "being fitted and held together." This is done by formation of joints. Obviously, formation of the joints depends on "the proper working of each individual part." Do you see the chain of events? If Satan could keep most individual members of a local church disinterested in spiritual maturity, in a sense, he can prevent spiritual maturity in the entire local body. I have a suspicion that this is exactly the strategy the enemy uses.

> I believe with all my heart that if every Christian would be conscientious of this principle—*the body of Christ is built on love*—it would bring a tremendous revival.

That is why the Scripture is filled with the expressions "one another" and "each other." Before His crucifixion, in the most intimate setting (Holy Communion), Christ said, "A new commandment I give to you, that you love one another, even as I have loved you, that you also love one another. By this all men will know that you are My disciples, if you have love for one another" (John 13:34–35).

As believers, we are called to:

– Be devoted to one another in love (Romans 12:10)
– Be of the same mind toward one another (Romans 12:16)

– Do not judge one another (Romans 14:13)
– Build up one another (Romans 14:19, 1 Thessalonians 5:11)
– Accept one another (Romans 15:7)
– Admonish one another (Romans 15:14; Colossians 3:16)
– Greet one another with a sincere love (Rom. 16:16, 1 Peter 5:14)
– Display the same care for one another (1 Corinthians 12:25)
– Be kind to one another (Ephesians 4:32)
– Be tender-hearted, forgiving each other (Ephesians 4:32)
– Speak life to one another (Ephesians 5:19)
– Be subject to one another (Ephesians 5:21)
– Serve one another in love (Galatians 5:13)
– Bear one another's burdens (Galatians 6:2; Colossians 3:13)
– Display sincere understanding for one another (Ephesians 4:2)
– Regard one another as more important than yourselves (Philippians 2:3)
– Abound in love for one another and love each other (1 Thessalonians 3:12, 4:9; 2 Thessalonians 1:3, 1 Peter. 1:22, 4:8; 1 John 3:11, 4:7, 4:11, 4:12; 2 John 1:5)
– Comfort one another (1 Thessalonians 4:18)
– Encourage one another (1 Thessalonians 5:11; Hebrew 3:13, 10:25)
– Live in peace with one another (1 Thessalonians 5:13)
– Seek good for one another (1 Thessalonians 5:15; Hebrews 10:24)
– Do not speak against one another (James 4:11)
– Do not complain against one another (James 5:9; 1 Peter 4:9)
– Confess your sins to one another (James 5:16)
– Pray for one another (James 5:16)
– Be hospitable to one another (1 Peter 4:9)
– Serve one another (1 Peter 4:10)
– Display genuine humility toward one another (1 Peter 5:5)

These are just a few references based only on the New

Testament epistles. Imagine how long the list would be if we included the entire Bible.

Now is the best time to declare before God three positive things:

- God, I realized that up until now I have just been a consumer in the Body of Christ.
- Dear Lord Jesus, please make me and mold me in such way that I may fulfill my role and destiny in Your Spiritual Body.
- Holy Spirit, please reveal to me the place, the function and the gift I have and most importantly, where I belong in the Body of Christ. Make me part of that special joint that only I was created to fulfill.

Let's pray this prayer:

> Father God, thank you for the gift I have in Christ. Now I am part of Your Eternal Family. I desire to be productive in the place you ordered me to be. My heart's desire is to be effective in the function You have given me. Lord Jesus I want to be organically connected with you in order to produce much fruit for God's glory. Holy Spirit please form me and mold me into the spiritual joint I have been designed to be. My chief desire is that, together with the rest of the members of the Church, we may work in unity for one cause only: that is the Body of Christ, to shine so the whole universe will see Your grand work. I pray in the wonderful name of Jesus. Amen!

Discussion Questions:

– After reading and re-reading this chapter what concept or idea stood out the most? Please explain why. Share your insights with a trusted friend or with your spiritual mentor.

– What is your overall impression about the section called: "Spiritual Identity Ignorance"? What aspect is new to you? Share your insights with a close friend.

– What is your overall impression about the section called: "Inability to Make a Meaningful Contribution to the Spiritual Body of Christ"? Share your insights with a trusted friend or with your small group.

– What do you think it is your place in the local Church? Do you know which is your spiritual function in the Body of Christ?

Notes

9. The Perils of Spiritual Immaturity–Part Two

[119] *Child,* νήπιος, népios – Strong number 3516: One who cannot speak, hence, an infant, child, baby without any definite limitation of age. By implication, a minor, one not yet of age (as in Gal. 4:1). Generally, in the Septuagint, used of a child playing in the streets (as in Jer. 6:11; 9:21); asking for bread (as in Lam. 4:4). Metaphorically a babe, one unlearned, unenlightened, simple, innocent (as in Matt. 11:25, Luke 10:21, Rom. 2:20). Implying censure (as 1 Cor. 3:1; Gal. 4:3; Eph. 4:14; Heb. 5:13). Synonyms: teknon—Strong number 5043: child, newborn child, infant. Antonyms: huios: Strong number 5207: a mature son or daughter. Spiros Zodiathes, 1993.

[120] δοῦλος, doúlos – Strong number 1401: someone who belongs to another; a bond-slave, without any ownership rights of their own. Accessed on August 11, 2014. http://biblehub.com/greek/1401.htm.

[121] δικαιοσύνη, dikaiosuné – Strong number 1343: righteousness: "divine approval," "God's judicial approval." "deemed right by the Lord (after His examination)," "what is approved in His eyes." Accessed on May 1, 2018. http://biblehub.com/greek/1343.htm.

[122] *Lawlessness.* Spiros Zodiathes, 1993.

[123] *Righteous.* Accessed on January 24, 2013. http://www.merriam-webster.com/dictionary/righteous.

[124] *Righteous*. Accessed on January 24, 2013, http://thesaurus.com/browse/righteousness.

[125] One micron is one-millionth of a meter. There are 25400 microns in one inch. The eye can see particles to about 40 microns. Accessed on August 12, 2014. http://www.engineeringtoolbox.com/particle-sizes-d_934.html.

[126] Timothy Keller, *Love and Truth.* Accessed on June 7, 2019. https://www.facebook.com/TimKellerNYC/posts/love-without-truth-is-sentimentality-it-supports-and-affirms-us-but-keeps-us-in-/910599765646577/.

[127] John Wesley's Explanatory Notes, Deuteronomy 6:6–8. Accessed on May 1, 2018. https://www.christianity.com/bible/commentary.php?com=wes&b=5&c=6.

[128] According to the Center for the Study of Global Christianity (CSGC) at Gordon-Conwell Theological Seminary, there are approximately 41,000 Christian denominations and organizations in the world. This statistic takes into consideration cultural distinctions of denominations in different countries, so there is overlapping of many denominations. Updated by Mary Fairchild, on December 19, 2017, Accessed on May 1, 2018. https://www.thoughtco.com/christianity-statistics-700533.

[129] *The Pareto principle*. (Accessed on August 12, 2014). http://en.wikipedia.org/wiki/Pareto_principle

[130] Stephanie Samuel, *Churches' Dilemma: 80 Percent of Flock Is Inactive.* Posted on Jun 26, 2011. Accessed on April 11, 2013. https://www.christianpost.com/news/authors-pastors-must-go-after-lost-sheep-to-increase-church-participation-51581/.

CHAPTER 10

The Building, the Builders, and the Process

And He gave some as apostles, and some as prophets, and some as evangelists, and some as pastors and teachers, for the equipping of the saints for the work of service, to the building up of the body of Christ;
— Ephesians 4:11–12

I would like to start with an anecdote about three mason workers involved in a massive building project who responded so differently when asked: "What is it that you are doing?"

Here is how the story goes:

> On a foggy autumn day nearly 800 years ago, a traveler happened upon a large group of workers adjacent to the River Avon. Despite being tardy for an important rendezvous, curiosity convinced the traveler that he should inquire about their work. With a slight detour, he moved toward the first of the three tradesmen and said, "my dear fellow, what is it that you are doing?" The man continued his work and grumbled, "I am cutting stones."
>
> Realizing that the mason did not wish to engage in a conversation, the traveler moved toward the second of the three and repeated the question. To the traveler's delight

> this time, the man stopped his work, ever so briefly, and stated that he was a stonecutter. He then added, "I came to Salisbury from the north to work, but as soon as I earn ten quid, I will return home." The traveler thanked the second mason, wished him a safe journey home, and began to head to the third of the trio.
>
> When he reached the third worker, he once again asked the original question. This time the worker paused, glanced at the traveler until they made eye contact, and then looked skyward, drawing the traveler's eyes upward. The third mason replied, "I am a mason, and I am building a cathedral." He continued, "I have journeyed many miles to be part of the team that is constructing this magnificent cathedral. I have spent many months away from my family, and I miss them dearly. However, I know how important Salisbury Cathedral will be one day, and I know how many people will find sanctuary and solace here. I know this because the Bishop once told me his vision for this great place. He described how people would come from all parts to worship here. He also told that the Cathedral would not be completed in our days but that the future depends on our hard work." He paused and then said, "So I am prepared to be away from my family because I know it is the right thing to do. I hope that one day my son will continue in my footsteps and perhaps even his son if need be.[131]

I hope this story may encourage us to pay more attention to the tremendous task we all have ahead of us—Building God's Church.

The Building and the Builders

The Lord Jesus gave men as gifts to the local church. These men, in a sense, are God's working *hand* for equipping disciple-makers who will lead others towards spiritual growth and maturity in local churches. Paul writes: "And He gave some as apostles, and some as prophets, and some as evangelists, and some as pastors and teachers" (Ephesians 4:11). What is Paul saying here? He is saying that the apostles, the prophets, the evangelists, the pastors, and the teachers are appointed by God to work His plans and purposes—to equip individual members to build Christ's Body through the guidance of the Holy Spirit.

Let's pray that God's mighty hand continues the work started two thousand years ago. My earnest desire is that all local churches will truly experience genuine spiritual formation. May the Lord Jesus—the One and Only CEO of the Church (Ephesians 1:22–23) be glorified.

What are the Builders' main objectives?

What are the main objectives of God's working hand? (See diagram 5.)

According to what Paul wrote in Ephesians 4:12, it is clear that these are:

– Equipping of the saints
– The work of service
– Building up of the body

Diagram 5

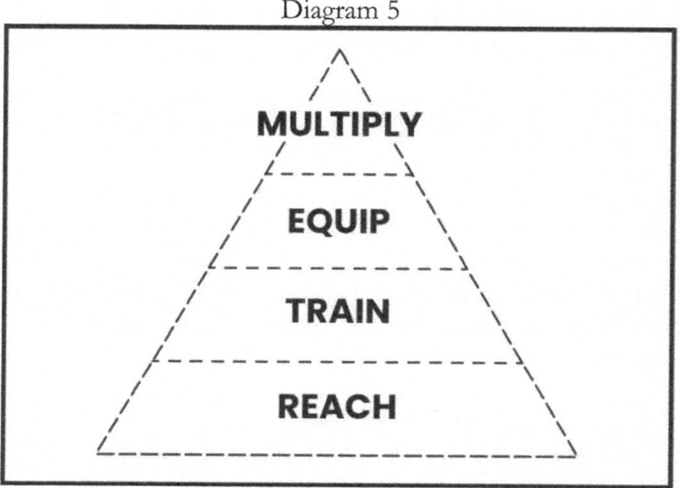

What is Spiritual Formation?

The late Robert Mulholland Jr., in his book, "Invitation to a Journey: The Road Map for Spiritual Formation," defines spiritual formation as: "The process of being formed in the image of Christ for the sake of others."[132] The late Dallas Willard, in his book, *Renovation of the Heart: Putting On the Character of Chri*st, wrote that: "Spiritual formation for the Christian basically refers to the Spirit-driven process of forming the inner world of the human self in such a way that it becomes like the inner being of Christ Himself."[133] Moreover, Richard Foster's Renovaré website states that: "Spiritual formation is a process, but it is also a journey through which we open our hearts to a deeper connection with God. We are not bystanders in our spiritual lives, we are active participants with God, who is ever inviting us into relationship with Him."[134]

Why does the church need spiritual formation?

The main reasons why spiritual formation is important are:

– People in the church need to be perfected
– The church needs to be served
– The Body of Christ needs to be built up

What is the aim of spiritual formation?

The apostle Paul didn't coin the term spiritual formation, but he was among the first to write about spiritual formation. The authors I mentioned above just expanded on the principles outlined in Paul's writings.

According to Ephesians 4:13, the aim of spiritual formation is three-prong:

– To attain the unity of the faith
– To attain the unity of the knowledge of Christ
– To experience spiritual maturity leading to the fullness of Christ

How do we assess spiritual growth in the church?

As with any project, the church's spiritual growth should also be assessed. How? By asking some important question, such as:

- Does the church take the Great Commission at its face value?
- Does the church facilitate discipleship?
- Does discipleship lead to spiritual growth and maturity?
- Are believers growing in the grace and knowledge of Christ?

The church is moving in an upward direction when the above questions are answered affirmatively. As believers continue in the process of discipleship, by the grace of God, the following spiritual milestones are attained:

1. Unity in the faith (Jude 1:3, Ephesians 4:5)
2. The experiential knowledge of the Son of God (John 17:3, Philippians 3:10–11)
3. Attaining the state of a mature man (Romans 8:14, 1 Peter 2:1–2)
4. Reaching the measure of the fullness of Christ (Ephesians 1:23, 3:19, 4:13, Colossians 2:9–10, John, John 7:38, 10:10)
5. Growing up in all aspects (Ephesians 4:15)

Let's analyze these aspects one by one.

1. Unity in the faith

Jude writes: "Beloved, while I was making every effort to write you about our common salvation, I felt the necessity to write to you appealing that you contend earnestly for the faith which was once for all handed down to the saints" (Jude 1:3). This job is not only for the few apologists out there. This is the responsibility of every believer.

Faith is the spiritual instrument which accesses God's grace. In God's economy, everything happens by faith: the salvation of unbelievers, the process of discipleship of believers, spiritual growth, any local or international ministries, any kind of activity of the local church.

Without faith, it is impossible to please God. The author of Hebrews is clear on this. He writes: "And without faith, it is impossible to please Him, for he who comes to God must believe that He is and that He is a rewarder of those who seek Him" (Hebrews 11:6). And Paul is saying that "whatever is not from faith is sin" (Romans 14:23).

2. Experiential knowledge of the Son of God

John writes: "This is eternal life, that they may know You, the only true God, and Jesus Christ whom You have sent" (John 17:3). This verse encapsulates the very essence of eternal life. "That they may know," does not mean accumulating more theological or intellectual knowledge about God and the Bible. This type of understanding refers to an intimate knowledge of God. In fact, in the Greek language, the verb "to know," as used in John 17:3 and Philippians 3:10 has a deeper meaning than what we can perceive in English. It refers to intimate knowledge, as the intimacy between a husband and a wife. Mary used the same word in Luke 1:34 (KJV) when she answered the angel Gabriel: "How shall this be, seeing I *know* not a man?" (See also Matthew 1:24–25).

"My people are destroyed for lack of knowledge. Because you have rejected knowledge, I also will reject you from being My priest. Since you have forgotten the law of your God, I also will forget your children" (Hosea 4:6).

The Apostle Paul understood the importance of the experiential knowledge. Because of this he wrote with great passion and deep conviction:

> That I may know Him and the power of His resurrection and the fellowship of His sufferings, being conformed to His death; in order that I may attain to the resurrection from the dead. (Philippians 3:10–11)

God passionately desires to disclose Himself to His children. It is essential to know Him for Who He really is: God of love, God of mercy, and God of grace in Christ. Having a distorted view of God is the major obstacle towards emotional freedom and spiritual growth. I like Tozer's statement: "What comes into our minds when we think about God is the most important thing about us."[135]

Even the Old Testament prophets hinted about this kind of knowledge. Isaiah wrote: "An ox knows its owner, and a donkey its master's manger, but Israel does not *know*, My people do not understand" (Isaiah 1:3). Jeremiah wrote: "Thus says the LORD, 'Let not a wise man boast of his wisdom, and let not the mighty man boast of his might, let not a rich man boast of his riches; but let him who boasts boast of this, that he understands and knows Me, that I am the LORD who exercises loving-kindness, justice and righteousness on earth; for I delight in these things,' declares the LORD" (Jeremiah 9:24). Daniel also wrote: "By smooth *words*, he will turn to godlessness those who act wickedly toward the covenant, but the people who *know* their God will display strength and take action" (Daniel 11:32).

The real crisis in the Old Testament period was that God's people didn't know their God. The Prophet Hosea wrote: "My people are destroyed for lack of knowledge. Because you have rejected knowledge, I also will reject you from being My priest. Since you have forgotten the law of your God, I also will forget your children" (Hosea 4:6).

I am afraid that, like the chosen people of old, the church also lacks the intimate knowledge (knowledge of the heart, experiential knowledge) of God and Christ through the revelation of the Holy Spirit.

3. Attaining the state of a mature man

God wants us to grow. Mature people in faith and understanding are those who are expressing God's nature and character in and through them. They indeed are ambassadors of Christ (2 Corinthians 5:20); they genuinely represent Christ well to the lost world.

To better understand the concept of spiritual maturity, let's take a closer look at two words used in the New Testament: *children* and *sons*. The word children—(Gr.) *teknon*[136], used in John 1:12, refers to infant children, or recently born babies. A newborn believer, character-wise, vaguely resembles the characteristics of their Father. This is the reason Peter wrote these critical verses:

> Therefore, putting aside all malice and all deceit and hypocrisy and envy and all slander, like newborn babies, long for the pure milk of the word, so that by it you may grow in respect to salvation if you have tasted the kindness of the Lord. (1 Peter 2:1–3)

In other words, it is our responsibility to desire the Word of God, and by it, we may experience spiritual growth.

On the other hand, the word *sons*—(Gr.) *huios*[137], used by the apostle Paul in Romans 8:14, refers to mature sons. Unlike the *teknon* kind of believers, the *huios* kind of Christians reflect more fully the character of their Father.

4. Attaining the measure of the fullness of Christ

We are the Church. We are called to reflect the fullness of Christ. This is the main reason why spiritual growth and maturity are significant. In most of his letters, Paul, writes with sincere care and passion for the church: "[The Church] which is His body, the **fullness of Him** who fills everything in every way" (Ephesians 1:23). When it comes to the individual Christians, Paul writes with confidence and authority: "We proclaim Him, admonishing every man and teaching every man with all wisdom, so that we may present every man complete in Christ" (Colossians 1:28). Paul's prayer for each of us is: "to know this love that surpasses knowledge—that you may be filled to the measure of all the **fullness of God**" (Ephesians 3:19).

Jesus Himself made a powerful promise to His disciples. Beside our salvation, He desires His disciples to experience life in abundance: "I have come that they may have *life*, and have it to the full" (John 10:10b). Let's be honest with ourselves and ask these heart-probing questions:

– Do we enjoy the abundant life promised by Jesus?
– If not, what is the cause of lacking it in our lives?

Could it be that, after we got saved, for whatever reason we did not get involved in the process of discipleship, and as a result, we don't have a proper spiritual formation of the soul? The Holy Spirit desires to bless us with streams of living water: "He who believes in Me, as the Scripture said, 'From his innermost being will flow rivers of living water'" (John 7:38). To get a complete picture of this concept, let's imagine for a moment the abundance of water flowing into the Niagara Falls. Let's contrasts this with emptying a bottle of water. There's a significant difference between the two, isn't it? This is what Jesus meant when He said—streams of living water. With this image in mind, let's examine our hearts:

- Do rivers of living water flow from our hearts? If not, why not?
- Is it just a trickle or only some drops of living water? Why is this?

In his letter to the Romans, Paul writes very convincingly: "For if, by the trespass of the one man, death reigned through that one man, how much more will those who receive God's abundant provision of grace and of the gift of righteousness reign in life through the one man, Jesus Christ!" (Romans 5:17). To reign in life means to be under the empire of this new life we received by grace. The King of this empire is the Lord Jesus. Is Jesus anxious, worried, hopeless, depressed, or defeated? Of course not. That is precisely the point. Christ intends for us to reign in life, to live without anxiety, to stop worrying, to live a satisfied and fulfilled life, to experience healing, deliverance, joy, and to live a victorious life.

If we don't reign in life, then we are under a different empire. This means that, while we are here on earth, we are not making the most of the "abundant provision of grace and of the gift of righteousness." I don't say these things to discourage people. I explain these things so I can encourage people to continue growing in discipleship. The bottom line is that Jesus desires us to reign in life through Him. This is part of our spiritual inheritance. If these aspects are missing from our discipleship, maybe it indicates that spiritual growth is missing from our Christian life. I encourage all of you to leave the childlike state, and (cf. Hebrews 6:1) "press on to maturity." (See also Philippians 3:13). Paul puts the dot on the "i" with these words: „As a result, we are no longer to be children, tossed here and there by waves and carried about by every wind of doctrine, by the trickery of men, by craftiness in deceitful scheming" (Ephesians 4:14).

5. Growing up in all aspects

Paul writes: "but speaking the truth in love, we are to grow up in all aspects into Him who is the head, even Christ" (Ephesians 4:15).

Before moving forward, I would like to make sure we are on the same page regarding the process of spiritual growth and maturity. It is a process. Spiritual maturity does not happen overnight. It requires a time of planting and watering (cf. 1 Corinthians 3:6), but only God (cf. 1 Corinthians 3:7) can cause growth.

Church history has proven that the more Christians get entangled into religious practices, the longer the process of spiritual growth and maturity takes. Trying harder to comply with all kinds of rules wears people out and prevents them from developing a genuine relationship with God by intimately knowing Christ (cf. John 17:3). The sad reality is that it becomes difficult for them to give up religion and start engaging in the process of growth. The hardest aspect of all is that it is challenging for religious people to see their spiritual immaturity.

Spiritual growth and maturity are the work of the Holy Spirit in the life of disciples. It is not about the accumulation of more information. Instead, it is the supernatural work of transformation performed inside us by the Holy Spirit. Paul captures this mystery in 2 Corinthians 3:18: "But we all, with unveiled face, beholding as in a mirror the glory of the Lord, are being *transformed* into the same image from glory to glory, just as from the Lord, the Spirit."

Trying harder to comply with all kinds of rules wears people out and prevents them from developing a genuine relationship with God by intimately knowing Christ (cf. John 17:3).

Spiritual growth and maturity are not conformity to a particular Christian denomination. It is the supernatural work of mind renewal by the living Word of God. Paul writes: "And do not be conformed to this world, but be *transformed* by the *renewing of your mind*, so that you may prove what the will of God is, that which is good and acceptable and perfect" (Romans 12:2).

When we were born again into God's family (cf. 1 Peter 1:23), we got His DNA. However, God's DNA in us is in a compressed form, like a *seed*. Therefore, it is absolutely necessary to abide in Christ (John 15:5), to present ourselves to God (Romans 12:1), to ask the Holy Spirit to progressively transform us into the image of Christ (2 Corinthians 3:18), and by God's grace, to move towards the fullness of Christ (Ephesians 4:13). These are the most important ways we can express His nature and His character in and through us.

When the individual members of Christ's Body experience growth in all aspects, something phenomenal happens: the Body of Christ builds itself up in love. This is the secret hidden in Ephesians 4:16. Paul writes: "from whom the whole body, being fitted and held together by what every joint supplies, according to the proper working of each individual part, causes the growth of the body for the building up of itself in love" This is the ultimate intention: For each part to function correctly within the spiritual body of Christ—the Church.

OK, Valy, you got my attention. What steps should I take?

I am glad you asked! Here are some ideas for those who would like to grow in the grace and knowledge of the Lord Jesus Christ.

Steps to move forward

Paul writes: "but speaking the truth in love, we are to grow up in all aspects into Him who is the head, even Christ" (Ephesians 4:15). In this verse, the apostle is giving us the two main directions we must pursue: *truth* and *love*. Let's briefly look into these two dimensions.

Truth

Christ told His disciples these memorable words: "I am the way and the truth and the life. No one comes to the Father except through Me" (John 14:6). I believe that Jesus wanted to reinforce the fact that He is the personified truth. Apart from Him, nothing reaches that level of truth. Why is this important? Because, Christ wants us to remember this fact for the rest of our lives so no matter the pressures or worldly philosophies, nothing will get us into its mold.

1. Experiential knowledge of the Truth

We must know the truth and be persistent. Continuation is one major component of discipleship. Jesus told the Jews who believed in Him to hold to His teachings. John writes:

> So Jesus was saying to those Jews who had believed Him, "If you continue in My word, then you are truly disciples of Mine; and you will know the truth, and the truth will make you free. (John 8:31–32).

The correlation between the Person of Christ—*truth,* and our *freedom* is very important. Christ is not talking about some philosophical knowledge, (as the Greeks believe), but instead *experiential knowledge* of the Logos (John 1:1), sent to us by God to give us the true *light* (John 1:4). To make sure those new believers understood precisely what He meant, Jesus continues: "So if the Son makes you free, you will be free indeed" (John 8:36). This is deep, and we just scratched the surface of it. We can spend an entire chapter just on this concept alone.

Marked by a deep experiential knowledge of the Incarnate Truth, some sixty years later, John writes: "I have not written to you because you do not know the **truth**, but because you do know **it**, and because no lie is of the truth" (1 John 2:21).

The Holy Spirit testifies: "This is the One who came by water and blood, Jesus Christ; not with the water only, but with the water and with the blood. It is the Spirit who testifies because the Spirit is the truth" (1 John 5:6). **We can conclude that the revealed truth is the only foundation for true love.** John, at an old age, writes: "The elder to the chosen lady and her children, whom I love in truth; and not only I, but also all who know the truth" (2 John 1:1). It cannot get much clearer than this, can it? **Love must be anchored in truth by all who know the truth.**

2. Sanctified by the truth

The heart of the Great Commission is discipleship. Discipleship is the vehicle the Holy Spirit uses to perfect the saints. The truth is essential in the process of sanctification. Sanctification is past, present, and future. Our sanctification had begun when we were born again (past tense), and it continues (present tense) until our physical death (future tense) or the return of Christ. If discipleship doesn't promote sanctification, it is not true discipleship.

In His Priestly Prayer, the last part of the Upper Room Discourse, Jesus prays for His disciples: "Sanctify them in the truth; Your word is truth" (John 17:17). This prayer is still in effect during the existence of the church. The Lord (cf. John 17:20) prayed for us too.

Paul also stresses the importance of holiness its connection with the truth. He writes: "and put on the new self, which in the likeness of God has been created in righteousness and holiness of the truth." (Ephesians 4:24). Please see the connection between righteousness, holiness, and the truth.

3. Speaking the truth

What separates humans from other creatures is our capacity to communicate and master languages. As Christ's disciples, speaking the truth must permeate all life's dimensions: family, church, community, and so on. Paul writes: "Therefore, laying aside falsehood, SPEAK TRUTH EACH ONE of you WITH HIS NEIGHBOR, for we are members of one another" (Ephesians 4:25). Unless our relationship with God is carried out into the tapestry of life, all of this is just a lovely religious theory.

4. Live in the truth

God's truth is the highest ethic in the life of Jesus' followers. John writes: "If we say that we have fellowship with Him and *yet* walk in the darkness, we lie and do not practice the truth" (1 John 1:6). Claiming fellowship with Christ while walking in darkness is an oxymoron. The truth in us is incompatible with anything that touches any form of sin (emotionally, physically, or spiritually). John writes: "If we say that we have no sin, we are deceiving ourselves, and the truth is not in us" (1 John 1:8). Truth demands nothing less than full transparency with God, ourselves, and others. This is foundational to our spirituality. Let's read slowly and carefully the following verse: "The one who says, 'I have come to know Him,' and does not keep His commandments, is a liar, and the truth is not in him" (1 John 2:4). That is a strong word. Why is that? Because, if we are truly His, we are bound forever in the truth. John writes: "For the sake of the truth which abides in us and will be with us forever" (2 John 1:2).

5. Love according to the truth

Truth is the most important ingredient of our love walk. John writes: "Little children, let us not love with word or with tongue, but in deed and truth" (1 John 3:18). There must be consistency in practicing truth in all spheres of our existence: speech, action, love.

There are so many truth-related connections we can make from Scriptures. Let me list a few without much elaboration:

– *Wrap yourselves in the truth*

> Stand firm therefore, having girded your loins with truth, and having out on the breastplate of righteousness. (Ephesians 6:14)

– *Stay strong in the truth*

> Therefore, I will always be ready to remind you of these things, even though you already know them, and have been ESTABLISHED in the TRUTH which is present with you. (2 Peter 1:12)

– *Work alongside the truth*

> Therefore we ought to support such men, so that we may be fellow workers with the truth. (3 John 1:8)

– *Preach the truth*

> Preach the word (truth); be ready in season *and* out of season; reprove, rebuke, exhort, with great patience and instruction. For the time will come when they will not endure sound doctrine; but *wanting* to have their ears tickled, they will accumulate for themselves teachers in accordance to their own desires, and will turn away their ears from the truth and will turn aside to myths. (2 Timothy 4:2–4)

There is no higher or nobler objective than preaching, teaching, and speaking the truth in love.

Truth and love must go hand in hand. If truth is separated from love, it kills. This is what the Law does. Paul writes: "who also made us adequate as servants of a new covenant, not of the letter but of the Spirit; for the letter kills, but the Spirit gives life" (1 Corinthians 3:6).

Love

Love without truth is sentimentalism at best and hypocrisy at worst. But when love and truth are working together, it is the very power of God transforming us more and more into Christ's likeness. Agape love is the very objective of Christian spirituality.

1. Walk in love

There is no better pathway for a born-again believer other than the path of love. Paul calls it the more excellent way (1 Corinthians 12:31). Agape love is superior to spiritual gifts, it stands far above sings and wonders. First Corinthians 13 describes the nature and character of God personified in Christ. In 1 Corinthians 13:4–7, to describe this kind of love Paul uses several action words:

– Love is patient
– Love is kind
– [Love] is not jealous
– Love does not brag

– [Love] is not arrogant
– [Love] does not act unbecomingly
– [Love] does not seek its own
– [Love] is not provoked
– [Love] does not take into account a wrong *suffered*
– [Love] does not rejoice in unrighteousness
– [Love] rejoices with the truth
– [Love] bears all things
– [Love] believes all things
– [Love] hopes all things
– [Love] endures all things [138]

Wow! Who can reach that standard of loving? Christ does. And He empowers His disciples to do it too. How? The Holy Spirit works it out through us, if we submit to God. Agape love is the very objective of Christian spirituality. Paul writes: "But the goal of our instruction is love from a pure heart and a good conscience and a sincere faith" (1 Timothy 1:5).

2. Pursue love

People all over the world pursue something: success, fame, money, power, and so on. Unlike the world, Christians are called to pursue love. I found it interesting that Paul urges his closest disciple, Timothy, among other qualities, to pursue love. He writes: "But flee from these things, you man of God, and *pursue* righteousness, godliness, faith, love, perseverance *and* gentleness" (1 Timothy 6:11). Also, before departing from this world as a martyr, Paul admonishes Timothy, once again, to pursue agape love. He writes: "Now flee from youthful lusts and *pursue* righteousness, faith, love, and peace, with those who call on the Lord from a pure heart" (2 Timothy 2:22). As I said, unbelievers have their dreams and goals in this life, but the highest goal of Christ's disciples is pursuing agape love.

3. Being united in love

More than any other group of people, Christians are required to be united. However, according to the Bible, they cannot live in *unity* without *love*. Paul addresses the church of Colossians with these words: "that their hearts may be encouraged, having been knit together in love, and attaining to all the wealth that comes from the full assurance of understanding, resulting in a true knowledge of God's mystery, that is, Christ Himself" (Colossians 2:2).

I like the way the Barnes' Notes on the Bible elaborates on the phrase "knit together in love":

> It means, properly, to make to come together, and hence, refers to a firm union, as where the hearts of Christians are one. Here it means that the way of comforting each other was by solid Christian friendship and that the means of cementing that was love. It was not by a mere outward profession, or by mere speculative faith; it was by a union of affection.[139]

4. Having a genuine love for one another

The market is assaulted with all sorts of fake pieces of jewelry which are nothing, but plastic covered with cheap imitation silver or gold. The most beautiful piece of jewelry disciples of Christ can wear is genuine love. Paul testifies about him and his companions that they have genuine love. He writes: "In purity, in knowledge, in patience, in kindness, in the Holy Spirit, in genuine love" (2 Corinthians 6:6). As followers of Jesus, we must weep in repentance and ask the Holy Spirit to cleanse us so that we can be pure conduits for His agape love (Romans 5:5). Peter writes: "Since you have in obedience to the truth purified your souls for a sincere love of the brethren, fervently love one another from the heart" (1 Peter 1:22).

The only way we can truly love each other is from the heart. Any different kind of "love", which does not flow from the spiritually regenerated heart, is not agape love.

5. Increase our capacity to love well

We are concerned with increasing our bank accounts,

investment portfolios, retirement accounts, and so on. But how many of us are concerned with expanding our capacity to love? Paul admonishes us with these words, "And may the Lord cause you to increase and abound in love for one another, and for all people, just as we also do for you" (1 Thessalonians 3:12). This verse is calling us to love not only our brothers and sisters in Christ but all people. This is what the Great Commandment (Mark 12:30–31) is all about.

There are so many agape love related connections we can make. Let me list a few of them without much elaboration:

– *Put on love*

> Beyond all these things put on love, which is the perfect bond of unity. (Colossians 3:14)

None of our clothes fall on us in the morning before going to school or work. We must be intentional and put the clothes on. Disciples of Christ are called to be intentional about "putting on love."

– *Keep on loving each other*

> Let love of the brethren continue. (Hebrews 13:1)

– *Sound love*

> Older men are to be temperate, dignified, sensible, sound in faith, in love, in perseverance. (Titus 2:2)

Talking and writing about love is not an easy task. We learn how to love well if it is modeled to us. I think that more than any time in Church history now is the time to see more role models in our churches. Mature men and women of God, mature people in faith, who know how to love well.

– *Do not forsake your first love*

> But I have this against you, that you have left your first

love. (Revelations 2:4)

It is so easy to get busy with things for God and forget all about God's love. Christ's words of "*correction*" towards the church of Ephesus should ring in our ears. The first love is God's love towards us. It is impossible to love based on our love. By nature, we are self-centered creatures, incapable of displaying sacrificial love towards others. "**We love, because He first loved us**" (1 John 4:19). That is the right order and the right motivation. We cannot afford to forsake our first love—the love "poured out within our hearts by the Holy Spirit." (Romans 5:5). We must go back, over and over again, to the only source of love we have—God's love.

I hope you can see how beautifully the *truth* and the *love* concepts are connected, leading to holistic spiritual growth.

Conclusions

I preached and taught many times from Ephesians 4:11–16. It is a favorite passage of mine. As I reflected over the years, there are a few call-to-action items that I would like to share with you:

1. We must bring back the lost art of discipleship into the local churches where God placed us as ministers of the gospel. (Matthew 28:19–20; 2 Timothy 2:2).
2. We must facilitate the ministry of spiritual growth and maturity in such a way that every individual member may partake of solid food (Hebrew 5:13–14, 6:1–3). The goal is that every disciple becomes adequately equipped and fully capable of edifying the Body of Christ in love (Ephesians 4:16).
3. We must realize that the price we are paying to remain spiritually immature is too high. We also must recognize that spiritual immaturity has tremendous negative consequences.

May all of us, like the third mason from the story at the beginning of this chapter, look confidently towards the sky and declare, "*I am a disciple-maker and, by God's grace, I am building His church.*"

Prayer

> For this reason, I kneel, and I am asking God to bless all ministers of the gospel, all spiritual leaders, and Bible teachers locally and around the globe. I pray that the Holy Spirit will empower them to keep on "equipping of the saints for the work of service, to the building up of the body of Christ" in such a way that each part shall work adequately for the edification in love and truth of the whole body. In Christ's name. Amen.

This chapter, no question about it, is challenging. It was challenging for me to write it. As you read about various concepts, I hope the Holy Spirit convicted you in some areas. In a small group or other discipleship settings, please try to answer one or more of the following questions. Please elaborate as the Holy Spirit leads you.

Discussion Questions:

– What aspects did you like the most from the section called: "Truth"? Please share your insights with a Life Group member.

– Please re-read the section called "Love." What aspects did you like the most from this section? Please share your insights with a close friend or your spiritual mentor.

– What is your place in the body of Christ? What is your role in the body of Christ? And what joint or ministry are you part of? What is your spiritual contribution supposed to be for the wellbeing of the Body of Christ? Please discuss it with your spiritual mentor.

– Assuming that you have identified your spiritual function in the Body of Christ, are you actively building the church in love and in truth? Please discuss your thoughts and experiences with your small group.

Notes

10. The Building, the Builders, and the Process

[131] Girard J.P. and Lambert S. *The Story of Knowledge: Writing Stories that Guide Organizations into the Future.* (The Electronic Journal of Knowledge Management Volume 5 Issue 2, 2007), 161-172. Available online at www.ejkm.com.
[132] Robert Mulholland Jr., *Invitation to a Journey: The Road Map for Spiritual Formation*, (Intervarsity Press, Downers Grove, IL, 60515, 1993), 15.
[133] Dallas Willard, *Renovation of the Heart: Putting On the Character of Christ*, (Hovel Audio, 2005), MP3 CD.
[134] *Spiritual Formation.* Renovare.org. Accessed on October 29, 2019https://renovare.org/about/ideas/spiritual-formation..
[135] A. W. Tozer, *Knowledge Of The Holy*, (Fig, 2017), 5.
[136] The word teknon also means a newborn baby. So it reveals the baby stage in our spiritual life.
[137] Huios means the child who's been marked as someone's son/daughter because of the similarity between the parents and the child, it is the similarity of facial features, character, and attitude.
[138] Valy Vaduva, *Fullness of Christ*, (Upper Room Fellowship Ministry, Livonia, MI, 2018), 188.
[139] Colossians 2:2. Accessed on October 22, 2019. https://biblehub.com/commentaries/barnes/colossians/2.htm.

CHAPTER 11

A Brief Literature Review

If the axe is dull and he does not sharpen its edge, then he must exert more strength. Wisdom has the advantage of giving success.

— Ecclesiastes 10:10

When for the first time I was compelled to look deeper into the aspect of spiritual immaturity I investigated the following books:

- *REVEAL: Where are You?,* by Greg Hawkins and Cally Parkinson
- *The Cross and Christian Ministry*, by D.A. Carson
- *The Great Omission: Reclaiming the Essential Teachings on Discipleship*, by Dallas Willard
- *Transforming Discipleship: Making Disciples a Few at a Time*, by Greg Ogden
- *12 Reasons Christians Don't Grow Even in Good Churches*, by Tony Green

Let's analyze the findings one by one. In the first book, *REVEAL: Where are You*?, Greg Hawkins, one of Hybels' senior assistant pastors, shares that he became aware that the effectiveness of the church service was wanting, and that Willow Creek Community Church [Willow] had become more of the place to be than a place to follow Christ. He approached Hybels, Willow's Senor Pastor, and asked for funds to conduct an in-depth study of membership to determine:

– Their state of maturity
– Their satisfaction with teaching and programs
– Their feelings about their church journey in general

The study was based on more than 11,000 completed surveys from Willow Creek and six additional churches of various sizes from different geographical locations. This research totaled an impressive 2.6 million points of data. The findings of this study shook Bill Hybles to the core of his being. I read somewhere that Hybels said that this was, "The biggest wake-up call of my life… and the worst day of my life." In the summer of 2007, Willow published the results of that self-study under the title: Reveal: Where Are You? The report's front cover says that readers will learn "surprising research findings that rocked Willow."

A spiritual continuum emerged from the research:

– Exploring Christianity—"*I believe in God, but I'm not sure about Christ. My faith is not a significant part of my life.*"
– Growing in Christ—"*I believe in Jesus, and I'm working on what it means to get to know Him.*"
– Close to Christ—"*I feel really close to Christ and depend on Him daily for guidance.*"
– Christ-Centered—"*God is all I need in my life. He is enough. Everything I do is a reflection of Christ*"[140]

The findings are absolutely astonishing! Here they are the most important points:

- Involvement in externally and internally focused church programs didn't necessarily translate into spiritual growth, which they defined as "increasing love for God and others."
- Spiritual growth is all about increasing relational closeness to Christ. Why is this? Very simple: "Because God "wired" us first and foremost to be in a growing relationship with Him not with the church."[141]
- The church is vitally important in the first two segments (Exploring Christianity and Growing in Christ), but as people grow into the latter two stages of spiritual growth

(Close to Christ and Christ-Centered), it becomes less and less important.

- Personal spiritual practices are the building blocks for a Christ-centered life.
- The church's most active evangelists, volunteers, and donors come from the most spiritually advanced segments. "These results caused us to reevaluate deeply rooted beliefs."[142]
- More than 25 percent of those surveyed described themselves as spiritually "stalled" or "dissatisfied" with the role of the church in their spiritual growth. This should make every pastor and church leader think deeply about what type of spirituality they promote.

Involvement in externally and internally focused church programs didn't necessarily translate

There was much more information that surfaced, but the most interesting aspects are listed below:

- Far too much emphasis was put upon church involvement, and far too little on encouraging personal growth through a personal and growing relationship with Jesus Christ.
- The church spends far too much time catering to seekers with their teaching and programs, what they called the "spiritual equivalent of diaper-changing", while letting "spiritual adolescents" fend for themselves.
- People in the church need, from the very beginning, to be fully instructed that it is their personal responsibility to be in a growing and vital relationship with Christ, for this is what would carry them long after the luster of church programs faded.

The leadership of Willow admitted: "We have been wrong. We need to rethink the coaching we give you as you pursue your spiritual growth." And:

> "We want to move people from dependence on the church to a growing interdependent

> partnership with the church. We have to let people know early on in their journey that they need to look beyond the church to grow . . . Our people need to learn to feed themselves through personal spiritual practices that allow them to deepen their relationship with Christ."[143]

I give pastor Hybels credit because he was sincere and indicated that the emphasis on programs and meetings did not produce disciples. Of course, a study does not address the enormous need for spiritual growth in all churches. However, Willow displayed a lot of humility to undertake a self-study and genuine vulnerability to publicize the results. Still, this is provoking us all to think more deeply about what it means to be the church. It is admirable that Hybels admitted that while they have "spruced up the worship, spiked up the sermons, and become great at organization" the same time they were failing to produce disciples. The real question is: Would there be more congregations with such passion and humility? Would the church in America wake up to Christ's original vision – Go therefore and make disciples? I pray that she would. Amen!

The second book that I consulted was *The Cross and Christian Ministry*. Dr. D. A. Carson writes so convincingly about the cross not only as God's redemptive tool but most importantly, the cross should stand as "the test and the standard of all vital Christian ministry."[144] This book is based on a series of talks Carson presented at the quadrennial world congress of IFES (International Federation of Evangelical Students). Mainly, the book is based on Carson's exposition on parts of 1 Corinthians.

Carson argues very convincingly that:

- The cross should be central to Christian preaching and Christian proclamation. His point is loud and clear, "The message of the cross may be nonsense to those who are perishing, "a stumbling block to Jews and foolishness to Gentiles" (1 Corinthians 1:23), "but to those whom God has called, both Jews and Greeks, Christ the power of God and the wisdom of God" (1 Corinthians 1:24)." I could not agree more with this author. Paul was a preacher of the cross (1 Corinthians 2:2), so should we be also.

- To really enjoy the gift of the Holy Spirit, one must appropriate the message of the cross. Carson writes, "The spiritual person is simply a believer, one who has closed with the message of the cross. Indeed, those who are most mature are most grateful for the cross and keep coming back to it as the measure of God's love for them and the supreme standard of personal self-denial."
- Factionalists display marks of wretched, unacceptable, spiritual immaturity. Carson writes, "Paul finds the Corinthians stuck at the "milk" stage. They are not growing in their understanding and application of the Word of God generally, and of the gospel in particular." Let me ask you – Why is that? I think you would agree that the main reason is because they failed to appropriate the cross in their daily lives. As a result, they remained fleshly (or carnal) Christians.
- Christian leadership means being entrusted with the mysteries of God. Paul, as a servant of God who embraced the cross (Galatians 2:2), has been entrusted with God's special revelations. In genuine humility, Paul calls the Corinthians believers to imitate Him (1 Corinthians 4:16). Besides Christ, Paul stands today as a giant example of what it means to be a true Christian leader. Christian leadership means living life in the light of the cross. If the first century Christians followed the crucified Messiah, so should we.
- The Cross makes us global Christians. We should not resume to an individualistic faith. Because of the cross and what God did through it for us, we "must adopt as our aim the salvation of men and women." Carson also writes, "I have become all things to all men so that by all possible means I might save some" (1 Corinthians 9:22, emphasis added). Right from the beginning (Acts 1:8), this exactly what Jesus wants the Church to be and do.

In conclusion, let me restate what Carson wrote:

> It is now commonplace to confess that evangelicalism is fragmenting. To the extent that this is true, it is

> utterly imperative that we self-consciously focus on what is central—on the gospel of Jesus Christ. That means we must resolve "to know nothing except Jesus Christ and him crucified" (1 Corinthians 2:2).[145]

Amen to that brother Carson! Since it is biblical, we should do just as Carson suggested!

The third piece of literature I investigated was *The Great Omission: Reclaiming the Essential Teachings on Discipleship* by Dallas Willard. He used to be a professor at the University of Southern California's School of Philosophy and, most importantly, a prolific writer. Professor Willard was a valuable contributing member of Renovare—The Institute for Christian Spiritual Formation. Willard wrote many books, among which my favorite works are: *The Divine Conspiracy: Rediscovering Our Hidden Life in God, Renovation of the Heart: Putting on the Character of Christ*, and of course, *The Great Omission: Reclaiming Jesus's Essential Teachings on Discipleship*. Oh, how much I enjoy reading Dallas Willard's books and articles! His writing style is deep and requires a lot of focused attention, but it is worth all the effort.

The Great Omission, unlike his other books, is a compilation of articles and speeches Willard has produced over the years. The chapters of this book are based on these articles. Each chapter builds on the preceding and form a nice flowing book. The book encompasses the most important subtopics of discipleship including apprenticeship to Jesus, spiritual formation, development of character, and the restoration of soul and mind. I can say that this book scratches where we itch – lack of spiritual maturity. This book addresses the subject matter that is nearest and dearest to anyone who loves Jesus and wants His Kingdom advanced via discipleship.

The book is structured in four major divisions:

- Chapters 1-5 in which Willard tackles the single most defining issue that individuals and the church today face—the biblical meaning of discipleship. In so doing, it identifies the "great omission" of which Willard speaks—the exclusion of meaningful discipleship from the church's spiritual life.
- Chapters 6-11 in which the author explains in general terms the spiritual formation that naturally and inevitably

accompanies such discipleship. It gives us a preliminary vision of the astonishing kind of people we can become as apprentices of Jesus.

- Chapters 12-15 are the "how-to" section of the book that introduces us to the means of discipleship and spiritual formation.
- Chapters 16-20, which contain the works of five friends of Jesus—historical figures who have contributed greatly to Willard's own apprenticeship to Jesus and who can contribute to ours as well.

For the purpose of my book, I will focus mostly on the first part of the book that deals with discipleship, or lack of it, in today's church. Right from the introduction, Willard spills out his heart, "We need to emphasize that the Great Omission from the Great Commission is not obedience to Christ, but discipleship, apprenticeship, to Him."[146] In other words, Willard admonishes churches and their leaders to go back to the original vision of Jesus–discipleship. I am as disappointed as Willard that most professing Christians can be "Christians" and never become disciples. The author names this The Great Omission from the "Great Commission" in which the Great Disparity is firmly rooted."

In the first chapter: "Discipleship", the author expresses his disappointment with the fact that most Christian institutions of our day consider discipleship "optional." Instead of focusing on fulfilling the vision of Jesus–making disciples; the churches today are filled with "un-discipled disciples." Ironically, "In place of Christ's plan, historical drift has substituted 'Make converts (to a particular 'faith and practice') and baptize them into church membership." However, the implications of non-discipleship are many and they are great. "Non-discipleship costs you exactly that abundance of life Jesus said he came to bring (John10:10)" But, by far, the most important negative effect is that a church composed of non-discipled people cannot influence the culture the way the first century church did. I hope that my readers agree that this is such a revelatory truth. Willard continues: "Thus, the very type of life that could change the course of human society . . . [discipleship] . . . is excluded or at least omitted from the essential message of the church."[147] Let me ask you—why is this? I believe this is cased because a non-discipled life is salt-less, in Jesus' own words, good only for "the manure pile" (Luke 14:35).

Even the title of the second chapter: "Why Bother with Discipleship?" is intriguing. In this chapter Willard conveys with precision and clarity four aspects why discipleship is a must, not an option:

- Forgiveness without obedience is unscriptural. It is an oxymoron to say that we trust Jesus for forgiveness of our sins and decline to follow Him as an obedient disciple. This makes us, according to Willard, "vampire Christians." It is like telling Jesus this: "I'd like a little of Your blood, please. But I don't care to be Your student or have Your character. In fact, won't you just excuse me while I get on with my life, and I'll see You in heaven."[148]
- Non-discipleship leaves us immature and defeated. Churches everywhere are filled with defeated congregants. The secret of spiritual victory is hidden somewhere else. Only by abiding in Christ's words one can know the truth and experience real freedom (John 8:36).
- Non-discipleship means lack of transformation. Only discipleship leads to genuine transformation. Only when we are walking with Jesus as His apprentices can we "remove the duplicity that has become second nature to us."[149] Only those believers who are mature in Christ are empowered to bring forth much fruit for God's glory (John 15:8). This is the only genuine badge for discipleship. Nothing more, nothing less, nothing else—but the fruit of the Spirit (Galatians 5:22-23).
- Non-discipleship means a powerless and defeated Christianity. Only a closer walk with Jesus prepares us to receive and exercise God's power. Willard writes, "We were meant to be inhabited by God and to live by a power beyond ourselves."[150]

The author's dilemma, as well as mine, is this: How can we be satisfied with a salvation that jumps into action when we die while here on earth we live a un-discipled, untransformed, and defeated life?? How can we call ourselves Christians and disobey the One who said: Follow Me? It does not make sense, does it?

In chapter three: "Who is Your Teacher", Willard elevates Jesus Christ as our Teacher above all teachers, professors, and scholars of this world. I like that! Jesus is not only our Savior; Christ is not only our Lord, the Son of God, the very Logos of the entire universe; Christ is also the wisest Teacher of all. If Christ is not seen by professing Christians as the Expert in every field it "is a simple lack of respect for Him."[151]

> Forgiveness without obedience is unscriptural. It is an oxymoron to say that we trust Jesus for forgiveness of our sins and decline to follow Him as an obedient disciple.

I am not sure about you, but I fully agree with that statement. Therefore, we must learn from Him three main aspects:

- The reason for our existence is in Him and from Him, "For in Him we live and move and exist…" (Acts 17:28).
- Our inner person is transformed according to His likeness (2 Corinthians 3:18).
- Jesus models us and teaches us how to live in the concrete real day-to-day life, we are invited to follow into His practices, take up His yoke, and learn from Him, "Take My yoke upon you and learn from Me…" (Matthew 11:29).

In other words, in all areas of life, from family life, school, profession, and Christian spirituality, Jesus Christ has supremacy. He is the Expert! Willard writes, "If you trust Jesus Christ as your teacher, He will teach you in all ways" (p. 22).

In chapter four: "Looking like Jesus", Willard explains that we are called to be "imitators of God" (Ephesians 5:1) and to "put on the Lord Jesus" (Romans 13:14). In other words, we are called to be like Jesus, to act like Jesus, and most importantly, to love like Jesus. The reality is that only as His disciples "living under the governance of heaven frees and empowers us to love as God loves."[152] Only in the context of discipleship we learn to open up to the transforming power of the Holy Spirit and to walk in the

Spirit (Galatians 5:25). Then we experience, externally, the gifts of the Spirit and internally the fruit of the Spirit. The bottom line is that "transformation into Christ-likeness is our direct, personal interaction with Christ through the Spirit."[153]

In chapter five: "The Key to the Keys to the Kingdom", Willard provides the reader with an 'airplane view' about spiritual disciplines, mainly about Sabbath with its companions: solitude, silence, and fasting. As disciples of Christ we are called to learn to practice these holy habits—called spiritual disciplines. Please observe that *discipline* and *disciple* come from the same Latin root, *discere*—"to learn."

Overall, the book demonstrates the author's knowledge of discipleship. I join the author in his deep desire that churches will go back to the basic vision of Christ–The Great Commission. I pray that it will be implemented as the number one priority of every local church–thus repenting of the Great Omission. If you pick up this book and study it, I hope that you arrive at the same conclusion—that Willard did a very good job with this work.

The fourth work that I studied for this chapter was *Transforming Discipleship: Making Disciples a Few at a Time,* by Greg Ogden. This work is another penetrating book on discipleship. Its author, Greg Ogden, writes with conviction from, both a practical and an academic perspective. He is executive pastor of discipleship at Christ Church of Oak Brook, Illinois. Ogden previously served as academic director of the Doctor of Ministry program at Fuller Theological Seminary in Pasadena California.

Right from the introduction, Ogden drives his point home quoting Bill Hull: "The crisis at the heart of the church is a crisis of product." Further down Ogden continues: "In all of my teaching through seminars and courses on making disciples Jesus' way, I still sense that a very small percentage of pastors and church leaders emulate Jesus' and Paul's models."[154] In other words, Ogden is saying that instead of focusing on fulfilling the Great Commission churches offer seeker-friendly programs. But, "disciples making is not a program but a relationship."[155] Programs don't offer the ingredients of genuine discipleship making. Ogden explains that only "when we bring together transparent relationships and the truth of God's Word in the context of covenantal accountability: for life change, then we have stepped into the Holy Spirit's sweet spot that makes life change possible."[156] Amen to that!

Ogden's book, *Transforming Discipleship*, is comprised of three parts:

– Part I: "The Discipleship Deficit"
– Part II: "Doing the Lord's Work in the Lord's Way"
– Part III: "Multiplying Reproducing Discipleship Groups"

In the Part I, the author focuses on the problem and tries to get to the root causes of why churches lack discipleship. For the purpose of this chapter I will focus my review mainly on the first part of the book. "Where have all the disciples gone?" is the primary question. Defining reality is the issue Ogden desires to address in chapter one of his book. As Max De Pree suggests to all leaders, the top priority for all church leadership is to define reality. We all must know where we are in order to determine with certainty where we are going. Otherwise, any path will take you to an unknown destination, like the refrain of "Any Road": "If you don't know where you're going, any road'll take you there."[157]

The sad reality is that one word sums up the state of the Church today—superficiality. "The Joint Statement on discipleship at the Eastbourne Consultation began with an acknowledgment of need:

> As we face the new millennium, we acknowledge that the state of the Church is marked by growth without depth. Our zeal to go wider has not been matched by a commitment to go deeper.[158]

I believe it was Chuck Colson who said: "the church is 3000 miles wide and one inch deep." According to many Christian thinkers this is the cause for the moral decay we see everywhere: in government, corporations, churches, and families. Ogden quotes Cal Thomas who writes: "The problem in our culture . . . isn't the abortionists. Isn't the pornographers or drug dealers or criminals. It is the undisciplined, undiscipled, disobedient, and Biblically ignorant church of Jesus Christ."[159]

According to Ogden, there are seven marks of biblical discipleship. If we sincerely compare these marks with our reality, we can easily identify the gap between the biblical standard and the state of our churches and ministries:

1. Passive recipients versus proactive ministers

The Bible describes a church full of proactive ministers, but today, the majority of churches are composed of just passive recipients.

2. Spiritually undisciplined versus spiritually disciplined

The Scripture describes followers of Jesus who were engaged in a disciplined way of living; however, today we see only a small percentage of Christians who live that way. Statistically speaking, according to Barna Research Group: "But not one of the adults we interviewed said that their goal in life was to be a committed follower of Jesus Christ or to make disciples."[160]

3. Private faith versus holistic discipleship

According to the Bible, the first century church was composed of believers who affected all compartments of life. What we see today are 'believers' who are trying to practice a private faith. This is far from what the kingdom of God is all about. Ogden writes: "Fundamentally we are kingdom people, which means that Jesus is Lord in our hearts, homes and workplaces; our attitudes thoughts and desires; our relationships and moral decisions; our political convictions and social conscience. In every area of our interior life, personal relationships or social involvement, we seek to know and live the mind and will of God."[161]

4. Blending in versus a countercultural force

The Bible talks about a community of believers as countercultural force. Acts portrays Christians as "men who have upset the world" (Acts 17:6). John Stott describes the church as a community of "radical non-conformity." It is so sad to say that in today's church, the believers' lifestyles and values are not much different from the secular culture. Ogden writes: "Many observers have concluded that the church, far from being countercultural, does not look much different from the unchurched." Barna observes: "The fact that the proportions of Christians who affirm these values is equivalent to the proportion of non-Christians who hold similar views indicates how meaningless Christianity has been in the lives of millions of professed believers."[162] What is astonishing to me is the one-sided freedom proclaimed by most Americans: "I want to do what I want to do when I want to do it. No one better tell me otherwise." This is what sociologist Robert Bellah found during his research included in Habits of the Heart. The fact that this study shows the true character of most Americans does not bother me too much. However, the fact that this is no different from the character of most Christians hurts my heart a great deal. The reality is that the disease of individualism and materialism plagues most American churches as well.

5. Church is optional versus Church is essential

The Bible pictures the church, more than anything, as a living organism with Christ as the Head of it. However, the cruel reality is that most believers view the church as an optional institution unnecessary for discipleship. It is sad to say, but the 21st century church is seen as a corporation or organization not as a living organism–the Body of Christ. Ogden challenges the reader with this penetrating question: "Unless there is a covenantal understanding of a believer's relationship with a community, how can people be formed into Christlike disciples?"[163] I found this to be such a good question!

6. Biblically illiterate versus biblically informed

The Scriptures picture the followers of Christ as spiritually knowledgeable individuals living transformed lives based on the revealed truth of God's Word. The reality today is that most believers are biblically ignorant people. According to CBN: "Some Christian leaders say this generation is the most Biblically illiterate in history. The problem: young Christians are guiding their lives by a popular culture instead of Scripture." The same aspect was found by Gallup: "Americans revere the Bible—but, by and large, they don't read it." Similar findings were reported by Barna: "60 percent of all American adults and 85 percent who described themselves as born again would affirm the statement: "The Bible is totally accurate in all that it teaches." Despite these affirmations, there is an appalling ignorance of the book we put on pedestal. For example, 53 percent of the adults in Barna's survey believed that the saying "God helps those who help themselves is a Biblical truth."[164]

7. Sharing your faith versus shrinking from personal witness

The Bible talks about believers who share their faith in Christ-experience with others. However, today many believers are intimidated individuals who shrink from sharing their salvation story with others. The book of Acts states clearly that we all are supposed to be Christ's witnesses. It is dramatic that in today's church environment it takes approximately 100 members to win 1.67 people to Christ in a given year. Please pause for a moment and think about this statistic.

In a nutshell, this is the state of discipleship today. Under these circumstances, the most challenging question is: "How can we grow self-initiating, reproducing, fully devoted followers of Jesus Christ?"[165] The answer is clear. We must return to the Mission Statement Jesus wrote for His Church once and for all: "Go therefore and make disciples of all the nations…" (Matthew 28:19a NASB). We must take seriously God's calling in our lives and swim against the flow as the countercultural community we are called to be. This requires a radical change, which is the most difficult things to do. According to John Kotter, in his book Leading Change: "the primary reason why change does not occur is that there is no sense of urgency."[166] Change, in its original sense—repentance, is the most urgent aspect of all. The church is required to assess her spiritual state and refocus her efforts, in other words, change her mind (metánoia) regarding the Great Commission.

In chapter two, Ogden digs deeper to expose the root causes of the discipleship malaise. According to Ogden, there are at least eight major causes for the discipleship malaise:

1. Diversion from the primary calling

According to Ephesians 4:12 the church leadership is called, "for the equipping of the saints for the work of service..." But pastors and church leaders have diverted from their primary calling. In the background, this is the plan of the enemy—Satan. Ogden writes:

> If I were Satan and wanted to fatally stunt the growth of disciples to maturity. What would I do? I would divert the leaders from fulfilling their God-given function of equipping the saints. Instead, I would distract them with other good and high-sounding activities engaging them in ministry. This is exactly what has happened. We have shunted our spiritual leaders into being program developers, administrators and caregivers.[167]

According to Ogden, one role consumes the pastors more than any other roles–pastoral care. This made the pastor "a responder" instead of "a saint equipper." This was exactly the temptation the first church leaders were faced with; the same dilemma to become "table servers" or continue to pursue God's commission of "preaching the Word." Thank God for the Spirit-given wisdom: they decided to stick with God's calling. Unfortunately: "We have an undiscipled church because its leaders have not made discipling their primary focus."

2. Discipling through programs

When churches replace 'person-centered' growth with 'programs' they fail to make disciples, thus failing the Great Commission. Only "proximity produces disciples."[168]

The natural question is: Why don't programs make disciples? According to Ogden, there are at least four major reasons why programs cannot make disciples:

i. Information does not necessary lead to

transformation

Odgen says that: "Programs operate on the assumption that if someone has information, having that information will automatically lead to transformation." One example is Elvis Presley. Attending church, summer camps, and memorizing 350 Bible verses each year as a child, was not sufficient to keep Elvis focused on a lifestyle pleasing to God.

ii. Programs are the one preparing for the many

Even though this is very good for those who work hard to prepare the program, the rest of the people are left with just a lot of unprocessed information. The classic example is preaching. Most of the stuff said in a sermon is forgotten by the time people meet in the hallway or the parking lot for discussion. Furthermore, on page 44, Ogden writes, "Preaching alone does not produce disciples."

iii. Programs are characterized by regimentation or synchronization

Most programs are designed to flow as a system which moves people through in a coordinated fashion, thus ignoring the specific growth rate of individuals. That is why programs cannot work when it comes to disciple making. In one of their studies, Barna concludes that: "Few churches intentionally guide their people through a strategic learning and developmental process that has been customized for the student."[169] Discipleship should not be confused with mass production. Ogden writes:

> Making disciples requires a customized approach. This means that a person's knowledge; character growth; obedience in thought, word and deed; discernment of unique ministry identity; and so on all need to be dealt with in the context of Jesus' radical and total claim upon an individual's life in the setting of community.[170]

iv. Programs have low personal accountability

Maybe some programs create the illusion of accountability, but in reality this is not solid at all. After some research, Barna concludes that: "Few churches have systems by which they measure what is happening in the life of church adherents. Few believers have lined up a trustworthy and competent partner who will hold them accountable to specific and measurable goals."[171]

3. Reducing the Christian life just to its eternal benefits

The sad part is that most believers do this, missing the joy and fulfillment of being a genuine student of Jesus. Dallas Willard in some of his essays and books points out that we reduced the spiritual life to a "bar-code" Christianity—we want abundance without obedience. In other words, instead of focusing on being conformed to the life of Jesus, we focus on the benefits that we receive by faith in Jesus. Maybe all of us have seen the bumper sticker: 'Christians aren't perfect, just forgiven." Willard comments that by this phrase we have reduced the Christian life to just receiving forgiveness. Then the question is: When is a Christian a Christian? Depending on the tradition, many believe that by reciting the sinner's prayer and walking down the aisle during an altar call, people become Christians. Willard challenges this position: "Should we not at least consider the possibility that this poor result is not in spite of what we teach and how we teach, but precisely because of it." The danger of reducing the Christian life to just embracing the gift of forgiveness is making obedience to Jesus and the spiritual transformation through discipleship unnecessary and irrelevant. Willard writes: "The most telling thing about the contemporary Christian is that he or she simply has no compelling sense that understanding of and conformity with the clear teachings of Christ is of any vital importance to his or her life, and certainly not that it is in any way essential."[172]

4. A two-tiered understanding of discipleship

In my opinion, this is one of the most dangerous views regarding discipleship. Most churches have made discipleship a special class for super-Christians, not for every believer. This is a sad reality which cannot be ignored – many consider themselves Christians, but have nothing to do with the quality of their Christianity. To this extent, Dwight Pentecost writes: "There is a vast difference between being a Christian and being a disciple."[173] For some, Christians and disciples differ in their level of commitment.

5. Unwillingness to call people to discipleship

The 'tragedy' is that most church leaders are reluctant to call their congregants to discipleship, thus failing to fulfill the Great Commission. The question is why?

According to Ogden there are a couple of reasons why church leaders shy away from discipleship:

- *Fear of losing people.* Many pastors are afraid that their congregants will leave their church for the nearby entertainment church if asked to become disciples.
- *Commitment to discipleship is frightening for leaders themselves.* Ogden writes: "Since discipleship is more caught than taught, as much model as message, it calls us to a level of self-examination that can be uncomfortable."

6. An inadequate view of the church

Many people have a very low view of the church and this affects it as a discipleship community. It is very concerning that many believers see church as being optional, not mandatory for the Christian life. "Robert Putnam, in *Bowling Alone: The Collapse and Revival of American Community,* makes the convincing case that the social capital of religious life is being undermined by privatized faith...

Putnam quotes Wade Clark Roof and William McKinney:

> Large numbers of young, well-educated, middle-class youth defected from the churches in the late sixties and the seventies… Some joined new religious movements; others sought personal enlightenment through various spiritual therapies and disciplines, but most simply "dropped out" of organized religion altogether… [The consequence was a] tendency toward highly individualized religious psychology without the benefits of strong supportive attachments to believing communities. A major impetus in this direction in the post-1960's was the thrust toward greater personal fulfillment and quest for the ideal self… In this climate of expressive individualism, religion tends to become "privatized" and more anchored in the personal realms."[174]

7. No clear pathway to maturity

We are forced to face the reality–most churches have no clear and public direction to spiritual maturity through well-thought discipleship. The well-known author, Rick Warren writes: "Instead of growing a church with programs, focus on growing people with a process. We need a process to go with purpose. Unless the purpose is flashed out in a process, then we don't have anything but nice platitudes."[175]

After extensive study in his book *Growing True Disciples*, George Barna reports:

> Relatively small numbers of born-again adults reported that their church helps them develop specific paths to follow to foster spiritual growth. Slightly less than half told us that their church had identified any spiritual goals, standards, or expectations for the congregation during the past year… Only one out of every five believers stated that their church has some means of facilitating an evaluation of the spiritual maturity or commitment to maturity of congregants… While many Christians were more than a bit cautious about

> the possibility, nine out of ten said that if their church helped them to identify specific spiritual-growth goals to pursue, they would at least listen to the advice and follow parts, if not all, of it.[176]

8. Lack of personal discipleship

The sad reality is that many believers in our churches have never been discipled in its the true biblical sense. Discipleship is a process that "takes place within an accountable relationship, over a period of time, for the purpose of bringing believers to spiritual maturity in Christ."

Barna writes:

> A majority (55 percent) of the adults who indicated their interest in advice on how to improve their spiritual life also said that if the church matched them with a spiritual mentor or coach, they would be more likely to pursue the changes suggested to them.[177]

In Part II of the book, Ogden writes about "Doing the Lord's Work in the Lord's Way". In Part III of the book he writes about "Multiplying Reproducing Discipleship Groups."

The bottom line is that if the Church doesn't turn things around, she fails the Great Commission, which states very clearly: "make disciples" not converts, else it becomes, as Willard puts it, the Church's Great Omission. My prayer is this: "O, God, open the eyes of Your Church to see clearly where she must go. Amen!"

The fifth work that I have consulted for this chapter was *12 Reasons Christians Don't Grow Even in Good Churches*, by Tony A. D. Green, a graduate of Dallas Theological Seminary and a psychologist. He is recognized as formidable multi-lingual speaker, conducting seminars in the Caribbean and in various parts of the world. Green does not shy away to ask WHY the 21st century Christians, who have abundant biblical resources, don't mature spiritually at the pace that the first century Christians did in spite of scarce biblical resources. The numeric growth that some churches experiences does not prove spiritual growth of believers.

Green compiled twelve reasons why Christians don't grow spiritually:

- *Lack of spiritual life.* Many of the church attendants did not experience "a real life-changing encounter with Jesus Christ!" They may know theology but, sadly to say, they are not born again.
- *Lack of spiritual growth.* Christians don't grow spiritually because of lack of intimate knowledge of the Word. This is sad but true. Believers don't make time for the Scripture.
- *Lack of genuine fellowship with other like-minded believers.* Fellowship with other believers is critical for one's spiritual growth. Green writes: "Christians who do not fellowship with other Christians soon grow cold and indifferent, and they lose their glow for Jesus."
- *Lack of empowerment through prayer.* Jesus left a strong impression on His disciples because of His prayer life. Christ took time to keep His intimacy with the Father kindled at all times. His disciples should do the same. Green admonishes his readers to pray if they desire to grow spiritually. He writes, 'a growing Christian . . . communes personally with God."
- *Lack of evangelism fervor.* Sharing the gospel should be part of the normal Christian life. A genuine child of God should have a genuine burden for the lost.
- *Stingy giving.* Lack of generosity denotes lack of spiritual growth. (See 2 Corinthians 9:6–8).
- *Lack of investment in the spiritual wellbeing of others.* As God's children we have the responsibility, not in a legalistic way, but in love, to care for others. Believers who don't invest in the lives of others don't grow.
- *Lack of worship.* We are created to worship God. When Christians worship God, they experience spiritual growth.
- *No exercise of faith.* We are supposed to live by faith. In other words, faith is required not only to get saved but to mature spiritually as well.
- *Cluelessness when it comes to exercising the spiritual gift(s).* Every believer has received at least one spiritual gift from the Spirit. (See Romans 12:6-8). It is sad to see so many

Christians who sit nicely in their pews Sunday after Sunday missing the real joy and the real spiritual growth because of lack of exercising their giftedness.

- *No involvement in missions.* Richard Wurmbrand, a well-known Christian leader from Romania, used to say, "Christians who don't go in missions are de-commissioned." Being involved in mission activities is another important ingredient for spiritual growth.
- *Lack of genuine self-emptying in order to be filled with the Spirit.* (See Eph. 5:18). In the process of being conformed into the image of Christ, believers are supposed to continually put off the old self in order to be filled with the Spirit (put on the new self.) Living spiritual lives is impossible without the Spirit of God being in control of our lives.

In conclusion, real spiritual growth occurs when believers advance from "genuine encounter with Jesus," to "enrichment from the Word," from "encounter with other believers in Christian fellowship," to "prayer life," from "evangelization of others," to "praise and worship," from "effective ministry to others," to "exercising your faith and spiritual gift." Then, from getting involved in a "mission program," to "daily emptying of self so that He may fill you continuously."

Dr. Paul D. Meier, in the forward of Green's book, concludes that the book is "biblical, inspirational, and encouraging. Definitely, an invaluable tool for the Christians who seriously want to grow to that next level of spiritual growth." I agree with Dr. Meier. This book is simple, easy to read, and could serve as a good tool for people interested to find out why Christians don't grow. It also provides simple aids in how one can grow spiritually.

Discussion Questions:

– After reading about the findings published in the "REVEAL: Where are You?," by Greg Hawkins and Cally Parkinson, what aspect surprised you the most? Why were you surprised? Please elaborate and share with a trusted friend.

– After reading the section based on "The Cross and Christian Ministry," by Carson, what concept or idea stood up the most? Why do you consider it important? Please share it with your spiritual mentor.

– What are your insights after reading the findings based on "The Great Omission: Reclaiming the Essential Teachings on Discipleship," by Dallas Willard? Please elaborate and share with your small group friends.

– What do you like the most from the ideas gleaned from the "Transforming Discipleship: Making Disciples a Few at a Time," book by Greg Ogden? Share your thoughts with your spiritual mentor.

– Which reasons from the "12 Reasons Christians don't Grow Even in Good Churches," do you notice more often in the local church. Please share your insights with your small group.

Notes

11. A Brief Literature Review

[140] Greg Hawkins and Cally Parkinson, *REVEAL: Where are You?* (South Barrington, IL: Willow Creek Association, 2007), 37.
[141] *REVEAL*, 39.
[142] Ibid, 45.
[143] Ibid, 64, 65.
[144] Carson, 9.
[145] Carson, 10.
[146] Willard, xiv.
[147] Willard, 11.
[148] Ibid, 14.
[149] Ibid, 15.
[150] Ibid, 17.
[151] Ibid, 19.
[152] Ibid, 25.
[153] Ibid, 28.
[154] Greg Ogden, *Transforming Discipleship: Making Disciples a Few at a Time*, (Westmont, IL: IVP Books, 2003), 16.
[155] Ogden, 17.
[156] Ibid, 17, 18.
[157]George Harrison, *Any Road.* Accessed on May 14, 2020. https://en.wikipedia.org/wiki/Any_Road.
[158] Ogden, 22.
[159] Ibid, 23.
[160] Barna, 8.
[161] Ogden, 28.
[162] Ibid, 30.
[163] Ibid, 33.
[164] Ibid, 34.
[165] Ibid, 37.
[166] Ibid, 38.
[167] Ibid, 41.
[168] Ibid, 42.
[169] Ibid, 45.
[170] Ibid 45
[171] Ibid 45
[172] Ibid, 47.
[173] Ibid, 49.
[174] Ibid, 51, 52.
[175] Ibid, 53.
[176] Ibid, 54.
[177] Ibid, 55.

CHAPTER 12

Options for Discipleship

The things which you have heard from me in the presence of many witnesses, entrust these to faithful men who will be able to teach others also.

— 2 Timothy 2:2

Let me share with you the back story of our core ministry—making disciples and equipping them for the kingdom of God. For many years, even as I worked as an engineer, I agonized in my heart for the work of Christian Discipleship to become a reality in the lives of believers across all denominations. Very frequently my prayer sounded like this:

> Father, God, my desire is to be a disciple of Christ and to make disciples. Lord, I want to preach and teach the Word in such a way that it would have a great impact on Your Church everywhere in the world. I want the nature and the character of Christ (Galatians 4:19) to be displayed in the believers in such a way that when nonbelievers look at Your children, they will see Christ. In Jesus' name I pray. Amen!

Many years passed by, and in 2004 I sensed God orchestrating my transition from the engineering field into fulltime ministry. This, in itself, is powerful story which I will probably share in another book. Now let me share with you how the Holy Spirit convicted my wife and I to go back to school.

In 2006, my wife and I attended a *Life in Christ Conference* in Atlanta, Georgia. During that conference, several speakers delivered special messages. Among the speakers were: Tim Elmore, a former disciple of John Maxwell, and Steve Pettit, a former disciple of Dave Stone. The atmosphere, the messages, and the experience were quite unique! After the conference, as my wife and I flying back home, we continued to discuss the special messages we just heard. You know how that goes: one thing led to another and then to another. I am just guessing that at 33,000 feet altitude we were closer to God. At some point, both of us felt something being communicated to us. It was not a voice in the plane, or a thunder; it was like receiving clarity in our thinking—a new level of understanding about what we needed to do next in our lives and ministry. I learned that when something like this happens, I better take notes. I got my personal journal out and I started to take notes based on what the Holy Spirit was impressing upon our hearts and minds.

In a nutshell, both of us sensed that God wanted us to go back to school. This sounded so funny, because we were in our late forties, and all four of our adult children were still at home. But I am telling you that the heart-impression was very strong, and both of us received pretty much the same guidance at the same time. I felt that the Holy Spirit was telling me:

> Valy, you should go back to school, not for more engineering or business training, but in the area of your ministerial calling—*spiritual formation.*

Elena sensed the Holy Spirit was telling her:

> Elena, you too should go back to school. Not for more business or training in applied economics, but in—*Christian Counseling*—the area of your calling.

We looked at each other greatly puzzled, not knowing what to make of all this stuff we freshly received from God during our flight back to Detroit. We got home tired but very excited about what we heard at the conference. And, like Mary the Mother of Jesus, we treasured in our hearts what the Holy Spirit communicated to us.

One thing I've learned over the years is that when God speaks, I better listen and act quickly. In the following months, I started researching options to obtain a Master of Arts in Spiritual Formation. From person to person, and from discussion to discussion, both my wife and I ended up contacting Spring Arbor University (SAU). SAU, a more than 100-year-old Christian university, is located, so to speak, in our very own back yard. By the end of 2007, both of us decided to take the leap of faith and go back to school in the areas of our calling. We applied for student loans, and in the spring of 2008, we were almost done with all the enrollment's forms. In the summer of 2008, we got the last recommendations, finished the necessary interviews, and received the green light to start the programs. In August of 2008, both of us were back in school. Praise God for His mysterious way of working!

I consider one factor extremely interesting. In 2006, right about the time when my wife and I had the unique discussion in that plane, Spring Arbor University started a new program called Master of Arts in Spiritual Formation Leadership (MSFL). SAU also offered Master of Arts in Christian Counseling (MA). I usually call these types of coincidences—*divine interventions.* Having adult children living with us would have made it almost impossible for us to go to school out of state.

For those of you who are not very familiar with the terminology—*spiritual formation* refers to God's master plan of forming, shaping, and transforming His children into the image of Christ. Spiritual formation—becoming more like Jesus—is the birthright of every born-again believer. My three years of training in Spiritual Formation and Leadership were almost one hundred percent about the process of transformation into Christ's likeness. I was exposed to teachings in this field from all sorts of angles and perspectives. I fully enjoyed that time. I can describe it using two simple phrases: It is ALL about Jesus, and Jesus is ALL about discipleship.

Year after year, credit after credit, book after book, project after project, and prayer after prayer stirred in me a deeper passion for Christ. Before completing the program, I poured my heart into writing my master thesis with this thought-provoking title—*Lack of Spiritual Maturity*. Actually, the chapter with the same title and *A*

Brief Literature Review, is based on my research paper.

Rejoicing over discipleship

I am glad to hear that some denominations, churches, and Christian ministries started to see that there is a need for spiritual formation. As a result of this, some churches increased their budgets and staff. However, even though there is a fresh interest for spiritual growth and maturity, make no mistake, **there is so much to be done**. We must hurry because we don't have much time! Christ is coming soon for a beautiful Bride who is ready for His return. The last book of the Bible tells us:

> Let us rejoice and be glad and give the glory to Him, for the marriage of the Lamb has come and His bride has made herself ready. It was given to her to clothe herself in fine linen, bright and clean; for the fine linen is the righteous acts of the saints. (Revelations 19:7–8).

I believe with all my heart that the Bride's preparation requires radical discipleship.

In the previous chapters of this book, I was trying to explain that in the New Testament era, when Jesus said "*make disciples*" the apostles understood that Christ's intent was not simply getting people to believe in Him (*convert* them), but to help these believers become what Jesus intended for them (*disciple* them) to full maturity. According to the *Westminster Dictionary of Theological Terms,* "a convert is someone who changes from one faith to another." But The Great Commission, as stated in Matthew 28:19–20, does not say "*make converts*", instead it says, "*make disciples.*"

Dallas Willard, professor of philosophy at University of Southern California, in his book, *The Great Omission*, writes:

> The last command Jesus gave the church before he ascended to heaven was the **Great Commission**, the call for Christians to '*make disciples of all the nations.*' But Christians have responded by making '*Christians,*' not '*disciples.*' This has been the church's *Great Omission.*"[178]

Similarly, Dietrich Bonheoffer, the author of *The Cost of*

Discipleship, considered the lack of discipleship—*cheap grace.*
Bonheoffer, writes:

> … the preaching of forgiveness without requiring repentance, baptism without church discipline, Communion without confession, absolution without personal confession. Cheap grace is grace without discipleship, grace without the cross, grace without Jesus Christ, living and incarnate.[179]

We must return to the complete gospel of Jesus, to the apostle's teaching, to the centrality of the cross and, once again, challenge each other with God's *ultimate intention.* (For the full description of the *ultimate intention*, please revisit the chapter titled: "Three Kinds of Disciples—Part Three."

The Back Story of the Advanced Discipleship Training

In the spring of 2010, while we were completing the master programs at SAU, my wife and I felt a deep urgency in our hearts to do something to help churches make disciples. We struggled and agonized for months. After much praying and seeking God's face, we felt very strongly that we should urgently design and offer an environment where believers can grow and mature in Christ. Thus Advanced Discipleship Training (ADT) was birthed. It took me three years to put together this platform.

ADT is for all believers who thirst after more of God in their lives, who desire to pay the price, who agonize to experience the fullness of Christ in their lives. The ADT platform can be used in small groups or life groups settings, weekly church classes, and online mentorship training programs.

I believe that every born-again believer who is intentionally engaged in the process of discipleship needs to grow in the grace and knowledge of our Lord Jesus Christ (2 Peter 3:18).

I firmly believe that any serious disciple must be mentored, at least in the following areas:

- How to study, properly interpret, and apply the Word of

God, in his or her one life, as well as how to help others do the same.
- Understand the true meaning of discipleship, its dynamics, and how to be a fruitful disciple in a fast-paced post-truth culture.
- Become very familiar with the process of spiritual growth and maturity.
- Self-awareness of the flesh and realizing that the flesh is a major obstacle towards spiritual maturity.
- Get a personal revelation of the cross, its meaning, its work, and its benefits, and totally embrace the cross.
- Understand one's spiritual identity and walking according with who she or he is in Christ.
- Having a correct world view when it comes to spiritual warfare, who the real enemy is, his modus operandi, and how to successfully fight against the enemy.
- Know his or her calling, giftedness, and spiritual function in the body of Christ, and how to be efficient for the kingdom of God.

The vision from God and the passion from the Holy Spirit to mentor, equip, and edify many willing disciples, was, is, and will be, the motivation for the Advanced Discipleship Training. ADT is structured into eight distinctive Discipleship Modules:

Module One

The Bible—The Foundation for Spiritual Growth & Maturity
Objectives:

- Aid disciples to gain more in depth understanding of the Bible and recognize the authority of the inerrant Word of God in every aspect of their lives.
- Equip disciples to study the Bible on their own, without relying on somebody else's interpretation; to increase one's knowledge of God in His way of working and strengthen one's personal faith.
- Help disciples become familiar with key principles and

practices in biblical hermeneutics (that is, interpretation), which seeks to discover contemporary relevance and meaning of the biblical text.

- Develop skills in the reading and interpretation of the Bible that enable contemporary disciples to study the text critically, to listen to the text carefully, and to engage the text faithfully.

Module Two

Discipleship—The Heart of the Great Commission
Objectives:

- Demonstrate, using Scriptures, that making disciples is a mandatory spiritual function of the Church not just an optional one. The *Great Commission* from Matthew 28:19–20 was, is, and is going to be the *vision* of Christ for His Church—Go, Baptize, Teach—*Make Disciples.*
- Demonstrate that discipleship is a ministry of multiplication, not just mere addition. Jesus Christ continues to call, even today, people from all ethnical groups to become His disciples despite all difficulties.
- Explore the main characteristics of a genuine disciple.
- Introduce disciples to the ministry of mentorship and properly equip them to use the Bible and other spiritual tools to make disciples who can make disciples.

Module Three

Maturity—The Goal of Discipleship
Objectives:

- Demonstrate, using Scriptures, that spiritual maturity is the very will of God not just a special privilege available only for the "select few." God ordained spiritual offices in the Church for this very purpose: "for the equipping of the saints" (Ephesians 4:12), so *all* could attain the "fullness of Christ" (Ephesians 4:13).

- Demonstrate scripturally that God did not *save* us only to go to heaven when we die, but to reflect the "image of Christ" (2 Corinthians 3:18) here on earth for the sake of others. The apostle Paul agonizes over this vision of Christ crying out, "My children, with whom I am again in labor until Christ is formed in you" (Galatians 4:19).
- Explore the main characteristics of each category of spiritual maturity:

  – Children in faith
  – Adolescents in faith
  – Adults in faith and spiritual parents

- Define and describe the process of spiritual formation, and provide the necessary tools for spiritual growth and maturity.

Module Four

The Flesh—The Major Obstacle Toward Spiritual Maturity
Objectives:

- Show, using Scriptures, that there are two ways or two patterns of living the Christian life:

  – According to the flesh (Romans 8:5a)
  – According to the Spirit (Romans 8:5b)

Therefore, directing disciples towards victory over the influences of the old man is a critical objective of this module.

- Define the flesh and explore the main characteristics of the flesh, which are:

  – The controlling flesh
  – The self-protective flesh
  – The victim-type flesh
  – The proud flesh
  – The idolater flesh

– The rejecting flesh

Part of this objective is to describe the process of laying aside the old-self and putting on the new-self.

- Demonstrate scripturally that God, in Christ, through the cross, provides full victory over the flesh. However, this requires personal appropriation of the cross in one's life.
- Probably the most important objective—Create the life-on-life context, grace based, non-judgmental environment, in which believers can be transparent and real.

These environments could be:

– Mentor-mentee relationships
– Small group
– Discipleship classes.

The essential aspect to be understood by every believer is that discipleship is not program, a platform, or a class. Discipleship is a lifestyle in which the cross is central, the Word of God is treasured, and the Holy Spirit has complete access to shape the lives of all committed disciples.

Module Five

The Cross—The Mystery of Suffering that Only a Few Embrace
Objectives:

- Demonstrate, using Scriptures, that (cf. Galatians 2:20, 1 Corinthians 2:2), the cross is central to Christianity and biblical spirituality. And, most importantly, show that the cross and suffering are part of the normal Christian life.
- Arrive at the biblical definition of the cross. To indicate the work of the cross, using Scriptures, in the

life of Christ's disciples for their own spiritual formation.

- Show, using the Bible, spiritual books, and personal examples, that *discipleship* and the *cross* are intimately connected. In fact, there is no such thing as a genuine disciple without the cross. This requires a personal appropriation of the cross in one's life.
- The most important objective—Provide the necessary guidance to every willing disciple how to appropriate the cross in his or her life, thus experiencing its deep meanings and blessings.

Module Six

Knowing Who We Are in Christ—The Key to Spiritual Victory
Objectives:

- Demonstrate, using Scriptures, that the true spiritual identity of each born-again believer is that of a *saint* not of a *sinner*. Also, to teach that discipleship plays a fundamental role in understanding the meaning of salvation, co-crucifixion, and spiritual victory, which are part of the believer's identity.
- Demonstrate, using the Bible, spiritual books, and personal examples, that what happened at spiritual-birth was a radical fact that influences not only what is going to happen with us after we die, but affects our identity and behavior here on earth.
- Demonstrate biblically that a correct understanding of our spiritual identity is fundamental for living successful, satisfied, happy, fun, secure, and peaceful lives. In other words, having a correct belief system about ourselves and a truthful relationship with God is the only way to fulfilling living and spiritual victory.
- Teach and model how to live according to who we really are in Christ, not according to how the culture tells us to live. Conform to 2 Corinthians 5:17 and Ephesians 2:10, who we are determines what we do, not the other way

around.

Module Seven

Free in Christ—Understanding Spiritual Warfare
Objectives:

- Demonstrate, using Scriptures, that spiritual warfare is real and it must be fought according to the Bible. Satan is a real being. One major principle in any war situation is to know who our enemy is and his modus operandi. Having a biblical view about the devil and his demons is a must. When Jesus sent His disciples to preach the gospel, He gave them power over the enemy (Matthew 10:1). The same is true today.
- Expose, using the Bible, spiritual books, and personal examples, the *modus operandi* of the enemy.
- Probably the most important objective—Properly equip disciples in the field of spiritual warfare. The facts that every believer must know, when it comes to the field of spiritual warfare, are:

  – To submit to God (James 4:7)
  – To resist de devil (1 Peter 5:9)
  – Not be ignorant of his schemes (2 Corinthians 2:11)
  – Not to give the devil an opportunity (Ephesians 4:27)

- Equip disciples to stand firm, learn about each piece of the armor of God, and challenge them to wear it and use each piece properly against the enemy. This is the only way we can experience freedom and victory in Jesus Christ (John 8:31–32, 36, Ephesians 6:10–18).

Module Eight

Fruits & Gifts—Developing a Genuine Intimacy with the Holy Spirit.

Objectives:

- Show, using Scriptures, that the presence of the Spirit, His manifestations, and the spiritual gifts are for the church of all ages, including the church of today. In his very first sermon after the Pentecost, Peter spoke these words: "For the promise is for you and your children and for all who are far off, as many as the Lord our God will call to Himself" (Acts 2:39). Therefore it is important to teach disciples that, cf. 1 Corinthians 12, and Romans 12:3–8, each believer has received at least one spiritual gift.
- The second objective is to demonstrate, using the Bible, spiritual books, and personal examples, that there is no genuine spiritual growth without the evidence of spiritual fruits in the believer's life. To teach believers that the real badge of disciples is to bear much fruit. "My Father is glorified by this, that you bear much fruit, and *so* prove to be My disciples" (John 15:8).
- The third objective is to mentor disciples into understanding their own calling and giftedness. To equip disciples to better serve the Body of Christ. To remind disciples to "kindle afresh the gift of God" (1 Timothy 1:6) Christ entrusted to them.
- Lay down a solid foundation upon which every willing disciple can develop a genuine intimacy with the Holy Spirit.

Ok, Valy, this sounds very good, but my life is very busy: I go to school, I work, I am raising a family, therefore I don't have time to add another "thing" on my plate. Besides, I go to church already, I support the local church and mission organizations. Isn't that enough? If I would ever consider enrolling in this kind of discipleship course, how long is going to take? These are some typical questions and some of the excuses I hear from people. Please hear my heart. These are valid excuses in the eyes of people, but not in the eyes of Christ. As I mentioned already, discipleship is not a program or a course. It is a lifestyle. I like to tell people that from discipleship we don't take breaks, go on vacations, or retire. If we accept the calling of Christ from Luke 9:23, we are going to be His disciples until we die, or He returns.

The question regarding the length of time, it is a very legitimate inquiry. Let me briefly try to address it. But before doing that, let me ask you: "How long did it take for the initial disciples to complete their training?" You may say: "Ok, I get it. I know that Jesus spent approximately three years in a half with His disciples." "But I don't think I can leave everything behind me and follow Christ the way they did." Trust me. I understand all of that. And I assure you that Jesus is not demanding you to leave everything and go to the mission field. Not everybody is called to do that. But everybody (cf. Luke 9:23) is called to become a disciple and live as a disciple. So, if you desire to take Luke 9:23 seriously, and you want to go through all eight modules of the ADT, as described above, you can do it in approximately three years. Of course, that depends on the amount of time you want to set aside weekly for the ADT. If you are under time constrains, you can take longer to do it. It is all up to you. You have complete freedom. You are not under any kind of pressure; you are not coerced to finish the training in a given period of time.

In the chapter titled "The Power of Intimacy with Jesus," of my book, *Fullness of Christ*, I shared: "Intimacy with Jesus requires not only quality time but a reasonable quantity of time." Christ, the Best Teacher in the universe, spent approximately 15,000 hours with His disciples. "In the secular world, scientists and sociologists found that nobody could be a pro, an expert at something in particular, without practicing at least 10,000 hours."[180] British researchers revealed that "it takes a person 10,000 hours of practice to become ace in a certain discipline."[181] Moreover, neurologist Daniel Levitin explained to Focus, a BBC science magazine, that "It seems it takes the brain this long (10,000 hours) to assimilate all it needs to know to achieve true mastery."[182]

Please keep in mind that Jesus considered that 15,000 hours are required to provide the necessary training of His twelve men. Scientists and researchers tell us that it takes 10,000 hours of practice for a person to become a pro in his or her field. And neurologists explain that the human brain requires this amount of time to become an expert in a specific area. My challenge is this: Why not consider Christian Discipleship the field worthy of our pursuit? It is going to take us our entire life to cultivate our intimacy with the Lord, and we will continue the journey in heaven.

I promise you that the Advanced Discipleship Training

platform is going to provide you with at least of 1,000 hours. You can use it as a lifestyle-model for the rest of your life. But the greatest benefit ADT provides is that it fully equips you to make disciples who are making disciples. The fulfillment you are getting when you start being an effective part of the Great Commission is not matched by any high-paying job out there. That is Jesus' promise to you.

What is the aim of ADT?

The main objective of any discipleship curriculum should be—*love.* Paul writes so directly: "But the goal of our instruction is love from a pure heart and a good conscience and a sincere faith" (1 Timothy 1:5). Similarly, during these eight modules of Advanced Discipleship Training, the aim is for *character development* and *spiritual formation.* We are not necessarily targeting the accumulation of more theological knowledge, as lofty as that may sound, but instead we are seeking to attain *genuine transformation* (Romans 12:2, 2 Corinthians 3:18) through the Word of God by the Holy Spirit. The Scripture states clearly, "And do not be conformed to this world, but be transformed by the renewing of your mind, so that you may prove what the will of God is, that which is good and acceptable and perfect" (Romans 12:2). In his letter to the Corinthians, Paul writes: "But we all, with unveiled face, beholding as in a mirror the glory of the Lord, are being transformed into the same image from glory to glory, just as from the Lord, the Spirit" (2 Corinthians 3:18).

Why is this important? This is vitally important because information alone does not transform us. More than that, knowledge makes us arrogant, but love edifies others. The Bible is bold about this: "Knowledge makes arrogant, but love edifies" (1 Corinthians 8:1). Therefore, any solid discipleship platform should state that its highest goal is *spiritual formation* and *personal transformation.* The Word of God and the Spirit of Christ transform people, not the discipleship program. As I already mentioned, ultimately, discipleship is not a program; it is a lifestyle.

ADT is not intended to be a **pass** or **fail** type of program. Therefore, all disciples who are diligent to go through all eight modules, and complete a final written paper, called—The Capstone Project, will receive a *Certificate of Accomplishment* from Upper Room

Fellowship Ministry.

Let's pray that Christians all over the world would get out of their comfort zones, and, through a solid discipleship platform like ADT, would becoming fully equipped to **make *disciples***, who in turn, would make other disciples. I fully agree with the legacy entrusted by Paul to Timothy before his martyrdom: "The things which you have heard from me in the presence of many witnesses, entrust these to faithful men who will be able to teach others also" (2 Timothy 2:2). Let us never forget that: **It is all about Jesus and Jesus is all about discipleship.**

Let me end this chapter with a prayer:

> Father God, I trust, pray, and believe that Advanced Discipleship Training will offer the necessary tools to other mentors to equip faithful men and women into the art of discipleship and spiritual formation. I pray that the Holy Spirit will convict multitudes of believers to become genuine disciples, to be fully trained and be ready to fulfill the Great Commission, so the Lord Jesus will return soon. In Christ's name. Amen.

Discussion Questions:

– Please slowly and meditatively read Luke 9:23. What do you think about Jesus' calling to discipleship? Is it valid for the 21st century believers? Please elaborate and share with your spiritual mentor.

– Please slowly and meditatively read Luke 9:24. What do you think "loses his life for My sake" really means? Please share it with your small group.

– What do you think is the greatest hindrance to the New Testament style discipleship? What do you think it should happen for believers to take the Great Commission seriously?

– What is your personal view on Christian discipleship? Have you worked with a spiritual mentor before? What are some of the highlights of your experience? Share your thoughts with a trusted friend.

– What do you think about the Advanced Discipleship Training platform? What changes do you consider doing in your life to enroll into such platform? Please elaborate and share your plans with your spiritual mentor.

Notes

12. Options for Discipleship

[178] Willard, front cover flap.
[179] Bonheoffer, 45.
[180] Vaduva, 167.
[181] *It Takes 10,000 Hours of Practice to Become a Genius*. www.infoniac.com. Monday, 24 Nov, 2008. http://www.infoniac.com/science/it-takes-10,000-hours-of-practice-to-become-a-genius.html. Accessed on November, 7, 2019.
[182] infoniac.com/science/it-takes-10,000-hours-of-practice-to-become-a-genius.html.

Appendix A

Bibliography for the Literature Review

1. Hawkins, Greg and Parkinson, Cally, *REVEAL: Where are You?,* (Barrington, IL: Willow Creek Resources, 2007)
2. Carson, D.A., *The Cross and Christian Ministry,* (Grand Rapids, MI: Baker Books, 1993)
3. Willard, Dallas, *The Great Omission: Reclaiming the Essential Teachings* on Discipleship, (New York, NY: Harper Collins Publishers, 2006)
4. Ogden, Greg, *Transforming Discipleship: Making Disciples a Few at a Time,* (Downers Grove, IL: IVP Books, 2003)
5. Green, Tony, *12 Reasons Christians don't Grow Even in Good Churches,* (Maitland, FL: Xulon Press, 2007)

Appendix B
Expanded Bibliography on Spiritual Formation and Discipleship

1. McDonald, Glen, *The Disciple Making Church: From Dry Bones to Spiritual Vitality*, (Grand Haven, MI: Faith Walk Publishing, 2004)
2. Barna, George, *Growing True Disciples: New Strategies for Producing Genuine Followers of Christ*, (Colorado Springs, CO: WaterBrook Press, 2001)
3. Rainer, Thom S. and Geiger, Eric, Simple Church, (Nashville, TN: B&H Publishing Group, 2006)
4. Stezer Ed, and Dodson, Mike, Comebacks Churches, (Nashville, TN: B&H Publishing Group, 2007)
5. Peterson, Jim, *Lifestyle Discipleship: The Challenge of Following Jesus in Today's World*, (Colorado Springs, CO: Navpress, 1993)
6. Hull, Bill, *The Disciple-Making Pastor: The Key to Building Healthy Christians in Today's Church*, (Grand Rapids, MI: Fleming H. Revell, 2003)
7. Bonheoffer, Dietrich, *The Cost of Discipleship*, (New York, NY: Simon & Schuster, 1959)
8. Foster, Richard, *Celebration of Disciplines: The Path to Spiritual Growth*, (New York, NY: Harper Collins Publishers, 1998)
9. Dieter, Melvin E., Hoekema, Anthony A., Horton, Stanley M., McQuilkin, J. Robertson, and Walvoord, John F., *Five Views on Sanctification*, (Grand Rapids, MI: Zondervan, 1996)
10. Gorman, *Michael, Cruciformity: Paul's Narrative Spirituality of the Cross,* (Grand Rapids, MI: Wm. B. Eerdmans Publishing Company, 2001)
11.. Stott, John R.W., *The Cross of Christ*, (Downers Grove, IL: IVP Books, 2006)
12.. Mulholland, Jr., Robert M., *Shaped by the Word: The Power of Scripture in Spiritual Formation*, (Nashville, TN: Upper Room, 2001)
13.. Nouwen, Henri J. M., Edited by Christensen, Michael J., and Laird, Rebecca, *Spiritual Formation: Following the Movements of the Spirit,* (New York, NY: Harper Collins, 2010)
14. Nouwen, Henri, *In the Name of Jesus*, (New York, NY: Crossroad, 1989)
15. Nouwen, Henri, *The Selfless Way of Christ*, (San Francisco, CA:

Harper Collins, 1991)
16. Mulholland, Robert M, *Invitation to a Journey,* (Downers Grove, IL: Inter Varsity Press, 1993)

Appendix C

Advanced Discipleship Training (ADT)

Basic Bibliography

Module One

The Bible—*The Foundation for Spiritual Growth & Maturity*

1. Henrichsen, Walter, Jackson, Gayle, "Studying, Interpreting, and Applying the Bible", Zondervan, 1990.
2. MacArthur, John, "The Sufficiency of Scripture," Audio CD, Grace to You, 1985, 1986.
3. MacArthur, John, "Why I Teach the Bible," Audio CD, Grace to You, 1996, 1998.
4. Arthur, Kay, "How to Study Your Bible," Harvest House Publishers, 1994.
5. Fee, Gordon, Stuart, Douglas, "How to Read the Bible for All Its Worth," Zondervan, 2003.

Module Two

Discipleship—The Heart of the Great Commission

1. Henrichsen, Walter, "Disciples are Made not Born," Victor, 1988.
2. Coleman, Robert, "The Master's Plan of Evangelism," Ravell, 2006.
3. Billheimer, Paul, "Destined for the Throne," Bethany House Publishers, 1996.
4. Oritz, Carlos Juan, "Accepted in the Beloved," Video 1, Cross Life Books, (n.d.)

Module Three
Maturity—*The Goal of Discipleship*

1. DeVern F. Fromke, DeVern, "The Ultimate Intention," Sure Foundation, 1999.
2. Stanford, Miles, "Principles of Spiritual Growth," Back to the Bible, 1997.
3. Whitall Smith, Hannah, "The Christian's Secret of a Happy Life," Spire, 1952.
4. Best, John, "Resolving Misunderstandings of the Exchanged Life," Abundant Living Resources, 1996.
5. Hudson, Taylor, Hudson, "The Exchanged Life," Website, https://www.wholesomewords.org/missions/biotaylor11.html.

Module Four
The Flesh—The Major Obstacle Toward Spiritual Maturity

1. Watchman, Nee, "The Normal Christian Life," Tyndale House Publishers, 1977.
2. Lord, Peter, "Turkeys and Eagles," The Seed Sower, 1997
3. Gillham, Gill, "Lifetime Guarantee," Harvest House Publishers, 1993.
4. Best, John, "The Cross of Christ: The Center of Scripture your Life and Ministry," Abundant Living Resources.
5. Gillham, Preston & Annabel, "A Study of the Mind," Booklet, Lifetime Guarantee Ministries.

Module Five
The Cross—*The Mystery of Suffering that Only a Few Embrace*

1. Solomon, Charles, "Handbook to Happiness," Tyndale House, 1999.
2. Edwards, Gene, "Exquisite Agony," The Seed Sower, (n.d.)

3. Stanley, Charles, "The Blessing of Brokenness," Zondervan's, (n.d.)
4. Trumball, Charles, "Perils of the Victorious Life," Booklet, Christian Literature Crusades.
5 Billheimer, Paul, "Don't Waste Your Sorrows," Christian Literature Crusades, 1977.

Module Six

Spiritual Identity—*Knowing Who We Are in Christ—The Key to Spiritual Victory*

1. Needham, David, "Alive for the First Time," Questar Publishers, 1995
2. Anderson, Neil, "Victory over the Darkness," Regal, 2000.
3. Vaduva, Valy, "Fullness of Christ," Upper Room Fellowship Ministry, 2018.
4. A.B., "Himself," Booklet, Christian Publications, Inc., (n.d.)
5. Oritz, Juan Carlos, "Liberated in the Beloved," Video #2, Cross Life Books, (n.d.)
6. J. Allan Peterson, Allan, "You Are Really Somebody," Booklet, Family Concern, (n.d.)

Module Seven

Free in Christ—*Understanding Spiritual Warfare*

1. Anderson, Neil, "The Bondage Breaker," Harvest House Publishers, 2000 or 2006,
2. Bevere, John, "The Bait of Satan,"Book and DVD, Charisma House,
3. Swindoll, Charles, "Finding Healing through Forgiveness," Audio CD, Insight for Living,
4. Stanely, Charles, "The Gift of Forgiveness" Thomas Nelson, 1991 or 2002.
5. Anderson, Neil, "Steps to Freedom in Christ," Gospel Light, 2004.

Module Eight
Fruits and Gifts—*Developing a Genuine Intimacy with the Holy Spirit*

1. Deere, Jack, "Surprised by the Power of the Spirit," Zondervan Publishing House, 1993.
2. Fortune, Don & Katie, "Discover Your Gifts," Chosen Books, 1987.
3. Bevere, John, "Intimacy with the Holy Spirit," – VIDEO, Messenger International, 2004.
4. Prince, Derek, "Gifts of the Spirit," Whitaker House, 2007.
Oritz, Juan Carlos, "Indwelt in the Beloved," Video #3, Cross Life Books, (n.d.)

Appendix D
Sample Lesson Plans
Advanced Discipleship Training (ADT)

General Instructions

Find the best time of day that suits you well for this activity. Some people prefer to read, listen, or watch a good book or an educational seminar when their minds are fully rested. They do it in a quiet and undisturbed environment. Whatever works best for you it is okay with me.

First, read the prescribed material without any "agenda" in mind. Just soak in what the author, speaker, or presenter has to say regarding various topics of study. Be open to let the Holy Spirit challenge your thinking. Write down any aha! moments.

Second, read the questions so you are familiar with what is being asked.

Third, read the prescribed material again, having the questions handy so you can jot down the answers to each specific question.

Fourth, be prepared to share what you have learned with your Life Group either via e-mail or in person during the next one-on-one meeting with your Mentor, or Life Group Leader.

Have a blessed time as you grow in the grace and knowledge of the Lord Jesus Christ.

Be blessed and become a blessing!

Module One
The BIBLE—The Foundation for Spiritual Growth & Maturity

All Scripture is inspired by God and profitable for teaching, for reproof, for correction, for training in righteousness; so that the man of God may be adequate, equipped for every good work.
— 2 Timothy 3:16-17

The Bible is an Incredible Book! No other book even comes close to the Bible. The Word of God is sweeter than honey to our spiritual mouth. The psalmist writes: "How sweet are Your words to my taste! Yes, sweeter than honey to my mouth!" (Psalm 119:103).

The Bible is not necessary a history book, however it contains important details of human history, especially the history of Israel. The Bible contains medical information, but it is not a manual of medicine. It contains specific geographical details about ancient cities, countries, and empires. It can be read as great literature, poetry, wisdom, and philosophy. The Bible is the main source of theological information. But the most important purpose of Scripture, as set forth by the Bible writers themselves, is to reveal the truth—Jesus Christ—the door to real freedom and liberty. I appreciate the statement below, which, I believe, it is attributed to C.S. Lewis:

> It is Christ Himself, not the Bible, who is the true word of God. The Bible, read in the right spirit, and with the guidance of good teachers, will bring us to Him.

The Bible is the Word of God that provides the standard for a meaningful life, and it is true food for man's soul. Nobody's education is complete without studying the Great Book—the Bible.

I like what Abraham Lincoln, the 16th U.S. President, said about this marvelous book:

> I believe the Bible is the best gift God has ever given to man. All the good from The Savior of the world is

communicated to us through this Book.[1]

Napoleon Bonaparte (1769-1821), the famous emperor of the French said: "The Bible is no mere book, but a Living Creature, with a power that conquers all that oppose it."[2]

Have you ever thought about successful investments? I have. In the end I realized that there are only two investments which we can make for eternity:

– The Word of God
– The souls of people

The psalmist writes "The law of Thy mouth is better to me than thousands of gold and silver pieces" (Psalm 119:72). Despite these wonderful benefits, the tragedy is that many Christians today are biblically illiterate. Why? I think that the main reason is that it takes time and discipline to know the Word of God.

John Chrysostom, (A.D. 347-407) puts it very well:

> "To get the full flavor of an herb, it must be pressed between the fingers, so it is the same with the Scriptures; the more familiar they become, the more they reveal their hidden treasures and yield their indescribable riches."[3]

In my early years as a junior disciple, I did not have too many resources to study the Bible. My "Discipleship Manual" was the Bible itself. From this great book I learned a few basic principles of studying, interpreting and applying the Bible:

- *The Guidance of the Holy Spirit.* No one knows the Bible better than its author—the Spirit of truth (see John 16:13–14). This is the reason why every disciple of

[1] The Bible, www.soulsupply.com, http://www.soulsupply.com/news/n/new-soulsnack-category-the-bible-130802. Accessed on November 12, 2019.
[2] The Bible is no Mere Book, www.selfeducatedamerican.com, https://selfeducatedamerican.com/2010/08/15/napoleon-in-exile-the-bible-is-no-mere-book/. Accessed on November 12, 2019.
[3] Lectio Divina. www.fisheater.com. https://www.fisheaters.com/lectiodivina.html. Accessed on November 13, 2019.

Christ should pursue a deeper intimacy with the Person Who inspired the Word of God—the Holy Spirit.

- *The Bible Interprets the Bible.* Not a single biblical passage can be interpreted by itself (see 2 Peter 1:20–21.
- *The Context of the Text.* The context of each verse, chapter, book, is vital important for a correct understanding of the Bible (see 1 Timothy 4:13, 1 Corinthians 10:11).
- *The Attitude of the Heart.* Understanding the Bible depends on our willingness to obey God's will (see John 7:17).
- *Literary Hermeneutics.* The Bible is to be interpreted first and foremost literally, in the most natural, most normal, most ordinary sense of communication (see 2 Corinthians 1:13). As A. W. Tozer once said: "If the simple meaning makes sense, you have the right sense."

I can tell you that these principles protected me from many "wolves in sheep's clothing" and saved me from erroneous interpretations of the Scripture.

This is the reason why I am so passionate to teach the Bible, disciple, mentor, and coach people into a greater intimacy with the Lord of the Bible.

Be blessed as you dig deeper in the Word of God and get to know various facts about the wonderful book we call—the Bible.

How to Study Your Bible
By Kay Arthur

We are going to spend time in the presence of a good book: "How to Study Your Bible," (Harvest House Publishers, 1994), by Kay Arthur.

Be prepared to share your insights with your Life Group, Life Group Leader, or Mentor.

1: After a careful reading of the book: "How to Study your Bible" by Kay Arthur, please answer the following:

Part I: Observation

1. Please write a short overview (or summary paragraphs) for this chapter.

2: How many steps does the process of Observation employ?

Please list these steps and briefly elaborate on them.

1.

2.

3.

4.

5.

Congratulations! Good Job!
Please share what you have learned with your Life Group during the next meeting in order to edify one another.

Part IV. Organization

15. Studying Topically by Subject

Topical studies require an enormous amount of work. But this kind of study is very rewarding. There are some important principles for doing topical studies.

15. Please list these principles and briefly elaborate on the steps.

1.

2.

3.

4.

Congratulations! Good Job!
Please share what you have learned with your Life Group during the next meeting in order to edify one another.

Module Two
Discipleship—The Heart of the Great Commission

And Jesus came up and spoke to them, saying, "All authority has been given to Me in heaven and on earth. "Go therefore and make disciples of all the nations, baptizing them in the name of the Father and the Son and the Holy Spirit, teaching them to observe all that I commanded you; and lo, I am with you always, even to the end of the age.
— Matthew 28:18-20

What is the mission of the church? Well, based on Matthew 28:18–20, the mission of the Church is to make disciples.

Discipleship defined:

According to Easton's Bible Dictionary, a disciple of Christ is one who:

– Believes His doctrine
– Rests on His sacrifice
– Imbibes His Spirit
– Imitates His example

See Matthew 10:24; Luke 14:26-33; John 6:69.

In other words, we can say that a disciple is believer who is committed to follow Christ wholeheartedly and is growing spiritually.

A disciple:

– Is obedient to God's Word (John 8:31)
– Is Loving (John 13:35)
– Is Fruitful (John 15:8)
– Is always prepared to share the hope of life in Christ (2 Timothy 4:2)

– Lives the Gospel (2 Corinthians 3:2-3)

Paul was sad that the believers in the Corinthian church were not growing in Christ-likeness.

He wrote:

> Brothers, I could not address you as spiritual but as worldly – mere infants in Christ. I gave you milk, not solid food, for you were not yet ready for it. Indeed, you are still not ready. You are still worldly. For since there is jealousy and quarreling among you, are you not worldly? Are you not acting like mere men? (1 Corinthians 3:1–3)

Immature Christians are worldly believers, who are controlled by their fleshly desires. Spiritually mature disciples are in tune with God's desires. They appropriate God's will, and in submission to the Lord, apply it in their lives.

What is the goal of discipleship?

To make disciples who can then make disciples (2 Timothy 2:2).

How? By teaching them to observe all that Jesus commanded (Matthew 28:20).

How long? Until we all reach unity in the faith and in the knowledge of the Son of God and become mature, attaining to the whole measure of the fullness of Christ. (Ephesians 4:13).

Why? To reach spiritual stability. Paul writes: "As a result, we are no longer to be children, tossed here and there by waves and carried about by every wind of doctrine, by the trickery of men, by craftiness in deceitful scheming" (Ephesians 4:14).

What? Spiritual growth. Paul writes: "But speaking the truth in love, we are to grow up in all aspects into Him who is the head, even Christ" (Ephesians 4:15).

What for? For the edification of the entire body. Paul writes: "From whom the whole body, being fitted and held together by what every joint supplies, according to the proper working of each individual part, causes the growth of the body for the building up of itself in love" (Ephesians 4:16).

Jesus brought clear understanding to what it meant to be a disciple when He said: "Everyone who is fully trained will be like his teacher" (Luke 6:40). The Apostle Paul echoed this way of life when he said: "My dear children, for whom I am again in the pains of childbirth until Christ is formed in you" (Galatians 4:19).

Disciple-makers are called to lead people to Christ and assist them in the process of growing and maturing spiritually. Disciple-makers have an intense love, concern, and lifelong care for those to whom they are spiritual parents. When we lead people to Christ, we are to stand by them, helping them grow until they are fully trained.

Making disciples involves bringing people into a personal relationship with Jesus and staying with them until their whole lives are in obedience to Christ Jesus.

Jesus is the Master. According to the Master's plan of discipleship these concepts are essential:

- We are called to make disciples, not just converts.
- Disciples are made in intimate, accountable relationships.
- Discipleship is a process, not a program.
- Making disciples involves helping another learn to obey all that Jesus commanded.
- Making disciples takes place in the context of loving, safe, confidential, and personal relationships. Transparency, community, and accountability are paramount factors in the process of discipleship.
- Making disciples occurs as each person assists others in their commitment to spiritual maturity.
- Making disciples includes helping others grow in God's Word, fellowship, communion and in prayer.
- Disciples must be taught the essential teachings of the Christian life in a systematic and sequential manner.
- Discipleship is the privilege and responsibility of every believer.

Growth in Christ-likeness is the ultimate goal. Enjoy the process of discipleship. Keep your eyes fixed on the Master (see Hebrews 12:1–2).

Disciples are Made not Born
By Walter A. Henrichsen

The source for this lesson is a book, called: "Disciples are Made not Born," by Walter A. Henrichsen, Cook Communications, 1988). Please read the book and follow the instructions. Be prepared to share your insights with your Life Group, Life Group Leader, or Mentor.

Chapter 1: The Kind of Person God Uses

1.1. After a careful reading of chapter 1, please list the nine characteristics of a genuine disciple of Jesus Christ. In your own words, briefly elaborate, on at least three of these characteristics.

1.
2.
3.

4.
5.
6.

7.
8.
9.

1.2. Which are true of yourself? Please explain why?

1.3. Which are not true of yourself? Please explain why not.

Congratulations! Good Job!
Please share what you have learned with your Life Group during the next meeting in order to edify one another.

Chapter 5: Principles of Evangelism

In this chapter, Walter A. Henrichsen presents eight principles of evangelism which are based on John 4.

5.1. After a careful reading of this chapter please list these principles. Briefly elaborate on two of them. Underline the principles that you consider to be the most important.

1.

2.

3.

4.

5.

6.

7.

8.

5.2. Which of these principles have you used, or are you going to use, in your personal evangelism outreach?

5.3. Please elaborate about your evangelism strategy.

Congratulations! Good Job!
Please share what you have learned with your Life Group during the next meeting in order to edify one another.

Module Three
Maturity—The Goal of Discipleship

We proclaim Him, admonishing every man and teaching every man with all wisdom, so that we may present every man complete in Christ. For this purpose also I labor, striving according to His power, which mightily works within me.
— Colossians 1:28–29

What is spiritual growth?

Spiritual growth is becoming more like Christ through a process called progressive sanctification, or discipleship, or spiritual formation. It is an imperative in our lives as Christians and should be the focus, without exceptions, in all churches and denominations. In 1995, God awakened me to the imperative of spiritual growth and maturity. The Holy Spirit guided me to put together this simple definition:

> Spiritual growth is the work of God through His grace by which God's children are transformed according to the image of Christ in the inner man and empowered to deny self and live in righteousness and holiness.

Later, I found out that within Christian spirituality, there is an entire field called—*spiritual formation.* During the Master of Arts in Spiritual Formation and Leadership (MSFL) program at Spring Arbor University (SAU), I learned that Christian spiritual formation is "the process of being conformed to the image of Christ for the sake of others." Dallas Willard writes that "spiritual formation for the Christian basically refers to the Spirit-driven process of forming the inner world of the human self in such a way that it becomes like the inner being of Christ himself." According to John Wesley's teaching to be sanctified means: "To be renewed in the image of God, in righteousness and true holiness."

As we grow in Christ, our moral condition is brought, by the Spirit of God, into conformity with our legal status before God. John writes: "But as many as received Him, to them He gave the right to become children [Gr. (teknion] of God, even to those who believe in His name" (John 1:12 NASB).

God desires all His children to reflect the character of Jesus Christ. Period! Paul writes: "For all who are being led by the Spirit of God, these are sons [Gr. huios] of God" (Romans 8:14 NASB). The likeness of the Father is what defines a mature son of God. Jesus used the word huios to clearly show the difference between children and sons (see Matthew 5:9, 44-45). Commenting on this Scripture W.E. Vine writes:

> "The disciples were to do these things, not in order that they might become children of God, but that, being children (note 'your Father' throughout), they might make the fact manifest in their character, might 'become sons.' Regarding Christian perfection, John Wesley writes: "Q: What is implied in being a perfect Christian? A: The loving God with all our heart, and mind, and soul. (Deut. 6:5.)"[4]

Enjoy your journey!

---

[4] Thomas Jackson, *A Plain Account of Christian Perfection*, (1872), article 17. (http://gbgm-umc.org). Accessed on April 20, 2011.

Ultimate Intention,
By DeVern F. Fromke

The source for this lesson is a unique book: "Ultimate Intention," (Sure Foundation Publishers, 1963), by DeVern F. Fromke. Please read the book and follow the instructions.

Be aware! This book contains short but very condensed chapters. Enjoy walking in the Spirit one day at the time. Be prepared to share your insights with your Life Group, Life Group Leader, or Mentor.

Chapter 2—The Proper Starting Point

In chapter two, Fromke explains that it is vitally important for Christians to have a correct view regarding God's plan. The author uses a diagram to illustrate his thoughts about our starting point:

A—With the Father
B—With Creation
C—With Man
D—With the Fall

After a careful review of this chapter, please follow the instructions.

2. Based on this diagram, please elaborate why is important to see God's work through God's prospective?

Congratulations! Good Job!
Please share what you have learned with your Life Group during the next meeting in order to edify one another.

Chapter 13. To Live by the Life of Another,

In this chapter, Fromke, writes about the call of Christians to live by Christ's life. He uses a diagram to illustrate the work of Christ's blood and the work of Christ's cross in order to access the power of Christ's life:

A—Resurrection Life
B—Reigning Life
C—Realizing Life

13.1. Based on the diagram from the book and your overall understanding, please explain the meaning of Romans 5:10.

13.2. What does '*We shall be saved by Christ's life*' mean?

13.3. Read Ephesians 2:6. What does '*And raised us up with Him*' mean?

13.4. Read Galatians 2:20. What does '*Christ lives in me. Living by Christ's life*' mean?

13.5. Read 5:17. What does '*Reign in life through the One, Jesus Christ*' mean?

13.6. Read Ephesians 2:10. What does '*Walking in the good works prepared by God*' mean?

Congratulations! Good Job!
Please share what you have learned with your Life Group during the next meeting in order to edify one another.

Module Four
The Flesh—The Major Obstacle Toward Spiritual Maturity

Beware of the dogs, beware of the evil workers, beware of the false circumcision; for we are the true circumcision, who worship in the Spirit of God and glory in Christ Jesus and put no confidence in the flesh.

— Philippians 3:2–3

Mainly, Module Four deals with the flesh. This module is one of the most important modules of the Advanced Discipleship Training (ADT). Understanding the conflict between the flesh and the Spirit is the cornerstone for genuine spiritual growth. I pray that the Spirit will reveal to you all that you need to know about your version of the flesh, so you will continue to grow in the likeness of Christ. I encourage you to pay close attention to this module.

The Flesh

The "flesh," according to A. W. Tozer, is the "veil" that prevents us from seeing God's face.

He writes:

> A veil not taken away as the first veil was, but which remains there still shutting out the light and hiding the face of God from us. It is the veil of our fleshly, fallen nature living on, unjudged within us, uncrucified and unrepudiated. It is the close-woven veil of the self-life which we have never truly acknowledged, of which we have been secretly ashamed, and which for these reasons we have never brought to the judgement of the cross. It is not too mysterious, this opaque veil, nor is it hard to identify. We have but to look into our own hearts and we shall see it there, sewn and patched and repaired it may be, but nevertheless, an enemy to

> our lives and an effective block to our spiritual progress.[5]

Tozer continues:

> Self is the opaque veil that hides the face of God from us. It can be removed only in spiritual experience, never by mere instruction. We may as well try to instruct leprosy out of our system. There must be the work of God in destruction before we are free. We must invite the cross to do its deadly work within us. We must bring self-sins to the cross for judgement. We must prepare ourselves for an ordeal of suffering in same measure like that through which our Savior passed when He suffered under Pontius Pilate.[6]

See: Romans 8:4-13, Galatians 5:16-21, 24-15. 6:7-8.

May God bless you as you explore the concepts included in this module.

---

[5] Tozer, A.W., "The Pursuit of God," (Camp Hill, PA: Christian Publications, 1993), 41.

[6] "The Pursuit of God," 43.

The Normal Christian Life
By Watchman Nee

During this module, we are going to use various resources, among which is a classical book: "The Normal Christian Life," (Tyndale House Publishers, 1977), by Watchman Nee.

This book requires a careful reading and studying of the various scriptures which are included in the text. We cannot cover all that Nee has to say in a week or two, so I hope that you will go back to this book over and over again. After a careful reading of the book, please follow the instructions. Be prepared to share your insights with your Life Group, Life Group Leader, or Mentor.

Chapters 3. The Path of Progress: Knowing

3.1. What does Romans 6:6, teach us? What must Christians know? Please elaborate extensively.

3.2. Please explain why it is so important to receive the revelation about the Exchanged Life as Hudson Taylor received. Please elaborate.

Congratulations! Good Job!
Please share what you have learned with your Life Group during the next meeting in order to edify one another.

Chapter 4: The Path of Progress: Reckoning

4.1. Based on your reading and understanding from the book and also based on Romans 6:11, explain in simple terms what *reckoning* means? Give a simple illustration to clarify your point.

4.2. Based on your reading and understanding from the book and also based on Romans 6:6, in simple terms, please explain the difference between the sin-principle and the body of sin.

4.3. Based on your reading and understanding from the book and also based on John 15:4 explain the meaning of *abiding* in Christ? Please give a different illustration besides the Vine-branch illustration in John 15.

4.4. What is your overall impression after reading "The Normal Christian Life" chapters 1-4? Share your sincere reaction.

4.5. What is the most difficult aspect to understand so far in these four chapters?

Congratulations! Good Job!
Please share what you have learned with your Life Group during the next meeting in order to edify one another.

Module Five
The Cross—The Mystery of Suffering that Only a few Embrace it

For the word of the cross is foolishness to those who are perishing, but to us who are being saved it is the power of God.
— 1 Corinthians 1:18

In Christianity the cross reminds Christians of God's act of love in Christ's sacrifice at Calvary—"the Lamb of God who takes away the sin of the world." The cross also reminds Christians of Jesus' victory over sin and death, since it is believed that through His death and resurrection He conquered death itself.

However, remaining at this definition only is not going to provide Christ's disciples all of the tremendous spiritual benefits the cross provides.

A. W. Tozer, in *The Old Cross and the New* writes:

> The CROSS is a symbol of death. It stands for the abrupt, violent death of a human being. The man in Roman times who took up his cross and started down the road had already said good-by to his friends. He was not coming back. He was going out to have it ended. The cross made no compromise, modified nothing, spared nothing; it slew all of the man, completely and for good. It did not try to keep on good terms with its victim. It struck cruel and hard, and when it had finished its work, the man was no more."[7]

I love how brother Nee explains this concept: "The cross is thus the power of God which translates us from Adam to Christ."[8]

---

[7] Tozer, A.W., *Man—The Dwelling Place of God,* https://www.worldinvisible.com/library/tozer/5j00.0010/5j00.0010.10.htm. Accessed on May 20, 2017.

[8] Watchman, Nee, The Normal Christian Life, (Wheaton, IL: Tyndale House, 1977), 47.

Furthermore, the cross is:

- The entire redemptive work accomplished historically (legally, theologically, and spiritually) in the death, burial, resurrection and ascension of the Lord Jesus Himself (see Philippians 2:8, 9).
- In a wider sense, the union of believers with Christ by grace (see Romans 6:4; Ephesians 2:5, 6).[9]

Moreover, the cross of Christ is one divine work. Period! However, for analysis and for better understanding on our part, it is important to see the work of the Cross from four angles. Two thousand year ago the Lord Jesus died on the cross and rose again. He is now, according to Acts 2:33, exalted at the right hand of God in glory. Nee writes: "The work is finished and need never be repeated, nor can it be added to."[10] Please keep this truth in mind.

Try to picture in your mind the 3D sketch of the cross. Each beam has four sides. If we look at the traditional cross, the two beams form four quadrants. Each of the four quadrants metaphorically speaks of the four spiritual dimensions of the work Christ did on the Calvary's cross two thousand years ago.

These dimensions are:

1. The Blood of Christ. The blood deals with sins and guilt. (Recovering what Adam lost in the Garden of Eden).
2. The Cross of Christ. The cross deals with sin, the flesh, and the natural man. (Recovering what Adam lost in the Garden of Eden).
3. The Life of Christ. The life made available to indwell, re-create and empower man. (Note: The life of Christ is bringing into us something that Adam never had, not even in the Garden of Eden).
4. The Working of Death in the Natural Man. The working of death makes all possible that the indwelling life may be progressively manifest.

---

[9]Vaduva, Valy, *Fullness of Christ*, (Upper Room Fellowship Ministry, Livonia, MI, 2018), 60–61.
[10] *The Normal Christian Life*, 206.

The fourth dimension is fundamental for the process of metamorphosis to take place in us and to produce more and more, the image of Christ in the inner man of God's genuine sons and daughters. The tragedy is that many Christians revolve around the first and (maybe) the second dimension of the cross and therefore deprive themselves of the tremendous benefits of the third and the fourth dimensions.

The cross and the suffering are part of the normal Christian life. We can declare that there is a tight correlation between the work of the cross and the spiritual formation in the life of Christ's disciples. In fact, scripturally speaking, there is no such thing as a genuine disciple without the cross. Those disciples who willingly embrace the cross in their lives experience its deepest meanings and blessings.

Paul freely invites the work of the cross into his life, thus leaving us an example to follow in his footsteps.

He writes: "that I may know Him and the power of His resurrection and the fellowship of His sufferings, being conformed to His death; in order that I may attain to the resurrection from the dead." (Philippians 3:10-11).

May God bless all of Christ's disciples who are diligently embracing the work of the cross in their lives.

Handbook to Happiness
By Dr. Charles Solomon

Among many other sources, the main resource for Module Five is a unique book, called, "Handbook to Happiness," (Tyndale House, 1999), by Dr. Charles Solomon. This book requires a careful reading and looking at various scriptures which are included in the text. We cannot cover all that Dr. Solomon has to say in a week or two, so I hope that you will go back to this book over and over again. After a careful reading of the book, please follow the instructions. Be prepared to share your insights with your Life Group, Life Group Leader, or Mentor.

Chapter 1: Experiencing the Cross of Christ

1.1: Based on your reading and understanding from this chapter, based on your own experiences, and based on the following bible verses: 1 Peter 2:13-21 and Hebrew 2:10-18, please explain the meaning of suffering from the Christian perspective. Share at least one personal experience in which you suffered for the sake of Christ.

1.2. On page 5, Dr. Solomon writes: "The Cross in the life of the believer involves brokenness and suffering, just as it did for our Lord." Do you agree with his understanding of cross and suffering? Briefly explain your opinion.

Congratulations! Good Job!
Please share what you have learned with your Life Group during the next meeting in order to edify one another.

Chapter 5: Intellectual Understanding—Then What?

After a careful of Chapter 5: Intellectual Understanding—Then What?, please follow the instructions.

1.1: Based on your reading and understanding from this chapter, and based on the following bible verses, Luke 14:26-27, John 12:24-25, and Philippians 3:10, please explain the meaning of Total Commitment.

1.2. In the context of today's culture, please explain how we can translate the Total Commitment concept in our day-to-day lives. Please share with the Life Group any difficulties you have encountered?

2.1: In the section called: Morbid Introspection, the author quotes Psalm 139:23–24. Based on this Psalm, please share with the Life Group, as much as you feel comfortable, one instance when God exposed the ugly side of your flesh.

2.2: Were you surprised to discover that side about your own flesh? Please elaborate.

Congratulations! Good Job!
Please be prepared to share what you have learned with your Life Group during the next meeting in order to edify one another.

Module Six
Spiritual Identity—Knowing Who We Are in Christ
The Key to Spiritual Victory

See how great a love the Father has bestowed on us, that we would be called children of God; and such we are. For this reason the world does not know us, because it did not know Him. Beloved, now we are children of God, and it has not appeared as yet what we will be. We know that when He appears, we will be like Him, because we will see Him just as He is.

— 1 John 3:1-2

In his book, "Victory over the Darkness", Dr. Neil T. Anderson explains that Christians don't mature in faith "because of unresolved conflicts in their lives." Therefore, they remain carnal just like those from 1 Corinthians 3:1–3 who were unable to receive solid food from Scriptures.

After many years of providing discipleship to Christians, the author found one main common denominator for all struggling Christians: "They do not know who they are in Christ, nor do they understand what it means to be a child of God." It is very naturally to ask: Why Not? How may Christians resolve their personal conflicts?

Anderson shares:

> Slowly I began to understand how to help people resolve their personal and spiritual conflicts through genuine repentance by submitting to God and resisting the devil (see Jas. 4:7).[11]

After many years of experience working with Christians in various discipleship settings, I can testify that discipleship, indeed,

[11] Neil T. Anderson *Victory over the Darkness,* (Ventura, CA: Regal Books, 2000), 16.

is the environment where believers can learn who they are in Christ. Not only that, but the process of Christian Discipleship is the way to go for believers who desire to grow spiritually.

Anderson writes:

> Discipleship counseling is the process where two or more people meet together in the presence of Christ, learn how the truth of God's Word can set them free and thus are able to conform to the image of God as they walk by faith in the power of the Holy Spirit", And, "Brokenness is the key to ministry and the final ingredient for discipleship counseling. Message and method had come together. [12]

May God bless all of Christ's disciples who are embracing diligently the work of the cross in their lives.

[12] "Victory over the Darkness," 17.

Victory over the Darkness
By Dr. Neil T. Anderson

Among many other sources, an important resource for Module Six is, "Victory over the Darkness," (Regal, 2000), by Dr. Neil T. Anderson. This book requires a careful reading and looking at various scriptures which are included in the text. We cannot cover all that Dr. Anderson has to say in a week or two, so I hope that you will go back to this book over and over again.

After a careful reading of the book, please follow the instructions. Be prepared to share your insights with your Life Group, Life Group Leader, or Mentor.

Chapter 1: Who are you?

1.1. Based on your reading and understanding from this chapter, please state the false equations in search for identity. Example: "Good Appearance + Admiration = Whole Person".

1.2. Please state God's Equation for wholeness and meaning.

1.3. Please list and elaborate on The Effects of the Fall. Share your insights with the Life Group.

Congratulations! Good Job!
Please be prepared to share what you have learned with your Life Group during the next meeting in order to edify one another.

Chapter 11: Healing Emotional Wounds from Your Past

After a careful review of Chapter 11: Healing Emotional Wounds from Your Past, please follow the instructions.

1.1. Please explain succinctly about steps we can take toward emotional healing.

– What is the sequence of events?

– What is the primary emotion?

– What causes the trigger?

– How do most of us manage emotional pain?

1.2. How are we supposed to resolve our primary emotions? (See Psalm 139:23–24, and John 8:31–32).

– First…

– Second…

1:3. What is forgiveness? Share with the Life Group the insights you discovered about forgiveness.

1.4. What are the steps toward forgiveness?

Congratulations! Good Job!
Please be prepared to share what you have learned with your Life Group during the next meeting in order to edify one another.

Module Seven
FREE in Christ—Understanding Spiritual Warfare

For our struggle is not against flesh and blood, but against the rulers, against the powers, against the world forces of this darkness, against the spiritual forces of wickedness in the heavenly places.
— Ephesians 6:12

The topic of spiritual warfare is considered a taboo subject in some circles. Sometimes this subject caused heated discussions and even divisions.

I pray and hope that you reached a certain level of maturity to understand that the domain of darkness is real and knowing our real enemy is the right of every disciple of Christ. Jesus Himself tells His disciples: "Behold, I have given you authority to tread on serpents and scorpions, and over all the power of the enemy, and nothing will injure you" (Luke 10:19). And Paul writes: "For He rescued us from the domain of darkness, and transferred us to the kingdom of His beloved Son" (Colossians 1:13).

Paul, Peter, James, and other writers of the New Testament wrote about the reality of spiritual conflict with the devil. They would have had no reasons to write to warn about the "domain of darkness" (Colossians 1:13), or to "resist the devil" (James 4:7), "Your adversary, the devil, prowls around like a roaring lion", if this stuff was not true.

Moreover, Paul writes: "But I am afraid that, as the serpent deceived Eve by his craftiness, your minds will be led astray from the simplicity and purity of devotion to Christ" (2 Corinthians 11:3).

So, let's approach this module thoughtfully and prayerfully, that God will give us understanding from His Word about our spiritual enemy—Satan. Also, let's ask the Spirit to properly equip us to "resist in the evil day" and be able to "stand firm" as Paul admonishes Ephesians in 6:13.

The Bondage Breaker
By Dr. Neil T. Anderson

We have several excellent sources allocated for this module. We are going to start off this important module with a unique book, *The Bondage Breaker*, (Harvest House Publishers, 2000), by Dr. Neil T. Anderson. This book requires a careful reading and looking at various scriptures which are included in the text.

After a careful reading of the book please follow the instructions. Be prepared to share your insights with your Life Group, Life Group Leader, or Mentor.

Chapter 1: You Don't Have to Live in the Shadows

1.1. Based on your reading and understanding of this chapter, please list the common misconceptions about bondage.

1.2. Why it is so important to have a biblical world view when it comes to demons?

1.3. Do you think that even believers can be affected by demons or not? Please elaborate and give examples from the Bible.

1.4. What is the enemy's most powerful weapon?

1.5. What is the Christian's most powerful weapon?

Congratulations! Good Job!
Please be prepared to share what you have learned with your Life Group during the next meeting in order to edify one another.

Chapter 11: The Danger of Deception

Self-deception is rampant in our churches today. False prophets and false teachers appear like mushrooms after the rain. And naïve and gullible Christians flock under their teachings. Immature believers, instead of taking responsibility for their own walk with the Lord and knowledge of Scriptures, seek shortcuts to spirituality though prophets. And the tragedy is that many of them are false prophets leading the sheep astray.

11.1. Based on reading and your understanding of this chapter, please list the three primary avenues though which Satan attempts to make us believe his lies.

1.
2.
3.

11.2. Please list the ways in which we can deceive ourselves.

11.3. What are some of the criteria to discern between real prophets and counterfeit ones? Please elaborate and share your insight with the Life Group.

11.4. Based on the Bible and your understanding of the section called: Spiritual Discernment, please answer—what is the motive for true discernment?

11.5. What are the means for increasing our discernment?

Congratulations! Good Job!
Please be prepared to share what you have learned with your Life Group during the next meeting in order to edify one another.

Module Eight
Fruits & Gifts—Developing a Genuine Intimacy with the Holy Spirit

And do not get drunk with wine, for that is dissipation, but be filled with the Spirit.
— Ephesians 5:18

Right from the beginning, let's pause and pray, and ask for a deeper understanding form the Scriptures about:

- What it means to walk by the Spirit
- How to ignite the gift (or the gifts) God has blessed us with for the edification of other people
- What it means to have the character of Christ in us

Concerning the Holy Spirit, right after Peter's sermon on Pentecost, Dr. Luke writes: For the promise is for you and your children and for all who are far off, as many as the Lord our God will call to Himself. (Acts 2:39)

Concerning spiritual gifts, Paul writes to the Corinthians:

> I thank my God always concerning you for the grace of God which was given you in Christ Jesus, that in everything you were enriched in Him, in all speech and all knowledge, even as the testimony concerning Christ was confirmed in you, so that you are not lacking in any gift, awaiting eagerly the revelation of our Lord Jesus Christ, who will also confirm you to the end, blameless in the day of our Lord Jesus Christ. (1 Corinthians 1:4–8)

We also know that (cf. 1 Corinthians 3:1-3) the believers in Corinth were immature and carnal. Therefore, manifestation of spiritual gifts in a church does not mean the believers are mature in Christ. Displaying the fruit of the Spirit in one's life is the real sign of maturity.

After describing the manifestations of the flesh (see Galatians 5:19–21), Paul introduces the fruit of the spirit.

He writes:

> But the fruit of the Spirit is love, joy, peace, patience, kindness, goodness, faithfulness, gentleness, self-control; against such things there is no law. Now those who belong to Christ Jesus have crucified the flesh with its passions and desires. If we live by the Spirit, let us also walk by the Spirit. Let us not become boastful, challenging one another, envying one another. (Galatians 5:22–26).

In other words, Paul is saying: "If we claim to be Christians, followers of Christ, and have spiritual (zoe) life from the Spirit, then let's prove it, by walking accordingly."

So, what are disciples of Christ supposed to do? We are to pursue the spiritual gifts and at the same time we must crucify all fleshly desires. We must let the character of Christ be manifested in our inner person by displaying the fruits of the Spirit in our daily walk in this world.

Enjoy this study! Be fruitful and multiply.

Surprised by the Power of the Spirit
By Jack Deere

We have several excellent sources allocated for this module. We are going to start off this important module with a unique book, titled, *Surprised by the Power of the Spirit*, (Zondervan Publishing House, 1993), by Jack Deere.

After a careful reading of the book, please follow the instructions. Be prepared to share your insights with your Life Group, Life Group Leader, or Mentor.

Chapter 1: The Phone Call That Changed My Life

Deere writes:

> Before that phone call I knew where I was going. My life was both comfortable and secure. I was in control and liked it that way. Most of the time I felt I knew what God was doing. But by the time I put the phone down on that cold day in January of 1986, all of that changed abruptly. I was no longer certain of where I was going and what I was doing, and I was beginning to wonder if I really knew what God was doing.[13]

1.1. Based on the Bible, on your own experience with the Holy Spirit, and based on your reading and understanding from this chapter, please share an event or an experience used by God to change your life's direction. Be as clear and as brief as possible as you share it with the Life Group so others may be edified as well.

Congratulations! Good Job!
Please share what you have learned with your Life Group during the next meeting in order to edify one another.

---

[13] Deere, Jack, "Surprised by the Power of the Spirit," (Zondervan Publishing House, Grand Rapids, MI 49530, 1993), 13.

Chapter 13: A Passion for God

For some reason, the Holy Spirit is the most neglected Person within the Holy Trinity. Maybe, (just maybe), some people desire the Holy Spirit to heal them, speak to them, but they don't necessary desire to cultivate a genuine intimacy with the Him. This is sad, isn't it? Who agrees to be used like that?

We cannot expect to have the spiritual results and effectiveness in ministry as spiritual giants, and not have the fired-up passion they had. I don't know about you, but I am motivated by men of God like A. W. Tozer.

I like what Lyle Dorsett, the author of a new book, "A Passion for God: The Spiritual Journey of A. W. Tozer," writes:

> From his conversion as a teen to his death in 1963, Tozer remained true to one passion: to know the Father and make Him known, no matter what the cost. The price he paid was loneliness, censure from other, more secular-minded ministers of the times, and even a degree of estrangement from his family. Read the life story of a flawed but gifted saint, whose works are still impacting the world today.[14]

After a careful reading of chapter 13: A Passion for God, please follow the instructions.

13.1 Based on the Bible, your own experience with the Holy Spirit, and your reading and understanding of this chapter, please explain how most people rationalize their lack of passion for God.

13.2. How do you rationalize your lack of passion for God?

---

14 "A Passion for God," http://awtozer.org/home/books/a-passion-for-god/. Accessed on November 11, 2019.

Please elaborate in greater detail and share with the Life Group.

13.3. What may constitute surrogates to a genuine passion for God and to real intimacy with the Holy Spirit? Please elaborate.

Congratulations! Good Job!
Please be prepared to share what you have learned with your Life Group during the next meeting in order to edify one another.

Upper Room Fellowship Ministry

In 1996, in response to God's calling and by the guidance of the Holy Spirit, *Upper Room Fellowship Ministry (URFM)* was formed in order to serve the body of Christ. It is a non-profit and non-denominational Christian organization.

Vision

Fully alive through mind renewal and spiritual transformation for God's glory.

Mission

Our desire is to assist believers to experience healing for the wounded heart, restoration for the soul, and spiritual growth in Christ. Our prayer and deep desire are that through the Holy Spirit you will experience Jesus Christ as your very source of life.

Through individual or small group meetings and retreats, our ministry is committed to create an environment where healing, restoration, and spiritual freedom can be experienced. Under the guidance of the Holy Spirit, URFM is making disciples and equipping them for the Kingdom of God. This organization ministers for the spiritual growth of all believers.

The goal is that every member of Christ's Body would attain the Ultimate Intention—*the fullness of Christ.*

Most Christians have been taught that Jesus Christ died for their sins. Some embraced Christ as their Lord. Only a few have been taught the truth that they died with Him and experience Christ as their Life. Consequently, even fewer find victory in their lives. Although they have been set free from their sins, they have not been set free from themselves.

Our desire and fervent prayer for all of Jesus' disciples are that they all will become everything that God intends for them to become, in other words—*the fullness of Christ.*

Meet the Author

Vasile (Valy) Vaduva was born in Romania, a beautiful country in Eastern Europe. Romania was, at that time, a communist country. The government was against the Bible and biblical Christianity. His parents were Christian Orthodox, but they were not born-again believers, so he did not grow up going to Sunday school and Bible stories were not read to him during his childhood. When he was twelve years old, during his summer vacation, his step-brother took Valy over to his apartment in Bucharest for a couple of weeks. One of the neighbors was a believer and gave him the most amazing gift ever: *a New Testament.* Since he had plenty of time left in his vacation, he read this interesting book at least three times during that summer. This was the first time Valy got in contact with the Word of God. *He recalls it as an awesome experience!*

A few years passed and he started high school. Little did he know that God orchestrates all things in great detail. God placed a Christian colleague in his class. Valy sensed that this boy was different from the other teenagers. He took a risk and witnessed to Valy about the Lord and invited him to attend his church. It was in the fall of 1976. At the first opportunity, Valy went to church and enjoyed the preaching and teaching from the Bible. After a while he gave his heart to Jesus, and then he got baptized in water. *His born-again (regeneration) experience was a very powerful one!* It was February 1977, just several days before the powerful earthquake which devastated downtown Bucharest. For several weeks, after the water baptism, he felt like he was flying. He did not feel like he was touching the ground when walking. He had never been that happy and fulfilled in his entire life!

Valy's friend from high school gave him a Bible. He was so excited! In a short amount of time he ventured into this marvelous and unique book, reading it from Genesis to Revelation. He fell deeply in love with the Word of God. He started witnessing to his own friends and relatives, including his parents. As a result, he endured a lot of persecution from the high school faculty and personnel, as well as from his classmates. However, God delivered him and gave him strength during these times of testing. In fact, those were great experiences with God. Valy sensed Jesus all the time alive in his life and being there for him in the midst of persecutions.

After a while Valy's pastor asked him to teach Youth Sunday School. He responded with great delight. Soon he realized that he loves teaching and preaching the Word of God. Valy wished to go to a Bible College, but his father strongly suggested that it would be better off for him to go into a technical field. That is why he attended the Polytechnic University of Bucharest and became a mechanical engineer. However, his passion for the Word of God remained in his heart throughout the years.

A couple of years after his born-again experience he met his future wife, Elena, at a prayer meeting. It was in the late 1970s. There was a group of people who prayed fervently. He wanted that kind of prayer life for himself as well, so he attended more and more meetings. He fasted several days. His strong desire was to get closer to the Lord. In one of those days, while praying with a close group of friends, he sensed the Lord's presence, because He touched him in a significant way. *He recalls this infilling with the Holy Spirit as a great and very powerful experience.*

After Valy got married, he and his wife started a small group Bible study in their apartment. This lasted almost a decade. Despite several encounters with the secret police and some persecutions, he enjoyed these times very much! It was very rewarding to the see the lives of these people being transformed by the Word of God!

In 1989, a popular revolution in Romania ended the 45-year communist regime. During that time, it was clear to Valy that it was the opportune moment to immigrate with his family to the USA. In the States he attended a Romanian Christian Church. Very soon he noticed the great need for Bible study, discipleship, and counseling among Christians, especially among the youth and young families. He felt strongly that religious services alone are not sufficient for spiritual growth. Something was missing.

In 1995, Valy and his wife heard a commercial on a Christian station about advanced training in discipleship and in Christian counseling. Immediately he and his wife enrolled and attended those classes. *The Exchanged Life*[15]teaching they received during that

---

[15] For a detailed explanation about this see, The Greatest Exchange Ever, section of the *Fullness of Christ.*

intensive training was marvelous! They learned about brokenness and the need of coming to the end of the self-life so that Christ's Life will be manifested in us and through us. The way that the co-crucifixion concept from Galatians 2:20 was explained to them was absolutely amazing! That was a spiritual revolution for Valy. He understood that he did not have to perform religious activities, start another Bible study, or anything like that. What he needed the most was the *Life of Christ*[16] to be manifested in his life. But there was a problem. He needed to surrender his own life in order to have His Life to the fullest; and, by God's grace, he did it! *The exchanged life experience was the chief of all experiences up until that time.* He testifies that this experience revolutionized his life, his ministry, his view of God, himself, and others.

In 1996, the Holy Spirit guided Valy and Elena to establish Upper Room Fellowship Ministry (URFM), a non-profit and non-denominational Christian organization dedicated to Christian discipleship, spiritual maturity, and growth ministries. However, he continued to work as an engineer in order to support his family. But the more time that went by, the more miserable and spiritually unfulfilled he felt. This situation culminated with an unforgettable experience which took place in 2002. A series of circumstances resulted in a very stressful condition that led to a devastating stroke. However, God is always in control! He bestowed His mercy upon Valy and rescued him from this trial with minimal intervention from the medical team. *God completely rehabilitated him without side effects!* More than 75 percent of his speech was restored in less than 6 hours. Wow! That was absolutely miraculous!

Even though the healing that took place was very important, the focus is not on that experience alone. Something else must be brought into the spotlight. A few hours after Valy was admitted to the hospital, the neurologist came to his bedside and asked: "What is your occupation?" Despite his speech difficulties, Valy replied quite proudly: "I am a preacher." Please notice that he did not reply "I am an engineer," even though this statement was true. After that he added: "I am going to get well from this condition with no side

---

16 For more about Life of Christ or Indwelled by Christ, see *Definitions for Deeper Spiritual Realities*, section of the *Fullness of Christ*.

effects because God called me to preach the gospel." Indeed, this was exactly what happened.

After a few more hours, his medical condition improved. This was visible to the entire medical team responsible for his care. They were surprised by Valy's swift recovery. He and his wife and their entire family glorify God for His miraculous intervention. They appreciate the friends, the church, and the hundreds of believers everywhere who prayed insistently on his behalf. Glory be to God for His divine healing in Valy's life!

After a period of recovery, he returned to his full-time job as an engineer, but his life was not the same. He no longer found joy in his career. The rest of the year, and into 2003, was a living nightmare. He was severely depressed. His doctor's efforts to treat him were unsuccessful. He felt that his life was torn apart by an internal spiritual battle: on one side, his engineering responsibilities and his role as the provider for his family; on the other side, his passion and deep desire to preach the Gospel of Jesus. However, not even during these circumstances did Valy find the strength to quit his job and start the full-time ministry that God called him to from his youth.

This difficult and painful battle lasted until mid-2004. At the beginning of July 2004, his boss came into his office and closed the door behind him. He said: "Valy, our department is going to taper down and close. All the engineers working in this department will be let go. Even I will have to find something else to do. The sad news is that you are the first to be let go. Starting tomorrow your job is eliminated."

Even though he expected something like this to happen, hearing "starting tomorrow you no longer have a job" roared like a thunder in his soul. After a few minutes he pulled himself together and went outside to call his wife. "Hey, I am calling to let you know that I am a free man!" "What do you mean?" she asked Valy. "Don't tell me that you are laid off." "Well, it's true," he replied, "but I am taking it from the hand of God. He freed me up to work for Him and His Kingdom."

Finally, Valy understood it! Starting in July 2004, he dedicated himself, spirit, soul and body for the work of the ministry. Gradually God healed the depression that lasted for over two years. Now, after almost fifteen years of intensively working for the Kingdom of God, he is very joyful and fulfilled. This is a sacred joy that does not come from the world; not from finances, earthly rewards, or comfort, but rather from walking in the central will of God.

As many of you know, working in full-time ministry requires a lot of time, effort, and the strength to fight spiritual battles. It also relies heavily on financial resources and a team of dedicated and talented people. However, once we decide to do God's will, the joy that comes from the Lord is incomprehensible and does not compare with anything this world may offer us. The devil is relentless in fighting against us and, unfortunately, at times he succeeds in deceiving us. We may be fooled into finding happiness and fulfillment in the things of this world instead of walking in obedience to the Holy Spirit.

Since he consecrated himself for the work of the ministry, Valy, is actively involved in mission trips in the United States and throughout the world. He currently offers personalized spiritual life couching sessions, mind renewal classes, transformation prayer ministry, and teaches Advanced Discipleship Training locally and over the Internet in English and Romanian.

Valy, his wife, Elena, their four grown children, and nine grandchildren live in southern Michigan.

Made in USA - Kendallville, IN
1208157_9781930529410
12.08.2020 0832